"Remember, You Can Make A Difference."

☆

For months before he ever heard of "America's Most Wanted," child advocate John Walsh carried a flier from the National Center for Missing and Exploited Children. It was a morgue photograph for an unidentified girl found shot dead in Banning, California, on May 1, 1987. He hoped that in his travels, he might find some sheriff, some social worker, or even a desperate parent who might help bring the girl's body home.

Little did Walsh realize that as host of "America's Most Wanted" he would do more than that. In ten seconds, he would help catch the girl's alleged killer, James Charles Stark.

AMERICA'S MOST WANTED™

How Television Catches Crooks

JACK BRESLIN

Harper Paperbacks

Harper & Row, Publishers, New York
Grand Rapids, Philadelphia, St. Louis, San Francisco
London, Singapore, Sydney, Tokyo, Toronto

S.T.F. Productions, a subsidiary of Fox Television Stations, Inc.,
has a trademark right to the name "America's Most Wanted."

 Harper Paperbacks a division of Harper & Row, Publishers, Inc.
10 East 53rd Street, New York, N.Y. 10022

First printing: April, 1990

Printed in the United States of America

HARPER PAPERBACKS and colophon are trademarks of
Harper & Row, Publishers, Inc.

10 9 8 7 6 5 4 3

To the dedicated men and women of America's law
enforcement community,

To the countless victims of crime frustrated in
their quest for justice,

And to those Americans who care to make
a difference.

Table of Contents

Acknowledgments

In the entertainment business one can easily lose touch with the realities of life—until you work on a film such as *Adam* and meet incredible people such as John and Reve Walsh. Six years ago I had the privilege of meeting them, and was proud to help educate America about missing children and recover 65 youngsters through *Adam*.

When I heard through the Fox grapevine that John Walsh would be the host of this new crime-fighting show, I wanted in. Now two years later, I am proud again to be part of a show that has not only made TV history, but has also actually made a difference in our country. This book is not a press release, but a look at an experiment that nobody expected to be the success it is today. I've tried to tell both the highs and the lows, and in fairness give both sides their way in evaluating the effort.

Without the help of the AMW staff, led by Stephen Chao, Michael Linder, Tom Herwitz, John Walsh, Glenn Weiss, Dan Kavanaugh, and Margaret Roberts, this book would still be only a memo. Many current staffers, especially Mickey McKenzie, Ray Mize, Joan Stair, Burke Stone, and Lisa Younger, took time away from their own hectic schedules to dig out files and memories to enlighten my work. Several former staffers, who have moved on in their careers, also gave me some wonderful anecdotes and insights into the show's early days, particularly Nan Allendorfer, Michael Cerny, Brian Gadinsky, Bill Oakley, Grace Vista, Mike Walton, and Tony Zanelotti. And without the usual expert efficiency and gentle kindness of Leslie Groves, I would still be months from finishing.

In researching this book, I also received incredible help from the hundred or so people whom I interviewed or pestered for information. A special debt is owed to many of the law enforcement officials who work with AMW on a daily basis, particularly Howard Safir, Bob Leschorn, and Bill Tsoodle at the U.S. Marshals Service, and Milt Ahlerich, Scott Nelson, Swanson Carter, Wiley Thompson, Rex Tomb, Dan McCarron, and Steve Markardt at the FBI.

If Barry Diller, Jamie Kellner, and Peter Chernin had not allowed me to do this project, I never would have gotten the insight into our criminal justice system that it has given me. And on many days, when I was depressed from that insight, I found encouragement from my friends and colleagues at Fox Broadcasting, especially in the publicity department. Thanks to Brad Turell and Michael Peikoff for the understanding in taking time off, and to the whole staff for being patient—Missy Burns, Monica Bouldin, Scott Boute, Antonia Coffman, Gregory Crawford, Joan-Ellen Delaney, Steve Elzer, Dom Giofre, Janine Jones, Sharan Magnuson, Lorraine Olivas, Holly Ollis, Cindy Ronzoni, Schuyler Samperton, and Andrew Shipps. And a special nod to Phil Gonzales, who helped catch crooks in my absence. Just because they have left the FBC family, doesn't mean I shouldn't be grateful to my former colleagues, and still friends, Ralph Hemecker, Paul McGuire, Rosemary O'Brien, Scott Penza, Tom Tanno, and Ann Whitney. And lots of gratitude to Jeff Mackler who happened to call me one day about an opening at some new company called Fox Broadcasting.

At Harper & Row, I would like to thank Ed Bell, Ed Breslin (we're probably related somehow), and Katie Smith for their foresight, editing, and patience in helping me meet their deadlines.

I have been fortunate to have been blessed with so many friends and family who have helped me throughout my life and career. On this project, I could never have made it without lots of love and support from Perry Ascher, Charlie, Debbie, and Kyle Bernuth (particularly with midnight computer questions), Debbie Bozeat, Chuck Connors (and Rosie), Skip and Brea Doyle (and company), Leslie Gallo, Fred Goodman, Mindy Green, Mary Manning, Jim Murray, Rick Remsnyder, Pat Schultz, Mary Rice Sternberg, Doug Stevenson (who minded my nest), and Dan Somrack. Without the help of George Barimo and Ben Shecter, I don't know where I would be today. And it wouldn't have been as fun without my parents, my sisters, Maureen and Carol, my aunts, uncles, and cousins, who give their love, from far away. And to Susan, Jenny, and Mark.

Jack Breslin
December 22, 1989
Los Angeles, California

Introduction

In 1987, there were more than 280,000 fugitives in the United States. They were wanted by the FBI, the U.S. Marshals, DEA, U.S. Customs, BATF, Interpol, all fifty states and thousands of local agencies.

John Emil List, David James Roberts, and Mark Austin Goodman were just three of those wanted men. But within two years, these three, and a hundred other or so like them would get caught in an electronic dragnet.

Their crimes, their faces, their descriptions, their habits and their tattoos would be seen on millions of television sets across America every Sunday night. Only within days, hours or minutes of their profiles, they'd be arrested thousands of miles from their alleged crimes, sometimes never knowing they'd been on television.

Others would know, however. They'd flee to Canada, Mexico, even Belize. They'd dye their hair, cover their tattoos, or knock out their teeth to hide from the law and its new television partner. But suddenly someone watching this show would recognize something about the person on the screen. They worked with the suspect, lived next door, worshipped at the same church that morning, recognized an unusual tattoo, or let them in their home to lay carpet the day before.

In the early months of 1987, the idea for this show hadn't even gone past early "development." That's a television term for an idea still being worked on. It hasn't been approval for scripts, casting or production. Every year thousands of projects never go past this stage. There are a lot of hurdles that an idea can stumble over on its way to being produced and broadcast. Some can fail with one network or studio, then wind up a hit for another. A lot depends on who pitches the idea and making others believe it can fly.

This idea did get out of the development stage. Other priorities came first, but it slowly made its way off paper into a "pilot" or experimental episode. Part of that pilot went on seven Fox-owned television stations as a hopeful trial balloon in February 1988. Helped by some amazing captures and encouraging rating numbers, it debuted nationally two months later on the 125 affiliates of Fox Broadcasting Company, and later to four independent stations in Canada. And within a year it would become one of the most controversial and successful shows on television. The road wasn't that easy, however.

In the beginning few people, even those who created it, ever thought it would work, much less become a national phenomenon. The fugitives who would be captured never dreamed they'd be caught by telephone tips from TV viewers or see themselves on a national crimefighting show.

Of those more than 280,000 fugitives being sought by various federal, state and local law enforcement agencies in early 1987, few would rate being even considered for a television movie about their lives and crimes. Roberts, Goodman and List were just three more wrinkled wanted posters on the thick stack nailed to the post office wall.

On October 24, 1986, Roberts had escaped from two prison guards while returning to Indiana State Prison in Michigan City, Indiana, after a medical examination in Indianapolis. He had been there since 1974, serving six life sentences, three of which were commuted from the electric chair. His crimes had shocked even the most hardened detectives. To this day, one 27-year veteran detective says Roberts is the only ice-cold criminal who ever made the hair stand up on the back of his neck. Still, Roberts maintains his innocence, saying he has been framed by the racially discriminating Indiana system.

Roberts was convicted in two separate incidents. In one, he was charged with burning down a home in New Whiteland, Indiana, after murdering a young couple in their living room. Their baby suffocated in the back bedroom during the fire. The murdered man, Bill Patrick, was a Sears tire salesman in Indianapolis. He had signed a deposition for court stating that Roberts, then on parole, had stolen four new tires and a muffler.

While Roberts was out on bond for the New Whiteland triple murder-arson, a 19-year-old Indianapolis woman was abducted in her car, raped twice, then locked in the trunk. Her assailant then left her infant son to die on the roadside in the subfreezing cold.

Roberts was arrested and charged with those heinous crimes. After five jury trials, he was convicted and sentenced on all counts in both incidents. He would file appeal after appeal, claiming his innocence.

Most everyone in Indiana, except his victims,

had forgotten about David James Roberts. Then he escaped.

Mark Austin Goodman had never killed anyone. Bank robbery and escaping from custody were his specialties—ten banks, ten breaks. That's how many the U.S. Marshals knew of when they went looking for him.

Goodman was like a modern-day Jesse James. He could rob banks, break into stores, steal cars. After he'd get caught, Goodman would pull the most bizarre escapes. He climbed over razor wire without a scratch, talked his way out of two jails, even crashed through a second-story plate glass window to elude the cops. One lawman credited Goodman with having "brass testicles."

Goodman had one problem, however. He could get out of jail, but he couldn't stay out. When he robbed several banks in Oklahoma, he used a disguised B.B. gun instead of a real one. A policeman in Edmond thought it could kill and shot Goodman in the act of robbery.

He was indicted on ten counts of bank robbery while still in his hospital bed, as he requested. Goodman recuperated from his wounds, and U.S. Attorneys prepared the solid case against him, which could get him a hefty prison term.

On Halloween, 1987, Goodman had a little trick in store for his keepers at the Federal Correctional Institution at El Reno, Oklahoma. It was only after two bedchecks that they found he was long gone.

John Emil List made a lot more headlines than Goodman or Roberts put together. Every cop in the state of New Jersey knows his name. The good citizens of Westfield wish he'd never lived there.

On December 7, 1971, police found the bodies of

List's wife and three teenage children neatly laid out on sleeping bags in the ballroom of his crumbling suburban mansion. Rags covered the women's faces and the children wore blood-caked overcoats. Upstairs was the body of his 85-year-old mother, stuffed in a hall closet. They'd all been shot in the head a month before.

In their gruesome search, the police also found detailed letters written by List, including one to his pastor, about his meticulous preparations for the murders. He'd excused the children from school, canceled the milk and the mail, closed his bank accounts, packed his suitcase, and shut the kitchen door behind him.

A month later, police found List's 1963 Chevrolet sedan abandoned at New York City's John F. Kennedy International Airport. The quiet, churchgoing insurance salesman had committed what he obviously considered the perfect escape. But why did he decide to wipe out his family? Was he so deeply in debt? Was he inspired on some twisted mission to save them from the world's hopeless morality? Or was he tired of his nagging wife, his overbearing mother, and his three growing teenagers?

Over the next 17 years, dozens of lawmen would be assigned to the case. They would follow hundreds of leads in Europe, Africa, and nearly every state in the Union. They would plead with Lutheran leaders to search their flocks and query insurance companies about new salesmen. They would send out flyers with computer-aged photographs to the media. Every few years, an eager rookie detective would retrace every minute detail of List's life for some new clue.

To most people in New Jersey, John List was gone—he'd gotten away with it. But the FBI, the Union County Prosecutors, and the Westfield Police

Department, particularly Chief Jim Moran, would never let him go.

Roberts, List, and Goodman. Three cases of men dangerous in their own right. They had all been charged with serious crimes, yet they were three distinct criminal types. Two had been previously convicted and sentenced. And in 1987, they were on the run with a television show not far behind.

1

"Okay, Next Stupid Idea..."

It was one of those nameless hospitality suites you wander in and out of at trade conventions. The room is hosted by polite, smiling folks offering drinks and eats. They hope you'll buy their product even if you aren't at the right show. It's a great place to network, scope out the competition, or just get a free meal.

Fox Executive Stephen Chao was wandering around one of those "bad parties" after the NATPE (National Association of Television Program Executives) in New Orleans during the early weeks of 1987.

Just a month before, the 31-year-old Harvard MBA had been given a job every television programmer would kill for. Fox CEO Barry Diller had given him free rein to set up a programming "laboratory" to use the seven owned-and-operated stations (O&O's) to test new shows. He would develop ideas, make pilots of the ones that might work, then try them out on the O&O's for network or syndication. The lab would give him "all the toys and resources" that a network would provide, with a fraction of the risk. The shows would be low-budget, low-risk. A good show could go on to be a hit on the up-and-coming Fox Broadcasting Company, while a flop would be dumped after a few weeks with relatively little harm.

Chao's area was a separate arm of Fox, Inc., from FBC, a fledgling network of small independent stations which had debuted the past October with Joan Rivers's late-night offering. His successful programming could wind up on the new network, which slated to debut its first night of Sunday shows in April. Though he sometimes spoke to the young mavericks starting up the bold venture to challenge the Big Three networks, Chao reported to Diller and Fox Television Stations chief Bob Kreek.

Browsing through the exhibits at shows like NATPE, one can get a sense of what's coming up in television in the coming year. There are hundreds of producers and syndicators peddling what they think are innovative new shows, along with plenty of proven prime-time hits for syndication. Nothing really interested Chao, who already built a strong reputation among his peers as an innovative executive, especially since he was relatively new to television. He could cut a tough deal and get the job done with no nonsense.

Looking over his résumé, you'd never expect Chao to have his own little programming laboratory. A native of Ann Arbor, Michigan, he had graduated from Exeter Prep and Harvard, where he majored in Greek and Latin. He worked as a reporter at the National Enquirer before going back to Harvard for his MBA. In 1983, he was hired by Rupert Murdoch to work in New York City with News America Corporation in one of the key areas of the billionaire's operation: mergers and acquisitions.

Chao was involved in Murdoch's purchases of Metromedia and 20th Century-Fox, his new ventures into feature films and broadcasting. Soon after the 1985 Fox deal, Chao found himself in Los Angeles working in the television production unit of 20th Century-Fox. Despite his lack of TV experience, Chao was the type of maverick executive who can truly "do his own thing," so he got his own laboratory. And Diller knew he would come up with some unusual products in an industry where every original idea has already been done or stolen.

At the NATPE show, Chao had been hanging around with Jim Platt, his successor in mergers and acquisitions at News Corp. in New York. Once a reporter at the St. Louis Post-Dispatch, Platt earned his MBA from Columbia, worked at a small Connecticut publishing company, then joined the Murdoch operations.

They were both MBA's, but far from stuffy academics or narrow-headed number crunchers. With different experiences from most TV folks in the room, Chao and Platt had a much different perspective on programming than the typical Hollywood executive clone. Chao confided in Platt that during his first month in the laboratory, he had been "thrashing around" desperately. He had begun developing a kid's show called "Doctor Science" and was toying with a few ideas, but nothing earth-shattering.

In their conversation, Chao asked his colleague if he has any possible development ideas. If he had said that to anyone else in the room, some would have babbled away, while others would call over their attorney. After all, many great shows have started as cocktail ideas, and many times the person who thought them up never got a dime, much less a production credit.

But these two men were on a different wave length, neither looking for credit, just trying to help each other out. In his travels in Europe, Platt had seen a few shows on television which reenacted crimes in cooperation with police, then asked viewers to call in with tips. Back in the States, he had noticed an article on these shows in the international section of *Electronic Media,* a weekly trade publication. Shortly before the convention, Platt had mailed the article to Chao as a possible show idea, but hadn't gotten a response.

So Platt brought up the crime show idea again, mentioning the success of local crime shows. But it didn't get much interest from Chao.

"Okay," Chao chuckled. "Next stupid idea?"

The two continued to bounce around more ideas, then passed through a few more forgettable hospitality suites before calling it a night.

Platt flew back to New York and Chao to Los Angeles. Before they left New Orleans, Chao asked if Platt could look into the crime show idea a bit more. Since News Corp. was then located in the same building as the *New York Post,* Platt looked through the newspaper's back files for some leads. He found articles about how the media, particularly *The Post,* had helped police capture criminals by readers' tips. He also wrote up some notes on how to Americanize the overseas shows, and sent the package on to Chao in Los Angeles. That was the end of Platt's involvement in the budding concept, since he would soon move to Fox's Boston station, WFXT, as promotion manager.

Chao looked over the pile of information that Platt had sent. In their research, the two had uncovered numerous citizen crimefighting groups which used the media to help law enforcement. Overseas, there were viewer-participation crimefighting shows in West Germany, the United Kingdom, and Australia, among others. But they couldn't find anything like that done successfully on American national television to that point.

The idea was intriguing, but Chao had several equally worthy projects on his desk. He had already gotten "Dr. Science" into development, was talking pitches daily from producers, and searching for more. He gave the crimefighting show the working title of "Electronic Roundup," and put it on his list of projects to mention to Barry Diller.

The chairman found the idea "appealing." Diller, one of the living legends of the entertainment industry, had heard nearly every breakthrough idea or "high concept" at least twice in his career. He hadn't seen this one before—it was good, it was fresh, it clearly intrigued him. So he told Chao to develop the idea further and find a producer to guide it.

In developing other ideas and listening to pitches, Chao had met with three to four dozen producers, with varying degrees of experience. He was also looking into serious documentary subjects for a "Frontline" type program. As a format-driven show, "Electronic Roundup" would need an imaginative producer with a variety of skills. The producers coming in and out of Chao's Hollywood office at Fox Television Center were either strictly news or strictly drama. None of the "available suspects" seemed right for the show, even though Chao would later admit that he didn't really yet have a clear concept of how the show would look or work.

As a guy who follows his gut instincts, Chao knew that he would know his producer when he saw the person. And again, he was right.

Like the group nurturing the infant FBC over at the Fox Pico lot near Century City, the team over at Fox TV Stations was a group of young, hungry pioneers. They shared everything and weren't afraid to yell for help. When Chao asked around for possible documentary producers, David Simon, another station group executive, suggested a Los Angeles producer named Michael Linder. When Simon was program director at KTLA, Linder had produced some specials and documentaries for the station as a free-lancer.

Chao put Linder's "reel" of sample works on his videotape machine. Not being a sports fan, he wasn't really moved by the title of the first industrial promoting a basketball school at Loyola Marymount University. But within seconds, he was hooked, thinking "this guy can put video together!" There were also samples from Linder's news reporting, entertainment packages from "Eye on LA" and "Entertainment Tonight," documentary segments and more industrials.

Chao was impressed. The reel was "pretty," but it was also interesting. Linder had a news background and obviously had a "special touch" for making entertaining, good-looking pieces on a tight budget. "Eye on LA," a local entertainment magazine on KCBS-TV in Los Angeles, was a proven training ground for hotshot young producers who had gone on to greater things.

By early March, Simon helped Chao track down Linder in Japan where he had been free-lancing for about two years. To himself, Chao wondered "what kind of fool" he might be for going to Japan to find an American producer for this "tacky little Hollywood show" that was still just a file folder of articles on his desk. He had some other documentary ideas to suggest to Linder, just in case he wasn't into catching crooks.

After a few trans-Pacific telephone conversations, Linder agreed to come to Los Angeles and work on some documentary ideas with Chao. The Fox executive promised nine weeks of work at least, depending on what ideas wound up in production.

Little did Linder realize that when he boarded that plane to Los Angeles, he was actually walking into his own little niche in television history.

2

From Hollywood to Washington

Fox attorney Tom Herwitz had enough work to keep him busy in the spring of 1987. As vice-president of corporate and legal affairs for Fox Television Stations in Washington, D.C., he was a corporate handyman. He did some legal work, occasional corporate development, a bit of industrial relations, lots of lobbying all over town, and plenty of Fox corporate events, such as feature film screenings and the White House Tennis Tournament.

Herwitz, 31, could never be pigeonholed as a stuffy legal type. Instead, he liked to dabble in a lot of areas. A native of Worcester, Massachusetts, he had graduated from law school at the University of Pennsylvania in 1981, then headed to Washington and two years of practicing communications law with the prestigious firm of Hogan and Hartson. Next, he decided to work with the folks who carried out the law: the Federal Communications Commission. As legal assistant to FCC Chairman Mark Fowler, he mingled with the most influential people in Washington. After three years, he wound up on the other side of the table from the government, when Fox hired him as a combination corporate attorney-lobbyist to protect its interests in D.C.

That spring Herwitz had a formidable battle looming on the horizon. The Big Three networks might cause problems with the FCC for the budding Fox affiliate family, being touted as the fourth network. That was one problem on his mind when he headed home one April night, assuming his work was done for the day.

One communications problem in any international company are time zone differences. No matter how long executives deal with their counterparts on the other side of the world or the country, they can't seem to learn how to tell time. That night Steve Chao was still wild with ideas at 6 P.M. in California, while Tom Herwitz was watching TV at home with his future wife, Laura, at 9 P.M., Washington time. So when Chao called all excited about getting the go-ahead for a new TV show it took Herwitz a few moments to switch from viewer to executive.

"Have you ever heard of these shows that catch criminals?" Chao inquired.

"Yeah, sort of," Herwitz replied.

"Would you like to help us develop it?"

"All right," Herwitz answered, though the only experience he had with actual TV production was trying to regulate what wound up on the airwaves.

"I'll send you some stuff," Chao said. "And you'll have to see if the F.B.I. will work with us."

Easier said than done, but what was a few more meetings and memos.

Back in Los Angeles, Diller had already decided that the show must be produced out of Washington. If it was done in Hollywood, it would probably wind up looking like a typical shoot-'em-up cop show. This would be different—dramatic, yet based on the facts, packed with action and emotion. It would later be called "reality TV" by some, "tabloid TV" by others, public service by most. Producing the show in the law enforcement capital would give the show credibility, since it wouldn't hurt being down the street from all the nation's top cops. After all, without their help, the show would never work. It would only show the crimes and profile the fugitives. Going after them would be the job of the police—if they liked the concept.

Meanwhile, there was a rumor that Orion Television was hot on a similar type of show called "Crimewatch," based in Los Angeles. Fox could protect its franchise by flying the flag next to the FBI, the Marshals, the DEA, and others. That kind of Washington credibility would be tough to match on a Hollywood back lot.

When Mike Linder first sat down with Steve Chao, he had a bag full of documentary ideas. Chao and his Fox colleagues were quickly building a reputation for being open to most any idea. They were anxious to break away from the traditional, stale TV fare that bored today's more sophisticated viewers. This new Fox network would offer an alternative.

Linder and Chao were fighting time. The producer was based in Japan, and so he needed an apartment or hotel room in LA. He could only be away from the Orient for so long before some of his clients started looking elsewhere. So Chao offered him a one-hour special commemorating the tenth anniversary of Elvis's death, and Linder went to work.

Within a few days, however, it became clear that the King's creator, Colonel Parker, had a stranglehold over the estate and the music. No music, no special. So much for that.

Chao and Linder now had a problem. They were committed to nine weeks of work and their best shot at a documentary had been shot down. Linder could either go back to Japan to think of something else, or Chao could give him another project. In LA tradition, they sat down over lunch to work something out.

Grabbing his well-worn file marked "Electronic Roundup," Chao began his pitch to Linder about this new crimefighting TV show. It wasn't a documentary, but it could become a series, and Chao needed an experienced producer such as Linder to make the pilot.

Later, Chao would recall that he thought Linder seemed "sort of unhappy" about the prospect. Perhaps because he had documentary instincts, he wanted to move the world with a solid documentary, not a weekly series.

What Chao interpreted as disappointment was really Linder thinking quietly. He didn't hesitate, since the idea of an interactive crime-fighting TV show appealed to him. He could draw on his news background to report the stories, and pull from his production talents for the crime reconstructions.

It was an intriguing idea, Linder thought. Reconstruct a crime exactly how it happened with the potential of learning more about that crime and perhaps catching the person who did it. He had seen a lot of Crimesolvers and Crimestoppers type shows, but the acting and production values were a bit "primitive." They were mostly done without professional actors and little news-style with handheld cameras. As a TV/video producer, Linder knew he could improve on that. And the shows overseas had already established a precedent that this type of show could work.

As a journeyman news reporter, Linder knew

there was a tremendous amount of frustration with crime in America. There wasn't much the public could do except take a "defensive posture." This type of show was fresh, and nobody had really tried to develop the full potential of this genre on a national level. Here was a chance to explore the human passions and emotions of crime and its victims while helping police capture the fugitives involved.

The Elvis special was out and "Electronic Roundup" was in. So in a way, television and America has Colonel Parker to thank for what would follow.

Michael Linder was a a journeyman in media. His senior year in high school he had started in radio at a 500-watt daytime farm station in his hometown of Harvard, Illinois. He worked there and at other small stations while going to school at Milton College, Wisconsin, and the University of Missouri, Columbia. After college, he worked his way up the market ladder through Cleveland, Detroit, Montreal, and finally New York. He'd been a programmer, manager, even pulled down air shifts.

What he really loved was news, especially covering the cop beat. As the morning man, he would sign the station off the air, then go over to the cops, the firehouse, and the sheriff's to go over their overnight blotter. Linder loved those crime reports, so full of passionate, dramatic stories that would only be told in a few seconds on the air or a few paragraphs in the press.

By his tenth year in radio, Linder had helped put some of the first FM rock stations on the air in Canada in the early '70s when progressive rock was just starting to happen. Soon he moved back to street reporting in New York, then in California, where he started his own news network for FM rock stations in 1976. This was the first time that anyone had customized news for a specific demographic group, but CBS and NBC would soon follow his lead.

By now he had done most everything he could in radio after 14 years, and it was time for television. Starting as a writer at KCBS-TV in Los Angeles, Linder became part of the team that developed the first two-and-a-half megablock of local news. He was knocking out copy for such network future stars as Brent Musberger and Connie Chung, while doing some general assignment reporting of his own.

Eventually he got the weekend beat for Channel Two, working with a young reporter named Krista Bradford, who would later be featured on Fox's "The Reporters." Linder liked the stories others turned down: gang wars, drive-by shootings, mediation attempts by local priests. He stayed ahead of the police on the Dorothy Stratten murder story in 1980, being the first to implicate Peter Bogdanovich in the love triangle that resulted in her death.

The next year, Linder started producing his own segments in the pioneering days of entertainment magazine shows. He helped KABC-TV get "Eye on L.A." off the ground, and was among the first producers on Paramount's "Entertainment Tonight." Among the specials he produced was an "Eye" travel piece on Japan in 1983, and Linder "fell in love with the place." Wandering around the Orient appealed to him more than sitting in dark editing rooms in Los Angeles. So three years later, he packed up and headed West.

His wide range of experience landed him jobs ranging from position papers for the Japanese government to new product videos for major corporations such as Canon and Mitsubishi, as well as topical radio broadcasts for the States. Linder could also live among the Japanese and jump off to explore

Micronesia, Hong Kong, Thailand, Indonesia, and beyond. The money was good, the travel fun, and the people fascinating. Then Steve Chao called.

Sure Linder loved to travel—but Washington? It would be another adventure, and this new show was intriguing, so off he went as the cherry blossoms began to bloom.

Herwitz had already called around to get some attention at the FBI. Through a friend at the White House, Dick Howser, former counsel to the President, he was able to set up a meeting at headquarters. The bureau itself was in a state of transition, being between directors. William Webster had resigned to become head of the CIA, and Judge William Sessions hadn't been appointed yet. Filling in meanwhile was John Otto as acting director, while supporting him was B. Oliver "Buck" Revell, chief of operations.

Herwitz had been at the FBI before, but not pitching a television show. Walking into Revell's office, he could feel the tradition of the Bureau surrounding him. On the carved oak desk was a pair of standing bronzed Smith and Wesson handguns with a plaque stating they had sat on J. Edgar Hoover's desk. Behind the desk was Revell, a bear of a man with 25 years in the bureau, starting as a field agent. The scene was impressive, perhaps imposing, even for an experienced lobbyist as Herwitz.

The meeting started cordially as Herwitz had already sent along a two-page description or "treatment" of the proposed show. Revell was impressed with how serious Fox seemed about the effort. Using the media to catch fugitives was not a new concept for the FBI. But this was Hollywood, famous for its sensationalism and hype. If the crimes were overdramatized, the show would lose contact with reality and be viewed as an attempt to sway, rather than inform the public. It could become both prejudicial for trials and be a disservice for operating procedures.

The FBI was obsessed with its image as pillar of law enforcement in America, sometimes getting in rivalries with other agencies. This show could help show the public how the Bureau operates, as well as inform viewers about specific cases. There could be severe ethical and legal problems, however, if these producers were irresponsible and careless with the facts. Fictional movies often attack the FBI, and show agents doing things that are totally false and illegal. If this show ever got on the air, the FBI would want to make desperately sure that it accurately depicted operations as they actually happened. Some producers and programmers would call that censorship; others consider it the price of cooperation.

Herwitz's original inquiries had gotten some attention on lower levels at the Bureau. Some were in favor of using the media to help catch fugitives, especially those making a trail of terror across several states. Others, even a few in public affairs, resisted, saying anything more than a description could be viewed as prejudicial. The criminal investigation area (CID) didn't want television exposing their secret operations.

Before the meeting, Revell had a chance to think about the idea. In fact, he took a different view. He believed that law enforcement has to seek out the support of the public. If this show could inform, not inflame, public sentiment against crime, it could help all law enforcement. Just don't skew the facts or prejudice the rights of the individual, even a mass murderer before trial. Use only information from the public record, or that which is appropriate before the case goes to court.

There was some potential in that two-page treatment, Revell thought. It could educate America about the amount of crime that's happening. But it could also help arrest some individuals hiding for years right next door to some unknowing TV viewer.

Herwitz would later recall that Revell was "very receptive and very nice," but committed to nothing. So the attorney broke away from his polished pitch for a moment.

"This could do for the FBI, what *Top Gun* did for the Navy," Herwitz joked.

Revell smiled.

"That was an interesting movie, but it had about as much to do with flying jet fighters as falling out of this building," he replied. "'We don't need that, thanks."

Herwitz decided to get more specific. He leafed through a folder with descriptions of the FBI's Top Ten Fugitives.

"Let's take a case—like Leo Koury," he said.

Revell's eyes lit up. Koury had been on the run for almost a decade for racketeering, extortion, and attempted murder. The FBI had followed thousands of leads and spent nearly a half-million dollars looking for him.

Herwitz had hooked him. Revell might be part of the system, but he was a cop at heart. He doesn't care about the *Top Gun* image, Herwitz realized, he just wants to catch criminals. This show could make his job easier.

Revell started asking how the show would approach a case. Where would the information come from? From law enforcement. Where would you film it? Where it happened. Wouldn't there be a problem with accusing the guy beforehand? Not if we worked from the public record.

Herwitz had sparked the imagination of the

number-two man at the FBI. It was next up to the Bureau's legal people, public affairs department, and the criminal investigators. The journey had only begun.

By early June, Linder had wrapped up his affairs in Tokyo and planned to be away working on this new show for a maximum of three months. Though it made sense for several reasons to produce the show in Washington, he preferred Los Angeles. Nothing was set except a commitment to shoot a demonstration tape or pilot episode. There was no staff, no host, no cases, no format, just an idea and a lot of enthusiasm.

Some were envisioning the show as centered around evidence in a case. For example, the host would hold up a piece of wood or a shoulder patch from the crime scene. Call us now and help us identify these clues: where were they made, and so forth. Not exactly gripping television.

In the time Linder had between his original discussions with Chao in Los Angeles and his actual arrival in Washington, he had plenty of time to develop the show in his mind. It was an exercise in the documentation of human passions and a chance for the audience to experience the emotional impact of crime—the acts, the perpetrators, the victims, the police.

Even TV news rarely captured the real emotion involved in crime. He often recalled an incident during his TV reporting days in Los Angeles which proved that very point. One day he and a camera crew were riding through Long Beach to cover a routine press conference somewhere. They got a call over the radio that there had been an officer-involved shooting about three blocks from where they were. They rushed to the scene and found what most would call an everyday robbery. Two guys had held up a gas station, then ran down an alley, directly into a squad car on patrol. The sergeant in the car got out and pointed his shotgun at the pair. They started to run, and one of them raised his gun to fire at the policeman. The sergeant ordered them to stop, and commanded the gunman to drop his weapon. He refused, and the policeman was forced to shoot the man in self-defense.

Linder and his crew arrived moments after the shooting. A bloody corpse lay on the sidewalk. The other robber had surrendered and was being taken into custody. The dead man had a ski mask half covering his face. In his hand he was clutching about $300 in small bills. This was a real image of crime, Linder realized. A man's life had been lost for his fistful of money.

Linder instructed the cameraman to give him a high shot from on top of the newsvan, showing the entire scene—a bloody body sprawled on the asphalt surrounded by the cops, bystanders, and press. He had the camera push in up the body, up his blown-away chest, across the half-masked face up to the fistful of dollars. The shot said everything there was to say visually about armed robbery, law and order, and the consequences. That image would come to mind many times for Michael Linder in the coming months.

The common problem of TV news in document-ing crime was that the cameras always got there too late. As a reporter, Linder had found himself stand-ing in front of a yellow police tape telling about what had just gone on inside. There was no way that a reporter could document the passion, the horror, or any of the other values involved in a violent crime that would merit media attention. The producer was fascinated with the possibility of going back to the scene of the crime with police cooperation. They would tell you exactly what happened. After all, they wanted to capture the fugitive, so why wouldn't they help? Then tell the whole story, from as many points of view as possible. It was a challenge that would top all of Linder's talents in news, video, and filmmaking, and those of the diverse team he would gather around him.

By the time Linder arrived at Fox's TV station WTTG on Wisconsin Avenue in Washington, Herwitz had obtained the "limited blessing" of the FBI. Linder moved into a small office on the first floor without even an assistant, much less a computer, VCR, or editing room.

Herwitz and Linder rode downtown to the Hoover Building for another meeting with the FBI. This time they met Milt Ahlerich and Scott Nelson of the Public Affairs division. Ahlerich, the assistant director for public affairs and the Bureau's chief spokesman, had discussed the idea at length with Revell. It had promise, but it was still strictly a research idea at that point. The FBI had decided "there would be some research undertaken" to determine if it would be involved.

On the positive side, the show would aid in "fugitive publicity," since the Top Ten List program falls under the responsibility of Public Affairs. As of February 1988, the FBI's "Ten Most Wanted Fugitives" had included 415 persons on its list since the program's inception in March 1950. Of the 388 individuals caught from the list, 114 of them were as a direct result of citizen cooperation. Another program called the FBI Crime Resistance Program under the care of Public Affairs was a successful Neighborhood Watch-type effort fostering citizen protection and cooperation with law enforcement.

Both Ahlerich and Nelson had chased crooks in

their years as field agents and they were privately sold on the idea. It was "doable," since there were plenty of FBI fugitives, even not on the Top Ten, who could be caught with the help of television. But there were still problems—legal, operational, and bureaucratic.

The G-men outlined the Bureau's concerns for the TV-men. The legal division was concerned about the amount of publicity that would be generated and harmful to ongoing investigations. There was a statutory requirement that states that the FBI cannot talk about ongoing investigations, except when it serves a law enforcement purpose. But this show would serve the purpose of law enforcement. Legal also warned about precautions in portraying anything from an untried case, except that of a prison escapee. But there was pretrial publicity on every local newscast and in newspapers every day. The material in the show would have to be directly tied to the original case and couldn't prejudice a fair trial.

Prime-time TV shows thrived on violence, especially gratuitous blood-and-gore without a purpose. How many thundering gunshots, exploding blood packs, and twitching bodies would this show plaster across the screen in a half hour of family viewing time?

The Criminal Investigation Division had a manpower concern. If the show was to be done accurately, the agents involved in the cases would have to be advisors every step of the way. Budgets and resources were tight already, so how could they spare five full-time agents assigned to a TV show?

Ahlerich and Nelson would later admit there had been "a lot of pushin' and pullin'" around the bureau for months before the first show aired. They argued that the CID had some 400 agents spread around the country looking for thousands of fugitives. This would add some 20 million extra sets of eyes to the hunt. They would have to work out lots of details, making all sides happy. An 18-year veteran, Ahlerich had been a field agent for 10 years, seven of them as head of an anti-truck hijacking squad in New York. Nelson had been supervisor of a fugitive unit for six years during his 21 with the Bureau. They both knew what it was like to track a fugitive for years. They knew this show would help.

Linder and Herwitz tried to answer their concerns. Without a preliminary tape, it was hard to explain exactly what the show would do. By the end of the meeting, they had at least gotten the feeling the FBI would help. How much would be a matter of time. Within a few days, Linder received a packet with the latest Top Ten fugitives, containing a poster and two-page press release on each. The rest was up to him.

Back at his tiny office, Linder started recruiting some help. He started calling around to local universities with TV-film schools to find a production assistant.

Meanwhile, down in South Carolina, a recent University of Maryland graduate named Mike Walton got a call from his former assistant in the radio-TV-film division up in College Park, Maryland.

"I got a call from some guy at Channel Five who wants a professor to recommend a PA for him," she said. "It sounds like he's from the news department and is doing some anti-crime show."

Anxious to get into any job that would get his career going, Walton took the information and called WTTG. He got Herwitz's office and spoke briefly with Leslie Groves, who promised Linder would get back to him shortly. Normally, Ms. Groves was Herwitz's legal assistant, but when the new show arrived she took over as a production coordinator. Later, after the show debuted, she would become a vital link with Herwitz as the Fox executive overseeing the production.

The next morning, Walton's phone rang again.

"Hi, this is Michael Linder in Washington. Where is area code 803?"

"South Carolina," Walton laughed. "But I'll be there tomorrow if you'll interview me."

Linder explained just what the show was all about. There would be one major story each week, produced on the road, with the live broadcast from Washington. It would be called "Most Wanted." In addition to the show studio, there would be a newsroom with a staff of reporters responsible for researching cases for future broadcasts and coordinating with law enforcement. Police would be in constant contact with the staff, either checking on cases or pitching new ones. Viewers would call in tips on a toll-free hotline staffed by trained operators with cops standing by. Walton told Linder about his college and production background. They agreed to meet in Washington the following week.

When Walton arrived at WTTG, he and Linder walked down the street to lunch for an informal job interview. By the end of the appetizers, Linder knew he had his first staff member. Back at the office, Linder gave Walton some more specifics about the pilot show.

Linder opened a thick volume of the *Academy Players Directory,* featuring thousands of actors and actresses. He pointed to Treat Williams.

"This will probably be our host."

Then he tossed an FBI Ten Most Wanted poster across the desk.

"This is the first guy we're going after."

Walton caught his breath for a moment when he saw the photograph on the poster. He would see that face every day at work and every night in his dreams for the next eight months. But for that moment, he was chilled by the haunting eyes of an escaped Indiana prisoner serving six life sentences for murder-rape-kidnap and triple murder-arson: David James Roberts.

3

Roberts: Charged, Convicted, Escaped

David James Roberts was born on January 25, 1944, in Perth Amboy, New Jersey. He was the third of eight children born to Mary and David Roberts, a self-employed semitrailer truck driver. Shortly after his birth, the family moved to Englewood, New Jersey, then to Boston, where young David started his elementary education. He was raised Catholic, and studied catechism with the church, but never attended parochial school as his brothers and sisters did. David got along with his teachers, and had no "intense problems." His best grades were in math, his worst in English. He played hookey once in the fifth grade because of a haircut given to him by his brother.

With the elder Roberts's attempts to better his trucking business and looking for highway construction jobs, the family moved to St. Paul, Minnesota, then to Chicago. He was a stern man, but a fair disciplinarian. They lived a "decent lifestyle," and the sons helped their father in his business. Young David attended three Chicago high schools through his junior year, maintaining a "B" average and playing basketball and track. He didn't get his high school diploma, deciding he liked working and making money "as an adult male would." As a youngster, he thought of studying medicine, but once he got out of school in 1961, he liked working at a local steel company for $5 an hour instead. He even once thought of becoming a deputy sheriff.

But Roberts's teenage days would change drastically in the next few years. The following year, his older sister was shot to death accidentally in their yard by a stray bullet fired by a passing vandal. In 1965, his father died of cancer. Family members would later recall that David didn't seem to care about anything after that. He started getting into trouble.

Less than a year after his father's death, Roberts was arrested in March 1966, for the kidnap and rape of a Gary, Indiana, woman, but he was never tried for the crime. A few days later, however, he did forcibly rob three women in Crown Point. He made two of them get in the trunk of a car, then attempted to rape the third, but she resisted. The women made such a ruckus that Roberts was apprehended shortly after he ran a red light and was chased on foot by police.

Roberts would admit that he committed the robbery after drinking with friends, but insists that he never tried to rape anyone. He was "intoxicated and one thing led to another," and can't remember if he even got any money from his victims. He pleaded guilty to robbery, however, and was convicted of armed robbery, sentenced to 12 years at the Indiana State Reformatory in Pendleton, a maximum-security facility for men under age 30. In 1966, his I.Q. was rated at 116, indicating above average intellectual ability.

According to his future wife, Connie, she met Roberts when they were both in the same wedding party. In an interview with the *Staten Island Advance* 22 years later, she said they had been acquainted "for one or two years" before his arrest. She said that he later told her that he had robbed the women because he had no money to buy flowers for a dinner celebrating the anniversary of their meeting.

September 26, 1969, Roberts claims was the beginning of his real problems, particularly with the State of Indiana. He would later state that one of the white prison guards (all card-carrying members of the Ku Klux Klan, he claimed when I spoke to him in an interview for this book) told him, "Dave, don't be on the yard when the shooting takes place because we're gonna shoot some of these niggers up."

A lay-down demonstration to protest prison conditions did occur, and the guards opened fire with shotguns on some 200 inmates in the recreational yard. Two inmates were killed and 45 wounded. Roberts was hit in the left arm and leg. He said he was shot again in the stomach while lying in a prone position and offering no resistance. After spending a year in the hospital and therapy, Roberts would need four operations and a metal plate to fix his fractured arm and a brace for nerve damage to his leg. In prison, he would also contract pulmonary hystoplasmosis from eating in the dining room where pigeon droppings would fall into the food.

While at Pendleton, Roberts earned his high school diploma. During the summer of 1971, he began taking classes by correspondence with Indiana University/Purdue University at Indianapolis in computers and electrical engineering technology. Roberts's sentence was commuted by order of Governor Edgar Witcomb, after he served six-and-a-half years. Released on parole to a work release center, he continued his education, becoming interested in environmental studies and health, but never earning a degree. Shortly after his release, he and Connie were married, and eventually they had a son.

Roberts tried to start his life over, dedicating himself to his family and work. He sometimes worked two or three jobs at once. He worked in construction, then as a job placement counselor for the Metropolitan Manpower Commission, City of Indianapolis, earning $7,900 a year. He resigned for a brief time to work as a quality control inspector for Allison Diesel, a division of General Motors, but was fired for coming late. He was rehired, but then fired for not including his armed robbery conviction on his job application. Roberts claimed that he only applied there to see if the firm would hire a black man.

Back at Manpower, his supervisor, George Phillips, described him as "nothing but a perfect gentleman and a good employee." He was liked by his co-workers and received several merit raises. Sometime during those days, Roberts decided to file a $100,000 civil suit along with 10 other inmates against 11 correctional officers and the State of Indiana for injuries received in the Pendleton incident. The original complaint was filed on September 24, 1971. Motions, countermotions, interrogatories, affidavits from both sides flowed through U.S. District Court in Indianapolis for the next three years until a trail date was set. Meanwhile, Roberts found himself in some more serious legal battles.

On October 10, 1973, a man pulled into a Sears tire store on North Alabama Street in Indianapolis. He told the salesman, Bill Patrick, that he needed four new tires and a muffler installed on his 1970 Buick. Patrick, 25, was a conscientious worker, having worked there about four years. Before that he had worked in construction, real estate, and general repair work. A former Army paratrooper in Vietnam, he was married and had two young daughters.

Earlier that morning, Patrick got a call from a
man asking the price of steel-belted radial tires. He
wanted to get the car aligned that day, and mentioned his wife and he had a charge, but he might
pay cash. When the man arrived, Patrick wrote up
the work order, writing down the name Robert Johnson with the address of 3359 Meadow Court. He
wrote down the license plate, took the keys from the
man, shook hands on the price, and put in the work
order. The bill came to $320.88.

Patrick worked to about 5 o'clock that evening.
At closing, there was still a set of keys and bill for
the '70 Buick, so the security guard went out to check
on the car. It was gone, new tires and all. Indianapolis PD Detective Jerry Quackenbush was working part time at Sears in security and got a call about
the missing car.

"Let's wait and see if the owner comes to pick it
up," he said.

But the salesmen had already put the unclaimed
cars inside for the night.

"You still have the keys?" the detective asked in
amazement.

"Yeah."

Of course, the owner didn't show up that night.
Quackenbush checked out the name and address and
both were phony. He ran the registration and up
came the name of David James Roberts, currently
on parole. From parole officer Dennis Kresak, the
detective learned that Roberts was working at Allison Diesel. Quackenbush went over to the plant,
checked around the employee lot and found the car.
He went and got a warrant for Roberts's arrest.
Going over to Sears, he laid out a dozen or so photographs for Patrick. The salesman picked out Roberts immediately.

Quackenbush went over to Roberts's home to arrest him.

Roberts claimed the whole incident was a misunderstanding. His story was that he had driven into a service station to buy gas. The attendant cleaning the windshield informed Roberts that his inspection sticker had expired.

"Oh yeah?" Roberts replied.

The attendant said that the station could do the inspection, so Roberts agreed. But once the car was on the lift, the mechanic informed him that he would need four new tires. The man went out to help someone else.

"There was this individual getting work done on his car," Roberts would explain 16 years later. "I started talking to the attendant about these polyester tires on the rack... This other guy says to me, 'Are you thinking of buying these tires?' I said, 'I'm thinking about it.'

"'Look,' he said, 'they're not radials and Sears has them at a better price to this place.'"

The two talked, and "one thing led to another," and they called Sears to get a price. Sure enough, it was about $150 cheaper than the service station. The man needed cash, and would put the work on his charge card. As long as the bill didn't go over $300, Roberts agreed to pay the man $200 cash once the work was done. The stranger would charge the difference, since he needed the cash.

The two went over to Sears, and the salesman filled out the work order. Roberts remembered the salesman (Patrick) writing down the license number as he took things out of his car and put them in the truck for safekeeping.

Roberts only recalls the name "Robert Johnson" because it was on the arrest record.

"This guy 'Johnson' had my phone number and

I had a phone number on him. I asked if this work could be charged and he (Patrick) said 'Yes.' He put the name of the guy whose name was on the charge, because it was Robert Johnson and he was standing right there."

By 5:30 P.M., Roberts got a call from "this Johnson" saying the car was ready and to come down. He met the man in front of the Sears store. Roberts's car was around the corner at a Phillips gas station, he said. Roberts walked over, inspected the new tires and the muffler.

"So I paid him, he gave me the keys, and I left."

Roberts was shocked when Quackenbush came to arrest him. It was very confusing. Perhaps stolen tires had been put on the car, Roberts thought. The detective explained the situation, since Sears wanted its money, but Roberts held to his story. (Roberts would later explain that Kresak was trying to work the matter out with Quackenbush and Sears, but couldn't reach the parolee to discuss it.)

"Instead, I was frightened, put out by Sears having me arrested, because I was fired at that point, because they said I had a record and they weren't made aware of it."

Upset with the situation and wanting to sue Sears, Roberts hired an attorney, who took the deposition from Patrick on January 15 in the Marion County Prosecutor's Office. The case had been slated for court in December, but was postponed to January, then postponed again.

Quackenbush would later remember Patrick being worried about the deposition, since he had never been through anything like it before.

"I told him it's nothing to worry about," Quackenbush recalled. "They'll ask you what happened, that's all. Just tell the truth, that's all you can do. But I told him explicitly, they'll ask for it, don't give them your address, it's not pertinent to the case. The prosecutor will probably object.

"Well, they did ask for it, the prosecutor did not object, and Patrick gave it."

It would prove to be a fatal mistake.

Both Bill Patrick and his wife, Ann, 23, had worked at their respective jobs at Sears until about 5 P.M. on Saturday, January 19, 1974. A baby-sitter watched their two children, Heidi, 1, and Anna Marie, 3, at home in New Whiteland, a small commuter-farming suburb of Indianapolis. There had been nothing unusual, except for a telephone call about 5:30 P.M., from a man asking if the Patricks were home.

The couple went out that evening at about 8:30 with some longtime good friends, Philip and Rita Sevier, leaving the girls at Bill's brother Buddy's house until they returned. The couples took in a movie at the Regency Theater in neighboring Greenwood, then stopped at the Pizza Inn for pizza and a pitcher or two of beer. For a nightcap, they stopped at the Green Acres Tavern at about 2 A.M., then headed back to New Whiteland. No one was rowdy or drunk; it was just a fun evening out with friends.

They stopped at Southcourt Trailer Park first to pick up the Seviers' two children, and continued on to the Patricks' home at 851 Princeton Avenue, a quiet residential street, less than a mile from the main highway. The Patricks had left the front porch light on when they left, but noticed it was off when they returned. Ann got in their car to go get the children from Bill's brother, Buddy. Bill opened the front door and entered the house. Ann returned a short time later, having left the sleeping Anna at Buddy's. That was the last time the Seviers, or anyone, would see the Patricks alive.

* * *

At about 4:30 A.M., the sun hadn't even risen on the misty, foggy morning of January 20. Gary Hilton was driving his girlfriend to her home at 719 Princeton. When he got to the next intersection, he noticed smoke coming from the Patrick house. He flagged down Johnson County Deputy Sheriff Mark Flint, who called the fire department.

Eight minutes later, two fire trucks roared up. The one-story wood frame house was fully engulfed. Deputy Flint was running around the house, beating on the windows to see if anyone was inside. He knew someone had to be in there. Flames were shooting out the windows and thick black smoke was coming out the front screen door. Two firemen quickly broke through a back window, but the intense heat of the fire pushed them back. There was an infant lying in the crib in the rear bedroom. Another fireman came in a bunker coat and oxygen mask and climbed into the house to get the baby. He handed the infant out the window to Flint. It wasn't breathing.

Flint rushed to a waiting ambulance on the street, now crowded with neighbors. It was only four minutes to Johnson County Memorial Hospital on North Franklin, and he administered heart massage to the infant, but there was no pulse or breath. At the hospital, one-year-old Heidi Patrick was pronounced dead.

Back at the Patrick house, the fireman had fought their way through the front door and battled back the flames through the living room. They worked their way down the hallway a few feet, then turned into the next room where most of the flames were coming from. It was a chilling, gruesome sight. On the floor were a man and woman. The female body was unclothed, lying by the leg of the couch. Lying parallel to the south room wall, the male body had pants on, and was covered with burned debris. Bill and Ann Patrick were both obviously dead.

By Bill's body was a five-gallon gasoline can, its paint partly burned off. On the carpet was a charred trail, probably from a flammable liquid, leading back into the living room. At the end of the trail was a spout from a gas can and a black leather glove a few feet away. About two feet inside the front door was a partially used pack of matches. There was a strong odor of gasoline in the house.

There was no sign of forced entry, but there had been a struggle in the living room. The front door had been found standing wide open with the screen door closed. There were barbells and weightlifting equipment in another bedroom. In the master bedroom there were several guns and a bow-and-arrow on a rack on the south wall. The TV room clock had stopped at 4 A.M. The bathtub was filled to the bath level with smoke skim on the water. Some clothing had been taken from the master bedroom closet, and several neckties were found knotted in a single strain.

More police would arrive, and the arson investigator and coroner would be called, all supervised by New Whiteland Town Marshal Winfrey Burton. They questioned the neighbors and bystanders. One witness claimed to have seen a black man driving a gold-colored car by the Patrick house between 3:30 and 4 A.M. A fireman at the scene would later admit seeing something similar.

The shocking news of the tragedy raced through New Whiteland and Johnson County like a prairie fire. Nothing like this ever happened here. Burton and his team were investigating the possibility of foul play, and county prosecutor Joseph Van Valer announced that the state fire marshal had joined the

inquest. To add insult to injury, someone had burglarized the vacant Patrick home on Sunday evening.

The Indiana State Police were meeting with
Burton and Johnson County Sheriff Jack Means behind closed doors on Thursday, January 24, as the
Patricks were buried in the local cemetery. Their
obituaries in the *Daily Journal* said William Patrick
had been born in Germany on August 27, 1948, had
resided in New Whiteland for 16 years and was a
member of the VFW and Lutheran Church. He was
survived by his mother, two sisters, and four brothers. His father had predeceased him. Elizabeth Ann
Patrick was born on December 17, 1949, in Johnson
County and had lived there all her life. She was a
member of the Whiteland Christina Church, and was
survived by her parents, four brothers, and four sisters. Heidi Patrick had been born on January 17,
1973, having died less than three days after her first
birthday.

By the weekend, police had interviewed more
than 50 people in the neighborhood. "Rumors were
getting out of hand," one official said, but would not
say there was yet evidence of a homicide. They were
looking for a "concrete motive" in the case, though
a "strange vehicle" had been noticed on two occasions
that morning and they were eager to talk to the
individual driving it.

In New York City on Monday, January 28, 1973,
Muhammed Ali beat Joe Frazier in Super Fight II.
But in Johnson County, Indiana, the frightened citizens read much more shattering news that morning,
though most had heard rumors already.

David James Roberts, 30, actually heard about
it two days before. Separated from his wife, Roberts
was at the home of his girlfriend, Cynthia Ayres, a
court probation officer he had met the previous au-

tumn at IUPUI. At 3:55 on Saturday afternoon, there was a knock on the door. Standing there was Burton, Means, and Detective John Lasiter. Burton read Roberts his rights and a warrant for his arrest for first-degree murder, and he was taken into custody once more. His car, parked nearby, was impounded.

Police had been watching Roberts since Wednesday. They had gotten a lead about the Sears tire incident in which Patrick was the salesman. When Roberts was brought into Greenwood City Court Monday afternoon, he was charged in the murder of Heidi, but not the parents—yet. The prosecutor charged that the suspect's motive was to keep from being sent back to prison on a parole violation.

"We have a triple homicide at this point," Van Valer told the press. "We have no hard facts to charge him (Roberts) in the death of the parents. It was a very sophisticated homicide, but a very poor arson job ... A hell of a lot of good police work."

(Roberts would challenge this motive later, saying he would have only been convicted on a misdemeanor, meaning six years at most. It was not something he would kill three people for and set their house on fire.)

Roberts said little at the hearing, standing with his arms folded, his head down. He was sent to Johnson County jail, then transferred to Marion County Jail (Indianapolis) without bail.

A few days later, the final autopsy report would state that Heidi died of carbon-monoxide poisoning and smoke inhalation. As for her parents the cause of death was consistent with death due to asphyxiation. There had been a homicide, but by means unknown. Both were dead before the fire. There was evidence of possible constriction by adhesive tape over the mouth or wrists, but it was not conclusive. On Bill's body, the autopsy found small abrasions and scraping injuries on the forehead, a bruise on the right eyebrow, a large scraping abrasion over the right eye to the jaw, and a slight bruise under the chin. Ann had bruises inside her neck structures, on her chin, and over her eye. She had internal injuries in the neck, which hemorraged into the voice box and lungs, due to strangulation or a compressive force. There was no evidence of smoke inhalation and carbon monoxide poisoning in their bloodstream, which contained alcohol, but not enough to be a factor in their death. It was speculated that the victims had been bound with neckties found in the house.

In jail, Roberts maintained that he had never visited New Whiteland until he was arrested on the murder charge. He told police that he had spent most of January 19 at different friends' houses in Indianapolis. In the afternoon, he had gone to a Shell Station to buy "$5 or $6 worth of gas," and got his car washed. He was starting a new job on the 22nd, so he hadn't worked the previous week.

During the evening, he bought some malt liquors at a store, then watched TV at friends until about 1 A.M. He returned to his room at the Fall Creek YMCA, where he was sleeping at the time of the murders, until about 8 A.M. He had no witnesses to corroborate that.

By September, the grand jury had indicted Roberts on nine counts of murder and one arson. His court-appointed attorney, Tom Jones, requested, and was granted, a habeas corpus hearing for reasonable bail in Johnson County Circuit Court in Franklin.

The prosecution claimed that Roberts had rented the gas can found at the Patrick home from an Indianapolis service station. He had been seen by a number of New Whiteland residents in the area on January 19. Strange as it may seem, a black man driving a gold or tan Buick had pulled into a Standard service station on Route 31 owned by Buddy Patrick, brother of the deceased, and asked for directions to Princeton Avenue, the prosecution. There were no blacks residing in New Whiteland, and few in Johnson County, though it bordered Indianapolis. Such a visitor would definitely be noticed.

Marcos Torres, an attendant at Patrick's station, had sold a dollar's worth of gasoline to a black man with a mustache, medium afro, and black leather jacket. The man asked him where Princeton Drive was and the attendant told him. He was driving a brownish-gold Buick with a vinyl top with the fender skirts missing off the back. Joe and Jim Remington noticed that the hub caps and fender skirts were missing off the car. Terry Patrick, also a brother of the deceased noticed a dent over the left wheel of the dirty car. The witnesses also noticed that the car had a mag wheel on the right front. But under examination by Jones, none of them, except Buddy Patrick, would swear under oath that the man in the car that afternoon was the accused, David James Roberts.

Two attendants from Cronkite Shell in Indianapolis also testified. They said that a man known to them as David James Roberts, who regularly bought gas there, had come into the station between 3 and 5 P.M. on January 19. He put gas in his car and in a five gallon can. William Clardy said that he wrote the words "$5 deposit this can" in yellow crayon on the can. James Tucker filled the can, put a nozzle on it, and wrapped paper towels around the spout. Both had also identified a mug shot of Roberts shown to them by Indianapolis PD Sgt. James Irwin. He had tracked the charred can found in the Patrick home to the station with the help of Quackenbush and others. But these two key witnesses could not identify the man in court as the man who rented the gas can, though Roberts was the only other black man in the courtroom.

Clean-shaven without a mustache, and dressed in sport coat and tie, Roberts listened attentively and took notes.

The hearing had lasted a day-and-a-half. At noon, on September 17, Johnson Circuit Court Judge Robert Young set bail at $10,000, despite the multiple murder charges, three of which mandated the death penalty upon conviction. Young would later maintain that "if there is not sufficient evidence to keep a defendant without bond, then bond must be set." A number of the state's key witnesses had failed to identify Roberts, he added.

Roberts was not out yet. On Jones's request, a change of venue was granted due to negative publicity and alleged threats from the Ku Klux Klan. The trial was switched to Angola in Steuben County in the northeast corner of Indiana, about 180 miles from New Whiteland. Roberts was transferred to the Steuben County Jail, since he couldn't get a bail-bondsman in Johnson County to help him. A week later, he would be able to get $1,000 cash and find a bondsman to put up the $10,000 bond. Freed until his trial sometime in 1975, Roberts returned to Indianapolis, his Manpower job, and eventually, his wife.

Glad to be out of jail, Roberts tried not to think about the coming trial. Within two weeks after his return home, he was contacted by his attorney, Sheldon Cohan of Gary, about the federal suit against the State of Indiana over the Pendleton shootings. Back in March, the Indiana Court of Appeals had ruled that state could not plead immunity in the case, reversing the Indiana Supreme Court's dismissal of it. The Attorney General's office wanted to take his depositions. Roberts was elated—they would finally get the suit underway. Previously, eight of the nine guards had been found not guilty of civil rights violations. One pleaded guilty and was given a one-year suspended sentence. The plaintiffs, now seeking a total of $1.3 million in damages, charged that undue force was used to quell the riot.

Roberts was also working three jobs: counselor with the Manpower Commission, loading produce at Ciado's Fruit at night, and doing maintenance work for his landlord. He had no spare time; his days and nights were full.

He advised Cohan that he "suspected some hanky-panky from state officials," considering he was out on bond on a multiple-murder/arson charge.

On November 7, the Roberts trial against the state with 11 other Pendleton inmates began in U.S. District Court before Judge S. Hugh Dillin. The trial was expected to last two weeks. The jury was selected, and the proceedings continued for six days. Roberts testified on the fifth day, November 13. Proud of his performance in court, Roberts was relieved it would soon be over. He would even claim later that "the court got into an uproar" over his testimony, and the spectators and attorneys wanted to shake his hand.

Five days later, Roberts would be severed from the case, and granted a mistrial. Another, much more serious problem, had developed that week outside of the courtroom.

It was bitter cold in the early morning of November 14, when "Helen" (name changed to protect the real victim) got off work. She was the night front desk manager at the Roadway Inn on the west side of Indianapolis, only a few minutes' drive from the famed Speedway.

At 19, she was a single mother, struggling to

support her six-month-old son, Jason. His father, whom she had never married, was serving in the U.S. Navy on a ship off Guam. Four years ago, she had given birth to another child by this man, but had given it up for adoption. Her mother and sister lived nearby and helped out when they could.

By the time she finished up the night books, it was a quarter after two in the morning. First, she had to pick up her son, at a baby-sitter's house. When she got to her car, a 1970 Malibu with a bench seat, she couldn't find the keys in her purse. She looked inside to see the keys still in the ignition. That afternoon she had been in such a hurry, she forgot to take them out. It was her first car in a while, and she had only had it eleven days.

One of the clean-up men said he would help her, but she waited 15 minutes before he came out. It was so cold, and the two or three minutes she stood by the car seemed like an eternity, until he got the coat hanger to open the lock.

By 2:30 A.M., she was picking up Jason. That afternoon before work, Helen had dressed her little son in a camino, white with yellow print and flowers, and yellow booties. She wrapped him in a warm blue blanket, laid him on the passenger side, and started home through the sleeping residential area. The only signs of life as she drove down 34th Street were a few gas stations, fast food places, and motels. She passed her mother's house at Mueller, but the lights were out so she didn't stop.

At High School Road, a main route through the area, she slowed down and stopped for a flashing red light at the intersection. As she passed the Clark Station at the corner, she noticed a man walking down the road from the parking lot.

Suddenly, the man was right next to her door. He had a gun and banged on the window. Helen was frozen with fear, as the man went around the passenger side and jumped in her car. Pointing the gun at her, he shouted, "Just drive!"

"I need a ride to 16th Street," he said, still holding the gun next to her side.

Now trembling, Helen tried to step on the gas, but hit the break instead. The car stopped. There was no one else around. She was helpless. All she could do was turn right down High School Road, as the man demanded. Her baby was on the seat between them.

She would describe him later as a black man, in his mid-twenties, six-foot, 160 pounds. He had a medium black afro and brown eyes. He was wearing brown pants, a plaid shirt, and a long brown overcoat.

He ordered her to turn on a side street. When Helen stopped the car, the man grabbed her, saying he was going to drive. She screamed.

Pulling her hair, he put the gun to her head.

"Stop screaming or I'll blow your ass off!"

She obeyed and switched places with the man as he slid over her and Jason to get behind the wheel. They headed back to High School Road and turned north.

"Do you have any money?" he demanded.

"No," Helen gasped.

He grabbed her billfold, opened it, spilling the change on the front seat. There was a dollar or two. No credit cards except a baby shoe store card and a bank machine card.

"Do you have a checkbook?"

"Yes."

"Where?"

"In the glove compartment."

The man reached over and opened the flap, taking out the checkbook.

"How much money is in this?"

"Forty dollars or something," Helen whispered as she opened up the checkbook.

"Write me a check for thirty dollars."

Helen started writing, barely able to hold the pen or write, numbed with fear and cold. She stopped writing.

"Who should I make it out to?"

"I don't know," he shouted, getting impatient. "Make it out to cash! How long have you had a checking account, anyway?"

"Year and a half, maybe," Helen mumbled, starting to cry.

"Make it out to Sherida Nelson."

"How do you spell the first name?"

"S-h-e-r-i-d-a. Can you spell Nelson?"

"Yes," Helen replied, finishing the check. She tore it from the book and handed it to the man. He stuffed it in his coat pocket.

They passed 39th Street, apartment complexes on both sides. There were lots of people living here, but no one could help her now. The man pulled into a little church parking lot by the Gateway Apartments. He drove through the lot, then back onto High School Road, pulling off into Village Apartments. He drove into the parking lot next to a trash bin. There was no one around.

The man turned and snarled at Helen.

"I'm going to get a piece of ass from you!"

She started crying again, upset and terrified. Jason was asleep on the front seat.

"Get in the back seat!"

Helen climbed over and the man followed her. He ordered her to take off her pants as he slid his down to his knees. Helen was lying half-naked on the back seat, her back shoved against the side of the car. He raped her.

She couldn't remember later how long it lasted. Finally, the man told her to put on her shoes and get in the front seat. Jason was still asleep there. The shoes were mixed up in the back with the diaper bag and everything. She fumbled around, and the man got angry.

"You better hurry up if you care anything about your baby."

They got back in the front seat, and the man drove them back onto High School Road. Even though he was kidnapping her and her baby and had just violently raped her, the man started chatting. He asked Helen about when she had gone to high school, about her family and other details.

Shocked and confused, Helen answered the man's questions. She was crying, wondering if she would live to see her family again. They drove maybe 25 minutes, past familiar landmarks, including her mother's house, still dark. He pulled into another apartment complex.

"Get in the back! I want another piece of ass."

He also commanded Helen to put sleeping Jason on the back seat, which she did. The man climbed over, and made her disrobe again. He repeated the brutal act again.

When he finished this time, the man got out of the car, saying he wanted to look in the trunk. He needed some tire tools, he said.

"Get out of the car and open the trunk. And don't run or scream because nobody here will give a damn."

Helen didn't scream. She just stood there frozen.

The man opened the trunk and took out a crow bar.

"Get in!"

"Can I take Jason with me?" Helen pleaded.

No, the man replied, he would take care of the

baby. Helen took Jason's seat out of the trunk, so she could fit inside. She got in and the man slammed the hood over her.

Helen pressed her ear to the back seat, desperate to hear Jason breathing. She heard the door open and slam shut. They started driving away. If only she knew Jason was okay. He usually sang to himself when he was sleeping. Faintly, she could hear her little man singing, softly.

For what seemed like a long time, they bounced on bumpy side roads. She could hear the gravel bounce off the car as they sped along. The car stopped, and she could hear the man get out.

"What are you doing?" she shouted through the back seat.

"I'm taking a leak."

Helen heard the passenger side door open and shut. She couldn't hear Jason anymore. She screamed. Where was he? She just wanted to pinch his rosy cheek.

"Please don't hurt my baby!" she pleaded through the seat. "Do something to make him cry so I can hear him."

"He's sleeping." And the car sped off.

Helen felt the car turn several times, going faster than before. She kept pleading with the man to make Jason cry. She had to hear her baby.

The man just rambled on about his three sons, how he had just gotten out of the state pen and had to hustle to make a living. Finally, he said he would let Helen out at the Watergate Apartments. They drove a little longer and stopped.

"Let me out!" No reply. She heard the man get out of the car. If only there was some way she could hear Jason, make him cry. Crawling lengthwise in the trunk, she kicked against the back seat. Maybe she could jar him awake.

Not a sound from inside the car. She could hear cars passing outside, but they seemed far away. Where was she? Where was Jason?

Groping around the dark trunk, she found a hook where the tire was. She took the hook and ripped out part of the trunk top. All she could see were her temporary license tags. The stereo speaker was hanging down, so she tore that out. Still, she couldn't see anything over the roof of the car. There was light from a street light, but she couldn't see the pole or the lamp.

She picked up the biggest piece of metal she could find in the trunk and started slamming it against the trunk lid. She screamed and banged— it seemed like hours.

There was somebody walking outside the car. She screamed for the person to let her out, but there was no answer. A moment later, there was.

"Lady, how did you get in there?" said another man's voice. It was much kinder than the one that belonged to the man who had just terrorized her and her infant son.

"A man put me in here!" she shouted.

Helen heard the man repeat her answer to someone else. She started screaming about Jason, was he in the car? They said there was no baby in the car. Helen was getting hysterical. She asked them four, five times where the baby was. They tried to calm her down, asking her if there was a latch inside the trunk. There wasn't, she replied, still pleading for her son.

She could hear them trying to pry open the trunk. Finally the lock gave. The trunk opened and daybreak poured in. Still dazed, she could see a fireman and a policeman standing there, staring at her.

Helen stumbled to the front seat. No Jason! She scrambled all around the car, calling his name. The fireman tried to calm her, while the policeman, Robert Hamlin, called for back-up. Within a few moments, another squad car arrived. Helen got in the car and gave the best description she could of the man who had kidnapped her, raped her, and now had her baby.

The police took Helen to the hospital to be examined. A report later would confirm she was raped, but there was no evidence of trauma. There was "semen in the vaginal bulb," it said.

Indianapolis PD Detective John Larkins had just started the day shift at 6:30 A.M. There was a call about a woman locked in a car trunk who said that she had been raped and her baby was missing. By 7 A.M., Larkins had gotten a helicopter, and along with Detective Jerry Campbell, he flew the victim around the area she described. They hovered low over the northeast and northwest areas of the city, trying to determine which apartment complex she had been raped in. Helen couldn't identify any of them, and they couldn't see a trace of her baby. By now, the weather had gotten colder and snow was blowing hard.

Larkins took Helen home, where her family was already waiting. Indianapolis residents were waking up to a media blitz, looking for a missing infant. A few hours later, Larkins returned to take Helen downtown to headquarters. Still no word on Jason. In the homicide office, Larkins showed Helen more than 900 mug shots, but she couldn't recognize her kidnapper-rapist. She did remember that he had a thin mustache, had a tooth missing, and spoke very intelligently. An artist drew a composite sketch from her description.

Meanwhile, some children walking to school on East 38th Place made a discovery they'd never forget the rest of their lives. Robert Glaspy's son ran back in the house, saying he had seen a body beside the road. Glaspy pulled on his coat and ran down the frozen street. He found an infant on the side of the road. It was a shady wooded road, not very often traveled.

Glaspy dashed home and called the police. Officer Melvin Soots arrived within minutes of his call. Glaspy got into the officer's car and they drove to where the body was lying—4508 East 38th Drive— near little puddles of frozen water. The infant was dead from exposure, still clutching blades of grass in its tiny hands. The autopsy would say it was placed on the frozen ground alive, and had crawled several hundred yards along the snowy roadside before it died.

Helen's family heard on the radio that a baby had been found on East 38th. The police chaplain arrived shortly afterward to take Helen and the family to the scene to identify her son. By the time she got there, the tiny street was jammed with police cars, an ambulance, and reporters. She didn't have to get out of the car to look. A friend of the family had gotten there first and identified the frozen infant as Jason.

This was one of the most heinous crimes in the city's history. The public was shocked and outraged. The police were baffled and searching.

Larkins went over to the service station at 34th and High School Road where the victim said she had been abducted. The night attendant was Frank Jessup, a local law student working his way through school. He told Larkins that a man had walked up behind him in the tiny store that night and scared him. Jessup turned around and looked at the man. He asked Jessup for change of a dollar, bought some potato chips, and left. Later, a convenience store clerk would make a similar statement, saying the man walked back south toward 34th and High School. Larkins showed Jessup hundreds of mug shots, but he couldn't identify any.

Back at headquarters, homicide was shifting through hundreds of leads from concerned citizens. Some would lead nowhere, but each had to be followed up.

Quackenbush was working at his desk in auto theft, when he overheard Larkins and Campbell talking about the case.

"We've gone through some old cases, and we don't know anybody who puts people in trunks," they were saying to another detective.

"What are you talking about?" Quackenbush asked.

"That murder last night. The guy raped her, put the baby out, locked her in the trunk of the car, and left her there."

Quackenbush knew of a man who had that same m.o.

Down in Johnson County, Sheriff Jack Means had been reading about the kidnap-rape-murder search in the local papers. It was banner headlines in all the local newspapers, especially the *Indianapolis Star* and *News*. The m.o. of a rapist locking a woman in a trunk was familiar to him too. He quickly called up an old friend, Detective Lt. Jack Coffey at Indianapolis P.D., who switched him to Larkins. Means told Larkins about a man who had been in the Johnson County Jail recently awaiting a change of venue. He had the same m.o. of the man Larkins was looking for. In fact, up in Crown Point, he had been charged with rape and convicted of a robbery during which he locked two women in the trunk of a car.

Following the leads given him by Means and Quackenbush, Larkins hunted through the files for the man's mug shot. It wasn't hard to find. He went over to Helen's, then to the service station attendant. They both immediately picked the same mug shot out of the lineup of photographs Larkins spread before each of them.

It was a photograph of David James Roberts.

Roberts remembered later being in a great mood that week. He was back at work, his testimony went well, and he had reconciled with Connie. But he had been upset to read about that little baby dying and its poor mother. Being a new father, he could understand her grief.

On Friday night, November 15, the couple decided to get a babysitter for their 14-month-old son. Roberts had a touch of the flu that his son had gotten, but this was the first chance they would have to go out since he had gotten home from Angola. They went to a nearby theater, and during the movie, Roberts would distinctly recall breaking a gold tooth on some popcorn. After the show, they were going to stop by Stouffers to get something to eat. Connie called to check on their son first, but she got no answer.

Their apartment at 4401 College Avenue was just a few blocks away, so they walked back. On the way, Roberts noticed a car following them. He remembered that his license had expired in jail. He told Connie that a car was following them, and they turned onto their street. It was still behind, never passing them. The couple stopped and so did the car.

Within seconds, one man, then two, came up to them. One identified himself as a police officer.

"Are you David James Roberts?" Larkins asked.

"Yes," Roberts replied.

The detective asked for some identification, and Roberts pulled out his expired license and some photo ID's.

"David James Roberts. You are under arrest for murder."

Connie gasped and began to cry. She began to holler at the police.

"Not again!"

Roberts tried to calm his wife.

"Is it in Marion County?" he asked the police.

"Yes," Larkins replied.

At least it wasn't Johnson County coming after him, Roberts thought. The police took him inside. They had already gotten a search warrant and combed the apartment when Roberts and his wife were at the movies. They found a pair of undershorts which matched the pattern that Helen said her assailant had worn. Under a mattress, they found a small automatic with the barrel protruding about an inch—same as Helen's description.

(In an interview with the *Staten Island Advance* 14 years later, Mrs. Roberts would accuse Larkins of duplicity that night.

"I was beside myself," Mrs. Roberts told reporter Laura Bruno. "The police were going into the house. The babysitter said they were in the house for 20 minutes. Larkins took me in a room and told me,'Don't you worry about anything—this is a scare tactic.' I told him I was getting an attorney and he told me, 'Don't get a lawyer—he'll be out tomorrow.' So I thought, maybe I'll wait."

Larkins told the *Advance* that Mrs. Roberts was uncooperative and "as cold-blooded as Roberts.")

Roberts was taken downtown for questioning. The police said they had an eyewitness to the murder he was accused of, and Roberts demanded to see the person. By then it was 11 P.M., and they couldn't arrange a lineup until Saturday morning. All dressed up for a night on the town, David Roberts instead spent it in jail.

Early the next morning, Roberts was brought to a holding cell for more questioning, then served coffee and doughnuts for breakfast. He was marched out on a line, chained to several other prisoners, still unaware, he would claim later, of the charges being filed against him. They went into another holding cell area, and one of the men with Roberts commented that there were "cameras out there" and "they were really trying to get somebody."

The suspect thought he was going to a lineup, not court. As Roberts would describe years later, his name was called and he stepped into the courtroom. The first person he saw was Connie in tears, trying to reach him in the commotion. With her was a friend of Roberts named Richard Hailey who had recently graduated from Butler University Law School. They talked frantically for a moment, then Roberts's name was called.

"Come on, Dave, we've got to go before the judge," Hailey said.

The three walked over before Municipal Court Judge Charles A. Wiles, and a litany of charges were read. Roberts was startled to hear the words "carnal knowledge."

He pleaded with the judge that he was not the man they were seeking. But the charges continued, as did the flashbulbs. One cameraman was even standing behind the judge, Roberts would recall, shooting photos of the accused. The case would be continued on November 25 and the suspect held without bond, the judge said.

Only the next day, Sunday, did Roberts first learn from his attorney in the federal case, Sheldon Cohan, that he was accused of "the city's crime of the century." He was dumbfounded. On Monday, he would be granted a mistrial in his case against the state, since a poll of the jurors revealed they all knew of the current charges against the plantiff, Roberts. (Ten other plantiffs in the case would be awarded a total of $43,000 in 1976. On July 7, 1980, the court dismissed Roberts's action for want of prosecution.)

Larkins was still continuing his investigation. The 17-year-old girl on Helen's check to the rapist had passed a lie detector test that she had nothing to do with the crime or the man. Monday afternoon, Helen "positively" identified Roberts as her assailant, and "did not hesitate" when she picked him in a police lineup. Both Hailey and a police legal advisor were present when the victim was given a card with the numbers of the men in the lineup, and she marked an "X" next to Roberts's number. Jessup was not allowed to see the lineup, since Hailey objected that the attendant had already seen some of the men in the squad room. None of Roberts's fingerprints were found in the car, but police pointed out that many were smudged and this "was not unusual." There was other evidence found in Roberts's apartment to link him with the crime, police said. A news photograph in the Sunday edition of the *Indianapolis Star-News* showed Larkins holding up a coat taken from Roberts's car.

Not only was Roberts front-page news, but also Judge Young was under fire for releasing him on $10,000 bond. The judge stood his ground, saying the evidence was not sufficient to hold him without bond. The media, particularly *Star* columnist Thomas R. Keating would criticize the city for hiring a convicted felon at Manpower. A Manpower official admitted there was "a very serious mistake in this case," and Roberts was suspended from his job, pending the outcome of the new charges.

Over the next three years, Roberts would probably set a record for most days in a courtroom. Indiana law stated that a defendant had a right to a speedy trial with 72 days. Following Roberts's Indianapolis arrest, Van Valer said the Patrick case would go to trial on May 12 in Angola and he would seek the death penalty. He was in for a surprise.

In February 1975, the selection of the grand jury which would hear Roberts's Indianapolis case, among others, was declared illegal. Another Marion County grand jury would indict him on two counts of kidnapping, one count of rape while armed with a deadly weapon, and one count of first-degree murder.

With Criminal Court Judge John W. Tranberg presiding, the trial began on June 2 in a packed courtroom. It was still news, a thorn in the public's psyche. Roberts would be represented by court-appointed public defenders, Michael Riley and Richard Sallee. The prosecutors for Marion County would be Charles Johnson and Patricia Woodward. The trial was expected to last a week.

On the second day of the trial, after the jury was seated, Johnson challenged the date of the indictment, saying it indicated the alleged crimes occurred on November 13, not the 14th, as reported elsewhere. He was overruled. Tranberg ordered the jury of seven women and five men to be sequestered due to substantial media coverage of the case.

The third day, the victim, now 20, took the stand. She broke down several times in describing the events of the morning in question. Riley had charged in his opening statement that the victim could not identify Roberts when looking at police mug shots that morning. But when Johnson asked her if her assailant was in court, she pointed to Roberts.

The fourth day, the prosecution failed to get the gun submitted as evidence because Tranberg ruled it had been obtained without a proper search warrant.

Roberts's attorneys attempted to get a delay to find witnesses to verify that he was at home on the night and morning of the alleged crimes. The accused maintained he had gotten home from work about 5:30 P.M., and his son was sick with an ear infection. At about 10:15 or 10:30 in the evening, he went downstairs to watch television with Connie, who was on vacation from work, but up making a bridal gown for a wedding. Roberts was ill and couldn't go to his night job. His wife gave him a cold tablet, and he fell asleep on the couch next to her until morning. She went to bed in the other room with their son about 2 A.M. Roberts never left the house, and Connie was willing to stand by her husband's story. He testified that he had never seen the victim until his probable cause hearing.

But they wouldn't need the extra time. The next day, June 6, Tranberg declared a mistrial.

In questioning Roberts, Johnson asked about a previous robbery conviction.

"Was it a guilty plea?" Johnson inquired.

Before Roberts could answer, Johnson asked, "Did the circumstances involve locking the victim in the trunk?"

Riley jumped to his feet. He argued for an immediate mistrial based on misconduct by the prosecution in the form of a statement that would prejudice the jury.

Tranberg told the court that a simple admonishment to forget Johnson's question would not remove it from the jury's minds. He dismissed the jury and set a new trial date of September 8. The victim would have to testify and relive the horror once more.

The Patrick murder-arson case wasn't moving very fast either. On July 3 in Angola, Judge John Burger delayed the trial to "the fall," citing pretrial publicity.

Johnson County would get their day with Roberts before Marion County. On November 7, more than two years since Bill Patrick met Roberts at Sears, the triple murder-arson trial began in Angola before Judge John R. Burger in Steuben County Circuit Court. Out in California, Patty Hearst was going on trial in San Francisco, and Lynette "Squeaky" Fromme was going to court in Sacramento for her attempt on the life of President Gerald R. Ford.

Twenty-five prospective jurors were excused before a jury of four women and eight men were seated. The first piece of evidence, a hair found in the gloves left at the crime, failed to point toward Roberts. The State Police crime lab tests could only indicate it has racial characteristics of "negroid." No latent fingerprints could be found on the charred gas can.

On November 15, both Cronkite Shell attendants took the stand. Neither could identify Roberts at the bond hearing more than a year ago. The accused looked remarkably different. He was dressed in a three-piece suit, had lost considerable weight, his afro trimmed and mustache gone.

William Clardy took the stand and identified the writing on the charred can as his own. Roberts's attorney, Tom Jones, reminded Clardy that he couldn't identify Roberts in Franklin, though he was seated at the defense table. Moments earlier, he had identified Roberts when questioned by the new Johnson County prosecutor, Charles Gantz. And did he know for sure that Roberts had rented that can, asked Jones.

"To be honest," Clardy replied, "I just don't know."

Gantz had Clardy step down and take a closer look at Roberts. Again, he was sure. Jones pushed the witness further. Was the man at the table, the same one who came into the station that day and put a $5 deposit on the can?

"I just know," Clardy said, shaking his head.

James Tucker also took the stand and identified Roberts. Jones pressed him also about not being able to identify him at the hearing. Now, Tucker said he was sure. Roberts looked more now like he did on the day in question.

The defense brought only two witnesses to try to undermine the credibility of the prosecution's witnesses and alleged motives. Roberts took lots of notes, but did not testify on his own behalf.

Roberts's attorney in the Sears theft case, Patrick Chavis III, testified that his client had passed a polygraph test about the incident.

To prove that Roberts rented the can at Cronkite Shell that day, the prosecution was using one of Roberts's canceled checks for $5 dated January 19, payable to the station. The defense called Roberts's insurance agent, Marshall H. Bluett, to challenge the check theory.

Roberts said when he was at the station earlier in the week, Bluett saw him and pulled in to get a check for an outstanding premium. Roberts gave him a check, but postdated it for January 19. Bluett deposited it, Roberts claimed, on the 15th, proving he was not at the service station on Saturday. Bluett testified he wasn't sure what day he met Roberts there, but it was "unlikely" that it was Saturday, since he passed there only on weekdays to pick up his wife from work. Roberts claimed the Cronkite check was also postdated.

In cross-examination, however, Bluett said it was possible he accepted a postdated check from Roberts. He had later gotten another check from Roberts, which he attempted to deposit, but the account was closed. He couldn't remember the day in question. In fact, all the checks mentioned were returned for insufficient funds. The service station owner said he would accept a postdated check from a customer he knew "very well," and Roberts was an "outstanding customer."

After six days of testimony, the case went to the jury at 7:40 on the evening of Monday, November 17. Just before midnight, they had reached a verdict. Roberts was guilty on all counts of murder, arson, and burglary. Sentencing was set for November 26.

Roberts, now a convicted murderer, was being rushed down to Indianapolis for his kidnap-murder-rape trial, which was beginning there the next day.

Roberts's attorneys were stunned at the verdict.

Albert Friend, an Angola attorney who assisted Jones, called the case "strange and bizarre" in an interview with the *Indianapolis Star*. He had a list of 21 "unanswered questions."

"It is my sincere belief that they have arrested and tried the wrong man," he said.

Jones added that the real murderer was still running around Johnson County.

"If ever there was a 'Rush to Judgment' this was it," Jones said. "Never in fifteen years of practicing law have I seen things as strung-out as this lawsuit."

Jones cited the fact that there were no signs of forced entry in the Patrick home. The Patricks could not have been surprised by anyone because Heidi had been put to bed and the bathtub was filled with water. Only one of the state's witnesses could truly identify Roberts. The state had brought in a man, then built a case without bringing in all the evidence.

Prosecutor Gantz had rebutted those accusations already in court. He had placed photographs of the three victims on the witness stand.

"If they hadn't been rubbed out," Gantz told the jury, "they would be here to tell us what happened. But Roberts did leave his calling card (the gas can).

"What do we do with people who murder citizens? What do we do to people who set fire to dead bodies and that fire kills babies? This man is pretty intelligent. It took an intelligent man to commit this crime."

It had been a "near-perfect homicide," Gantz continued, and the victims died with only the slightest traces of what caused their deaths. The checks and dates didn't coincide with the defendant's claims. The polygraph that Roberts passed in the theft didn't eliminate motive because Roberts's attitude in the case would be Patrick's word against his. And the variables and procedure made the test unreliable.

"That's the man who killed the people in New Whiteland," Gantz said, pointing at the accused. "Where was he from about eleven P.M., January 19 to about four-thirty P.M. on January 20, 1974? He was right there in the Patrick house doing his dirty work."

Now it was back to Indianapolis. On November 19, Roberts's attorneys Sallee and Riley asked for a delay based on the publicity from Angola. Judge Tranberg would take it under advisement until he determined if a proper jury could be seated. The next day, six men and six women were seated. The prosecution couldn't mention the triple murder-arson conviction. Again, the defense motioned for time, citing Roberts's emotional stress.

The victim told her tale of horror once more on November 22. A section of her testimony was:

Johnson: Is your attacker in this courtroom?
Victim: Yes he is (hand pointing at Roberts).
Johnson: Are you trying to say that our client looks like the man that night?
Victim: I'm trying to say he is the man. I'll never forget him.

Sallee made an intensive, slow cross-examination of the victim, including:

Sallee: How do you know for sure that he is the man?
Victim: I'll never forget him. I spent two hours with him. He raped me twice and killed my baby.

When George Jessup, the station attendant, took the stand, Riley challenged his description of the man he saw that night. Jessup stated that he knew the person's height because he (5'11") was at the same eye level as the man. Riley had Jessup stand back-to-back with Roberts, and the accused (6'3") was 4–5 inches taller than the witness.

The prosecution tried to call three women from Crown Point who claimed to be raped by Roberts in 1966, but was denied. When Larkins took the stand, the defense argued that a suspect, William Morton, who better fit the description of the rapist, had been ruled out too quickly. Larkins countered that he knew the man in question. He was "a cool cat" and was not very articulate, as both the victim and Jessup stated the man they saw was.

The prosecution brought two surprise witnesses, a couple who said they had seen Roberts in a bowling alley near 34th and High School the night of the crime. The defense challenged that the couple was "anti-negro," and volunteered their testimony a year after the crime.

The defense also challenged the victim's description fitting Roberts. Six witnesses, including the defendant's wife, took the stand to state that he did not have a mustache at the time of the alleged crime, as the assailant did. Roberts did not take the stand to deny his guilt as he did in the first trial. His appearance could prompt questions about the Patrick murder-arson conviction.

The prosecution brought an employee of a local costume shop who testified that at least a dozen false mustaches were rented in October 1974. Johnson even ripped a fake stash off a witness to demonstrate how easily it could fool people.

The "final visceral arguments," as reported by the *Indianapolis Star*," included Prosecutor Woodward mentioning that the baby died clutching blades of grass in its tiny hands. The defense pleaded to the jurors' sense of humanity. Riley described how inmates at the state prison had constructed the electric chair from the scaffolding of an old gallows. He also told how an inmate facing execution has his head shaved and his pants slit before being electrocuted.

The defendant showed little emotion during the closing statements, while the victim sat, clutching her hands and holding back tears, according to the *Star* report.

"He (Roberts) is sitting in the chair of innocence and the state wants to put him in the chair of death," Riley told the jury, as he rolled an empty chair in front of them to symbolize the chair of death.

"The death penalty is the ultimate judgment, and only God has the power to take someone's life."

The defense stood on the victim's testimony.

"That is the man," Johnson said, pointing to Roberts. "Would you ever forget the man who raped you twice and threw your baby out in the snow to die? There has been the strongest possible identification (from the victim) of Roberts.

"You have only one possible verdict. If there has been a case in Indiana where the death penalty is called for, this is it."

The jury got the case on at 11:45 on Tuesday morning, November 25, but not for long. Their emotions would get the best of them.

After deliberating for eleven hours, the jurors recessed and were taken to their rooms at the Indianapolis Athletic Club for the night. They resumed at 9:30 the next morning, Wednesday, November 26.

At 2:45 in the afternoon, a woman juror had been taken to the hospital when she started breathing in "great gulps." A second had broken into tears during the deliberations. A third complained of stomach pains and her doctor sent her to the hospital. A fourth had trouble breathing in the crowded jury room.

Judge Tranberg called in the remaining jurors and decided there was an insufficient number of them to continue. It was another mistrial! Roberts hung his head and cried. The victim sat motionless, tears rolling down her cheeks. It still wasn't over.

More than two years would pass before the Indianapolis case would be finally decided. But just a month after the second trial, the Angola jury sentenced Roberts to death for the Patrick murders-arson. He was saved from the electric chair when a judge reduced the sentence to five life terms after ruling that a portion of the Indiana death penalty statue was unconstitutional.

On January 14, 1977, after four-and-a-half hours of deliberation, a jury found Roberts guilty on all counts. The jurors stated that the victim's testimony—her third time on the stand—and the ID by Jessup were the most crucial pieces of evidence. Roberts did not take the stand in his own defense. He was convicted on the charge of simple rape, since no evidence of a gun was ever introduced in the trial.

Hearing the verdict, Roberts pounded his fists on the table and was shaking his head as it was read. He then broke into tears.

Before being sentenced for 21 years for the rape and a life term for the murder (six total with the Patrick murder-arson), Roberts addressed the Marion County Criminal Court on January 28.

"I would like to say at this time that though I stand before you convicted by a jury, I do not, I repeat I do not stand here before you a guilty man," he said. "I never saw that diabolic, lying (victim's real last name) girl before in my life outside of this courtroom, and I not only did not rape her, but as a rationally sane individual and father of a young child myself, I am not capable of committing such a crime.

"It would seem to me that after winning such cases as the Scottsboro Boys in this country it would suffice the judicial system of this country for the next four hundred years.

"I am not guilty of the crime. I did not commit it. I feel that this court has tied my hands and gagged my mouth by denying me the motions I have put forth. I'm just not, I'm just not guilty of the crime.

"If the court had given me a chance to affirm my innocence, I feel that I could have proven that I am not guilty of it."

The ordeal was finally over for Helen who had to relive the horror that night five times on the witness stand (probable cause hearing, the grand jury, and three jury trials), enduring intense, humiliating cross-examination. Her life was even threatened in

July 1975, before the second trial, according to a report in the *Indianapolis Star*. After three harassing phone calls, two from a man who said she better not testify in the next trial, the police gave her round-the-clock protection.

The legal system made little sense to her. Why did she have to sit in a packed courtroom and look at the man accused of the crime, and made to look like a liar? In an interview with the *Star* during the second trial, only a few days before the jury would be deadlocked, the victim told a reporter that she did it for her baby. She wore a picture of her baby on a chain around her neck.

"I don't like being talked to like a liar," she said. "That makes me angry. They kept on trying to put words in my mouth. I guess the cross-examination Friday was the worst. After all, I'm not the one on trial.

"People tell me how brave I am . . . I don't know if it's bravery or not. It's not for me, anyway, it's for him. I keep telling myself, he's the one who suffered.

After the ordeal, she underwent several months of counseling at a mental health clinic, and learned to talk about her experience. She put off going to college, and was still working as a hotel receptionist. The threats made her "paranoid." She was living with her sister, and seldom went anywhere alone. Her phone was tapped and she had police escorts.

Helen wanted to have another baby someday. She would, after getting married, changing her name and living out of state. The thought of that night still brought tears and trembling years later, but most important, she was confident in herself.

"I feel pretty good about myself now."

Roberts went back to the Indiana State Prison in Michigan City, where he was already serving his other five life sentences, three commuted from death.

Over his next decade, part of it on death row, Roberts would put some of his time to good use. Studying the penal codes, he became a well-versed cell-house lawyer, often counseling inmates during administrative hearings at the prison. He would be elected head of Lifers United for Penal Progress, Inc., by his inmates at Michigan City. As an entrepreneur, he made up to $2,000 a year doing income tax returns for inmates until corrections officials shut down his illegal private enterprise within the prison. He also kept in excellent physical shape, despite his lung problems and injuries from the Pendleton shooting.

Roberts would be busy filing appeals, some 20 petitions between September 1976, and August 1978, according to court transcripts made available by his current attorney. His federal suit against Indiana had been dismissed in July 1980, for his failure to prosecute.

He read everything he could get his hands on, especially about forensic medicine. One article about blood testing prompted him to hire a private investigator to locate the semen sample, which was never tested in the kidnap-murder-rape case. Roberts alleged that the investigator discovered that Detective Larkins had removed the sample from the IPD property room. (Larkins denies the charge, saying the evidence never reached the property room, having been destroyed by the court after Roberts's appeals were exhausted.)

An Indiana probation officer, Irene Washington, made a haunting comment about Roberts, based on an extensive interview with him following his sentencing in January 1977.

"This worker concludes that this defendant is either guilt-free due to innocence of these crimes, or due to his being completely psychopathic, and able to hide the fact from his psychiatrists and friends."

By autumn of 1986, Roberts had enough of prison life. He planned to escape.

It seemed like another hospital visit for Roberts. Prison officials were well acquainted with the lifer's chronic lung problems, which he blamed on his incarceration. He had been in the prison hospital for a short time, and the doctors suggested more tests to determine what was causing his persistent cough.

On the morning of Friday, October 24, two guards, Sergeant Dale C. Frazier and Mario P. Rodriguez, were assigned to drive Roberts, now 42, for diagnostic tests at Wishard Memorial Hospital in Indianapolis, about a three-hour drive south. According to prison regulations, the prisoner was handcuffed and chained to leg shackles for the entire trip. He was strip searched before leaving the institution for the trip.

Roberts's stop at the hospital was routine. An hour or two of tests, a stop in the bathroom, and they were headed back north to Michigan City. The inmate was searched again.

During the ride back, the trio stopped at a McDonald's restaurant drive-through window in Lafayette. The congenial Roberts, who had been making friends with the officers throughout the trip, convinced them to loosen his waist chains so he could eat his food. As they neared the prison, somewhere on U.S. Route 421 in the cornfields of LaPorte County, the guards stopped to tighten the chains.

From out of nowhere, Roberts pulled a .38-caliber derringer pistol and ordered the guards to remove his handcuffs. Forcing the guards to handcuff themselves together and taking their handguns, Roberts drove the car in the opposite direction toward Illinois. He repeatedly told the guards that he would not hurt them if they cooperated, and even apologized for "ruining everybody's day."

He stopped finally at the South Shore Railroad station in Hammond, Indiana, and got out to make a call from a pay phone. Using a hidden key, the guards unlocked the handcuffs and jumped out of the parked car. They flagged down a passing motorist and escaped to call prison officials.

That was the last time Indiana officials saw Roberts. Within an hour, they launched a three-state manhunt, particularly west toward Chicago.

On April 27, he would be placed on the list of FBI's Ten Most Wanted Fugitives. A federal warrant had been issued at Hammond, charging him with Unlawful Interstate Flight to Avoid Prosecution for the crimes of escape and kidnapping.

4

A Little
Too Real

For the half-hour pilot Linder knew he wanted
to do one of the FBI's Ten Most Wanted fugitives.
But which one? How much information could he get
on them? Would the case agents or the local police
help find him film at the crime scenes? How fresh
was the trail and could he actually be caught? And
would the case and the fugitive make for compelling
television that viewers would watch and want to help
police catch the person?

He, Chao, and Herwitz were having daily hour-
long conference calls discussing cases. Chao, being
the programmer concerned with ratings and staying
on the air for a long time, was leaning toward a
"batting average." Without a good batting average
of profiles versus captures the show would have no
legitimacy since the public and police would think it
couldn't work. Who would want to watch a show that
never caught anyone?

Cases without a known suspect were out because there was nothing for people to grab on to.
How could someone have seen the person if no one
was sure what he or she looked like? The police would
get tired of checking out pointless leads and lose faith

in the show. Fugitives were more tangible because
viewer tips could lead more directly to captures.
Chao argued that the more fugitives caught, the better the batting average, the more credibility and
viewers. People watching the show could help directly in the fight against crime by their tips directly
leading to fugitive captures. There wasn't any magic
number of shows or specific average in mind. Yet
those involved knew that if no one was caught in the
first six or so shows, it wouldn't stay on the air very
long. Just like a major leaguer, if the show batted
between .200 and .300, it would probably make the
next season's roster. Any higher, it might make
the All-Star team or even the Hall of Fame.

There was another factor imposed by trying the
show out in Chao's programming laboratory. The
show would only be broadcast as an experiment on
the Fox owned-and-operated stations, namely in
New York (WNYW), Los Angeles (KTTV), Chicago
(WFLD), Boston (WFXT), Washington (WTTG), Dallas (KDAF), and Houston (KRIV). Either the fugitive
had to be wanted from one of those markets or there
had to be a strong chance he was hiding out there.
For example, someone who committed a murder in
Dallas and could be hiding in Chicago might work.
But profiling someone wanted for prison escape in
Florida who most likely was in San Francisco would
be a waste of time and money.

The concept of the show was to be a national
dragnet, and the seven stations, though all top ten
TV markets, covered only 25 percent of the country.
That could be a serious problem in the long run, but
for the time being, picking three suitable cases for
the pilot was the major concern.

The geography and time immediately ruled out
most of the FBI Top Ten fugitives. Donald Eugene
Webb was wanted for murder and attempted bur-

glary out of Pittsburgh. James Dyess was wanted for murder out of Jackson, Mississippi, and David James Roberts had escaped from prison in Indianapolis.

Accused armed robber Ronald Glyn Triplett was wanted out of Detroit, and was captured in May. His replacement, Darren Dee O'Neall, was from Seattle. The case of Leo Koury, wanted for violations of the RICO (Racketeer Influenced and Corruption Organizations) Act, extortion, and attempted murder, had been on the list since April 1979, and could be dead by now.

Prison escapee and kidnapper Danny Michael Weeks was wanted by Houston authorities, so his case was a possibility. Victor Manuel Gerena was wanted for armed robbery and other charges in New Haven, Connecticut, which was between New York City and Boston. Alleged terrorists Claude Daniel Marks and Donna Jean Willmott were charged with attempting to free a comrade of the Fuerzas Armada De Liberacion Nacional (FALN) from federal prison in Leavenworth, Kansas; their warrant issued from Chicago.

In addition to Walton, Linder had also borrowed Bob Curry, a CNN veteran, from the WTTG news staff as a researcher and associate producer for the pilot. He had Curry gather some preliminary articles from Chicago newspapers about Marks and Willmott.

But as Linder read through the two-page press releases on each fugitive, something jumped out at him when he studied the Roberts report. This was a man who had escaped from jail less than a year ago. He had a record of tremendous crimes, especially the killing of two infants in separate incidents; one by fire, the other by ice. One of the infants died in a house fire, which Roberts set after killing the parents. The other was left at a frozen roadside in the dead of winter, after he raped the mother and locked her in the trunk of her car.

Of the Top Ten fugitives staring up from the desk at him, Linder knew Roberts was certainly the most dangerous, and probably would strike again. He was also the most apprehendable. He had escaped from prison in Michigan City, Indiana, which was near Chicago. Interest could be generated in the Chicago market since Roberts was convicted in Indiana. And who knows, he could be hiding out in Chicago. It was worth the chance. Roberts was "Most Wanted"'s number-one case.

Curry started researching the Roberts case. The Indianapolis Police Department cooperated and opened its files. They also helped locate the scenes of the crimes in Indianapolis and nearby New Whiteland, Indiana. Indiana Corrections officials gave their version of Roberts's escape from custody in April 1986, and would allow filming at the Indiana State Prison in Michigan City, just a few miles from the sand dunes of Lake Michigan. Curry also did some pre-interviews with the principles by phone, who gave a lot of details not provided in official reports or newspaper accounts. He also found a 1978 NBC documentary on multiple killers which featured an in-prison interview with Roberts.

By early June, Linder started auditioning cameramen in Washington. It was a difficult job because the producer was accustomed to a more film-oriented talent pool in Los Angeles. Here in Washington, most camera crews were strictly TV news, mostly shooting talking heads or staged events. He went through dozens of local cameramen, and was almost ready to head for New York. But then along came a very talented local man, Vic Pimentel, with an eye for the subjective as well as the objective perspective, and soundman Craig Gibson.

Walton, meanwhile, was shopping around the Washington area for wardrobe. You can't really buy prison uniforms in a store, so they would improvise with work shirts. It was also difficult to buy or rent a policeman's uniform, since local authorities didn't approve of such costumes, so he found something similar.

This was television the hard way. Linder, Walton, Curry, and crew were basically starting from scratch. It was a handmade pilot—small staff, no-name cast, low budget ($68,000). They were asking the police for an awful lot of help for a program that may or may not ever be broadcast. There was no precedent or history to support this type of show and there were plenty of risks involved. The sales pitches worked, however. People in Indiana involved in the case were quite willing to cooperate, since Roberts was the state's most wanted fugitive. Many people still remembered how his crimes and trials shocked the entire state for years. Some of his victims feared for their lives as long as he was at large.

On the fifth of July 1987, the "Most Wanted" crew arrived in Indianapolis ready to work.

The first few days were a little rough since the crew was trying to make mini-movies far away from Hollywood. The usual production services that one takes for granted in film locations such as Los Angeles, New York, Florida, or Chicago, did not exist in Indianapolis.

Through the contacts that Curry had made, Linder found a county prosecutor and two Indianapolis police detectives willing to be interviewed. From newspaper articles, Walton managed to find a car resembling the one that Roberts had stolen in the rape-murder-kidnap case. He also found a props company to provide a wrecked car and a smoke machine for the winter scenes. A local casting agency helped find actors to play the two prison guards, the female victim, and other principals. To play Roberts, they located an Ohio actor named Kevin Speece, who would resemble the fugitive when disguised with a mustache. A local actress, Sherry Heistand, would play Roberts's rape-kidnap victim.

Linder scouted locations and lined up interviews, which were done the first afternoon. Detectives John Larkins and Jerry Quackenbush both agreed to on-camera interviews. Larkins was responsible for tracking down Roberts in the Indianapolis kidnap-rape-murder case. Quackenbush was involved in his arrest for stealing the tires from the Sears store, which was the motive for the Patrick triple murder-arson in New Whiteland. They also interviewed former Johnson County Prosecutor Joseph Van Valer and Investigator Ed Jones of the Indiana State Police.

Doing interviews resembled news reporting so the impact really didn't sink in that first afternoon. Then late that night, in the pouring rain, they searched for the intersection of High School Road and 34th Street where Roberts abducted his victim. It's one thing to read about a crime, but to see the gas station, the stop sign, the corner—everyone felt an emotional chill. If they had only been here at two in the morning thirteen years ago, maybe it wouldn't have happened. It was for real now.

In the morning of the second day, Linder and crew met their actors. Wishard Memorial Hospital where Roberts was examined the day of his escape allowed the team to film there. Speece was bound in handcuffs and leg shackles borrowed by the Indianapolis P.D. Led by the two actor guards, he was chained and led up and down the corridors. They let "Roberts" go to the toilet unattended, where some theorize he got his gun. A Celebrity Ford station wagon was rigged with chicken wire across the front seat to resemble a prison vehicle, and off drove the "prisoner" and his "captors."

Later that night, with the smoke machine trying to create a winter chill, the crew went to work rigging lights at the Clark Station they had visited the night before. The actors wore winter coats in brutal Indiana summer heat and humidity, trying to act chilled.

The service station attendant allowed the crew to film Roberts stopping in the station to buy potato chips, as he did that night. It took several rehearsals to get everything perfect as it happened—Roberts running up to the car, pulling his gun, opening the door, jumping in, and yelling, "Just drive!"

It looked real, a bit too real. After the final take, a Ford Bronco ran the light, and came spinning back. The driver looked out and stared for a moment at what he thought was a man kidnapping a woman at gunpoint on a lonely street corner late at night. Then he saw the cameras, laughed, waved, and drove off. For the rest of the filming, the crew would make sure everyone passing by would know this was only make-believe.

Pimentel quickly demonstrated his ability to get the best shot possible, even at a little physical risk. In one scene, Roberts demands that his victim write out a check, payable to a third party. To film that shot from the victim's point of view, the cameraman sat on the driver's side with his body dangling out the window as the actress drove, and did the same on the passenger side to get Roberts's POV.

Now came the scene that would give everyone nightmares for weeks to come. The car was driven into a church parking lot, and Roberts locked his victim in the trunk of the car. Several angles were filmed from inside the trunk, the back seat, and front. Walton checked the shot list against the case file for other exteriors and drive-bys. Next, the baby would be left at the roadside.

A baby hired through a local casting agency was dressed in a yellow jumper, as was the victim. The car (driven by Walton) drove up and Speece walked around with the baby, placing him on the grass. The baby cries and rolls over without prompting for the camera as the car drives away. For the first time, something happened that occurs on almost every segment filming done for the show. From a film-making perspective this was an incredibly perfect shot, Linder and Walton would remark later, but it was chilling to see how real they had made this terrible, sick crime. Everyone would have nightmares for weeks to come.

For the filming of the triple murder-arson in New Whiteland, the "Most Wanted" crew got some unexpected cooperation from the locals. The fire department in neighboring Greenwood offered to burn down an abandoned house for the filming. The crew would get their burning house, and the department would get some training time. This area was still haunted by what happened that January night some 14 years ago, and everyone was willing to help catch the fugitive convicted of the crime.

When Linder arrived at the dilapidated farmhouse that morning, it was covered with trees and brush. He mentioned to the fire chief that there weren't any trees in front of the Patrick house on the night of the fire. "No problem," was the reply, along with "do you need any furniture?"

Upon returning with the crew that evening, Linder found that the chief had sent the department rookies out to clear out the front of the house. Inside he found plenty of used furniture and carpet laid for the fire. They had also propped up the sagging porch, all so "Most Wanted" could burn it all down. The Greenwood F.D. had brought three pumper trucks, four other apparatus, more than 50 firefighters. They even brought portable water vats to hose down the house so the crew could film as many times as they wished.

While the department got their gear ready, Linder rehearsed the scene with Speece. The actor would walk through the door, pour out the gasoline, back out the door, throw in his gloves and the empty can, then toss a match. Walton readied the scene's critical prop, a gas can found at the scene which later linked Roberts to the crime. Pimentel mounted his camera right at the door at the edge of the flames.

In goes Roberts, down goes the match, up goes the house. Within minutes the blaze was out with the firefighters asking Linder if he wanted a second take. This time a little more gas so there would be a little more flame. Finally, after four fires and four dousings, the shot was finished. There was even an air of confidence, like the fire had cast a spell to catch Roberts.

Walton was amazed that all the firemen asked for were the sodas the crew had put on ice for them. After some coaxing, Linder got them to accept a $250 check for the Firemen's Benevolent Association. This was something that the "Most Wanted" crews would often find in filming their segments. It was more than warm hospitality and great cooperation. They just wanted to help catch this man, nothing else.

The next two days would later remind Linder of the early days of Hollywood filmmaking back in 1914 or so. A small group of silent actors and a crew would go out, find a location, and make a movie before dark.

To film the escape scene, Linder found a quiet road alongside a cornfield, similar to the location where Roberts pulled a gun on the prison guards. The car was rigged again with chicken wire, and the camera set. Only one thing was missing: the fast food. According to the escape report, the guards had stopped for a quick lunch on the way back to the prison, and loosened Roberts's cuffs from the leg irons so he could eat. When they stopped to restrain him, Roberts pulled a gun. So off went Walton to find a fast food outlet, the closest being 45 minutes away. He returned to find his colleagues "mildly upset," sitting in an Indiana cornfield in the heat of July. But he was soon forgiven, since he brought enough for everyone's lunch—and several extra takes.

Again, some people driving by, including two police cruisers, had to be assured that this scene— a man holding two others at bay with a gun and demanding they disrobe—was only a film crew.

Before heading north to Michigan City, the crew filmed more interviews with defense attorneys and prosecutors involved with the case. They also stopped by the FBI Indianapolis field office to check some facts with the agents assigned to the Roberts case.

Some members of the Patrick family, still devastated by the tragedy, agreed to be interviewed off-camera. Nobody really knows what happened that night, Linder would remark later, only what was gathered from the evidence. Hearing someone tell the details of a loved one's murder is something you must witness to understand. No matter how long ago the crime took place, they slip into almost a transe, somehow trying to bring the person back. It was a form of therapy for these surviving victims of a horrible crime to talk it out despite years of pain.

(Before any case is considered for the show, the

reporter assigned always consults the families of the victims, and the victims themselves, if they had survived the crime. If a fugitive profile will harm these families in any way, the shoot is dropped. These brave people would prove valuable assets to the show, even suggesting cases for broadcasts. Catching these fugitives becomes a lifelong quest for justice, even if it won't bring back a loved one.)

At the prison there was more reality in store for the crew. The Indiana State Prison here is an imposing fortress, built in the late 1800s. To get inside a film crew must remove their shoes, be frisked, break down the camera gear, then sit in a holding area surrounded by steel bars. But it was worth the effort. Several officials, guards, even inmates had off-the-record stories about Roberts which would enhance the profile. They told how he was a cameleon who could talk so smoothly and convince you of most anything. He could talk to you and physically change his face at the same time. Only with photographs and that documentary could you really see the man's ability to look different from one moment to the next.

After filming at the prison, the crew filmed Roberts's departure from the kidnapped guards at the Hammond, Indiana, train station. Five days of filming completed and the profile "in the can," Linder and crew headed to Chicago's Midway Airport—a route that would later prove ironic—and flew back to Washington.

Back in Washington, Herwitz had been making some calls on other federal law enforcement agencies, namely the U.S. Marshals Service (USMS), the Drug Enforcement Administration (DEA), the U.S. Customs Service (USCS), and the Bureau of Alcohol, Tobacco and Firearms (BATF). The response was excellent, but again their top priority fugitives didn't fall into the geographic restrictions dictated by the show being tested on the owned-and-operated (O&O's) stations.

Linder needed three, maybe four more cases for the pilot episode. Building on Herwitz's original contacts, he followed through with the agencies. Over at BATF, Jerry Rudden of Public Affairs brought the idea to his staff. The mandate of the Bureau of Alcohol, Tobacco and Firearms is to assist local and state law enforcement officers in enforcing federal firearms laws and to assist these jurisdictions with problems involving firearms. It also limits interstate traffic in firearms, keeps track of manufacturing, and has a national tracing center which tracks some 35,000 firearms annually. The agency also collects taxes on alcohol and tobacco, being the second biggest revenue producer in the government after the Internal Revenue Service.

Traditionally, BATF has been the premier agency in all bombings, except those which occur in a federal building or aircraft. For example, in the past five years, the agency has investigated 68 bombings of abortion clinics and solved 90 percent of these cases. Linder was greatly interested in a bombing case, but the BATF was leary about showing "how-to" cases. Showing pictures of explosive devices can give viewers, especially children, dangerous ideas. They had plenty of fugitive cases involving firearms violations.

Wanting to find the case in the area, Rudden contacted Special Agent Richard Pederson who suggested profiling gun fanatic Ray Alan Minnick, who had allegedly robbed several banks and fired on Maryland policemen. Minnick "was really a crime waiting to happen," Pederson told Linder, and was most likely still in the Baltimore area, which would fall into the Washington viewing area.

According to BATF, Minnick had an incredible arsenal of high-powered weapons. If cornered and outnumbered, Minnick would probably try to shoot it out. He had been spotted several times, but when agents arrived all they found was hundreds of guns he had left behind. Minnick felt a need to be surrounded by guns in his home, in his car, and on his person, Pederson said. Agents tracked him to a farmhouse about 50 miles south of Cleveland five months before, and they found more than 150 firearms on the property.

Curry researched the case thoroughly with BATF, while Linder wrote a working script from the material. They would shoot in Baltimore where Minnick had last lived, and reconstruct the shootout with the Howard County police near the city.

Minnick also raised a pit bull, so Walton had to track one down for the filming. But in late July, America was caught up in a pit bull scare, so he found a terrier breed which looked similar.

Once up in Baltimore, Linder asked the local BAFT bureau for some firearms as props. He was amazed when the agencies rolled out a shopping cart filled with dozens of weapons—Uzis, sawed-off shotguns, armor-piercing shells, automatics, machine guns—many allegedly from Minnick's own collection.

Sometimes during filming the crews get some unexpected advice from the locals about the case. Baltimore was no exception. As Linder and crew started filming some walk-bys with the Minnick actor on a city residential street, a lady yelled from a second-floor window.

"He always wore a hat," she shouted.

"Excuse me?" asked a startled Linder.

"The man who walked his pit bull, the gunman you're looking for. He always wore a hat."

Linder thanked the woman and put a hat on the actor.

Arranging the filming with the Howard County police, Linder and his crew reconstructed the attempted liquor store holdup by Minnick and two accomplices. For the high speed chase following the failed robbery, the police had arranged for filming right through some of the fields which Minnick raced through that night with Howard County police in pursuit. Again, the neighbors were very polite, offering electrical outlets for lighting and lemonade for the thirsty crew and actors. Of course, the folks remembered the night being reconstructed, and offered some valuable tips. The officer who had encountered the heavily armed Minnick that night was also interviewed for the segment.

While Linder and crew were out filming, Chao and Herwitz were discussing a problem which was getting bigger as the amount of film being shot increased: a host.

With more hour-long conference calls, the three went through lists of possibilities—politicians, crime authors, military men, journalists, actors, actresses. They needed somebody who could not only speak clearly and follow cues, but also someone with credibility. Someone who would convince people to call in and would reassure law enforcement about the serious nature of the show.

Chao contacted best-selling author and former Los Angeles Police officer Joseph Wambaugh. The choice was considered perfect since he had a national image as a crime author and former cop, but he rarely appeared in public. In fact, Chao found the author somewhat of a recluse, who only communicated by Telex. Wambaugh was flattered by the offer, but wrote back saying he didn't think such a national dragnet would work in America.

Another strong candidate was U.S.Attorney Rudolph Guiliani (later the Republican candidate for mayor of New York City), who had recently resigned his job as New York City's tough Mafia prosecutor. Guiliani had a great image as an Elliot Ness–type crimefighter, but he might be uncontrollable off-camera, Chao thought. There were indications that Guiliani had political ambitions and might use the show as a launching pad. He was out.

Herwitz suggested some other politicians not currently in office who had a good camera presence and established a following, such as Virginia's Chuck Robb, former governor and son-in-law of the late President Lyndon B. Johnson, or Bob Curry, former governor of Oklahoma. Again, the possibility of a politician using the show for future office nixed that prospect.

A few former police chiefs and military leaders, including P.X. Kelley, former commandant of the U.S. Marine Corps, were also suggested. Good image, but what about on-camera experience. Then came a list of actors who had played famous cops: Treat Williams (*Prince of the City*), Ed Marinaro ("Hill Street Blues"), Brian Dennehy (*Best Seller*), and Brian Keith.

But the sentiment was leaning toward a "real person" involved with fighting crime instead of an actor who had played a cop. Several media consultants sent tapes of TV news crime reporters from Miami, Chicago, and New York. Linda Ellerbee, famous for her work with ABC and NBC News, was a strong candidate, but committed elsewhere. Ike Pappas, who would later host "Crimewatch Tonight" was also considered. Herwitz had lunch to discuss the idea with Watergate journalist Bob Woodward, an

editor with the *Washington Post*, but he politely declined the offer.

It was agreed that a journalist would make the
show set look too much like a newsroom, taking away
the personal touch. The show needed someone that
viewers could identify with, so they would believe
that they could participate in the law enforcement
process. That person hosting the show had done
something to make a difference in crime and so could
they.

Finally, came the idea of having a person who
was a victim of crime. The first candidate to surface
was actress Teresa Saldana, who had played herself
in a television movie about her near fatal stabbing
by a crazed fan, her incredible recovery and continuing work with the organization "Victims for Victims." Ms. Saldana came to Washington for an
interview, but unfortunately was too well known as
an actress and celebrity to fit the "everyday working
look" the show was looking for.

During one of those marathon conference calls,
Herwitz struck a gold mine.

"How about John Walsh?" he said. "You remember the TV movie *Adam*, and there was another one.
Plus he's done some specials on child safety for HBO,
and he's a crusader for legislation. I've seen him all
over."

Chao and Linder immediately recalled the powerful TV movie *Adam* about the tragic kidnap-
murder of Walsh's six-year-old son, Adam, in 1981.
They also remembered reading somewhere about
Walsh's continued fight for legislation to protect
missing children which had resulted in two federal
laws and hundreds of state laws. And if they weren't
mistaken, he was a young, attractive man with a
convincing camera presence. Viewers would identify
with him as someone just like them whose life had

been devastated by crime, but was working within the system to make a difference.

It was a brilliant selection, they agreed. Now all they had to do was convince Fox—and Walsh.

Herwitz contacted the Adam Walsh Child Resource Center in West Palm Beach, Florida, that day to reach Walsh. Walsh's wife, Reve, had established these centers after Adam's death to help educate parents and children about safety, track missing children, and monitor legislation. Herwitz quickly found out what a hard man Walsh can be to locate sometimes, considering his heavy schedule of speaking appearances, legislative testimonies, and family responsibilities. Nancy McBride, Walsh's assistant at the center, was enthusiastic about the idea and sent Herwitz some videotape copies of the HBO special ("How to Raise a Street Smart Child") and PBS documentary ("Parents' Greatest Fear"), press conferences, and interviews with Walsh on national TV shows.

Walsh called the next day and spoke for nearly five hours with Linder and Herwitz about hosting the show.

Neither man had ever spoken to Walsh before. In the first three sentences, Herwitz would later recall, Walsh told them about Adam and moved him tremendously. Linder had already looked at the tapes and "with one look" knew that they had found an attractive, sensitive man with a quality in his voice that said "commitment and passion." He also noticed that Walsh had a good voice-over voice. He would be appealing on TV because he was "an everyman, an ordinary guy who had been hit hard by crime and that would be important to the audience," Linder said later.

Walsh didn't commit right away, however. He had a host of questions. Over the past seven years he had received numerous requests to host TV shows and specials about crime and missing children, some being responsible, others sensational. He was also very sensitive and skilled in working with the media, and realized that even the most well-intentioned efforts can be misguided.

With his working for missing children and victims' rights, Walsh maintained a schedule that rivaled any corporate executive, flying up to a half-million miles a year around the country. He would have to be allowed to continue that work despite the TV production schedule.

Walsh was impressed with Linder and Herwitz, but he had reservations.

"I don't envision myself as the host of a television show," he said. "I'm not a celebrity, I'm the father of a murdered child."

Linder and Herwitz agreed that he could maintain his schedule. They would work around it. The host would be needed only three days a week, probably weekends, since the show would be taped very close to its Sunday broadcast.

They also discussed Walsh's relationship with law enforcement. In lobbying for legislation to protect missing children after Adam's death, Walsh had taken on the FBI on Congressional testimony and the media. He had criticized their lack of responsibility in tracking missing children. All that had changed now, he assured them. The laws were changed and Walsh had been working with the FBI for several years, even serving as a consultant to the Justice Department.

"We've buried those hatchets years ago," Walsh assured Herwitz.

The discussion continued about different aspects of the show. Content of the segments and treatment of victims was very important to Walsh.

"That's why we want you to host the show," Linder said. "You're a victim's advocate and a children's advocate."

"Thank you," Walsh replied. "But I won't move to California or host a show that's based there. My family comes first."

"No problem," Linder said. "We're in Washington."

Walsh agreed to do the pilot episode and decide later if he'd host the show as a weekly series. The following week, he would met Linder in Fort Lauderdale, where "Most Wanted" was filming a segment about some drug smugglers with the Broward County Sheriff's Department.

Having watched the Geraldo Rivera special on drug busts, Linder remembered being impressed by the Broward County Sheriff's Department in Fort Lauderdale. He contacted them for a possible pilot case, and sure enough, Sheriff Nick Navarro (later featured on Fox's "COPS") had a drug smuggler case with some incredible video footage.

On June 4, 1987, U.S. Customs agents and the Broward Sheriff's Office had tracked a Piper Aztec airplane with two men suspected of drug smuggling coming into the country across the Everglades. Officers pursued the plane, which was flying erratically and without lights, in the air that night using infrared tracking, but the suspects eluded them. Finally, the plane landed on the Sawgrass Expressway near a toll booth plaza. One suspect was captured and convicted; the other fled into the swamps and was still at large and wanted for questioning.

Navarro agreed to provide a helicopter so Linder could shoot some "on-camera bridges" while flying over Fort Lauderdale with Walsh to introduce the segment. He'd also provide a videotape of the night tracking of the suspect's plane.

At one o'clock in the morning of August 5, 1987, Linder and crew met John Walsh in person for the first time in the lobby of a Fort Lauderdale hotel. Everyone was impressed with Walsh being "so alive, almost at a fever pitch all the time," Walton would later recall.

"I watched Linder and him talking and I said, " 'This is it,' " Walton said months later. "He's a working man, he's at a fever pitch, he cares about this and he knows television."

Linder and Walsh talked for about an hour, then parted to get some rest. They would be back up at 5 A.M. to shoot a sunrise show opening with Walsh introducing the segment. Linder gave the prospective host some script to look over, but the exhausted Walsh fell asleep before he could look it over.

The crew and Walsh met on schedule in the lobby and departed for the airport where the deputies and helicopter pilot would meet them. The cops were late, however, so the crew wired Walsh up for rehearsal. Though Walsh stumbled a little with his lines and his voice was a bit scratchy at 5:30 A.M., Linder knew he had his man.

While they were waiting, Linder asked Walsh if he would like to see a short sample of the show so far. The producer popped a rough cut copy of the Roberts segment into a portable VCR deck on the back of the rented station wagon and Walsh watched the monitor. Within seconds, he was riveted to the end of the five-minute piece.

"It's worth it, Michael, if we just catch one of these guys," Walsh said. "I'm the father of a murdered child and here's a guy who killed two kids. Wouldn't it be great if we caught just one guy?"

Linder, his staff, and America would hear Walsh

say that a thousand times over the next two years.

Standing there on the airport tarmac, Linder also realized how comfortable Walsh was talking about his son's murder. He wouldn't break down on camera talking about brutal crimes or victims. In fact, he would be quite good.

At that point, Walsh would later recall, he was convinced of the integrity of the program. Some trusted friends in Hollywood had warned him about the Fox network. It had already failed with the Joan Rivers show and George C. Scott's "Mr. President." It had lost a lot of money and had a tabloid reputation with Rupert Murdoch as its owner, they cautioned him. But the Roberts segment touched something inside him.

"That changed my whole opinion of the show once I saw the Roberts segment," Walsh would say later. "It brought tears to my eyes looking at what this guy had done to two families."

Roberts, of course, would have a different story for Walsh in the year to come.

The Broward cops finally arrived and Walsh did his bridges high over Ft. Lauderdale. And he wasn't the only one who was on a high that morning.

Walsh, Linder, and Herwitz would continue their discussions about the show in the coming months. Walsh suggested a toll-free number, which was already being worked on. In his experience with *Adam* and its sequel *Adam: His Song Continues* on NBC, Walsh realized the power of television. Following the broadcasts, photos of missing children were shown and thanks to viewers calling on a toll-free hotline, 65 were recovered.

Having worked with law enforcement, Walsh was concerned that the show would foster cooperation. Some cases might involve several jurisdictions

on the local, state, and federal levels, and the show
would have to be careful about possible rivalries.

He was also concerned with legal dangers—civil
liability, pretrial publicity, and treatment of victims.
Herwitz, the corporate attorney, quickly reassured
him. Those matters were already being considered
by some of the nation's best legal minds as consultants to the show.

The show would be controversial, but Walsh was
no stranger to that. The critics said nobody would
watch *Adam*, or "Street Smart," but both shows won
exceptional ratings and numerous awards. Most important, Walsh stresses, they raised the conscious-
ness and awareness of the American public about
missing children and family safety.

"I wasn't adverse to taking a chance," Walsh
would recall later. "I thought this would be a project
that the other three networks wouldn't tackle. Only
maybe somebody like Fox would have the guts to do
it."

Walsh agreed to be the host.

The pilot needed a West Coast segment. Curry
had returned to WTTG when his leave was up, so
Linder hired Ralph Stein to research more segments.
From the California Highway Patrol, the show got
the case of accused car thief Peter Miller. Based in
Los Angeles, Miller, police said, would take ID plates
from wrecked cars and put them on expensive cars
that he either rented or stole. He would then sell
them to an unsuspecting buyer.

Linder and crew went to Los Angeles for a week,
filming the segment in the Beverly Hills area where
Miller allegedly stole a red Ferrari from a Budget
Rent-a-Car dealer. In hopes of Miller being caught,
the dealer lent "Most Wanted" several cars for free.

To finish up the pilot filming, the show obtained

a tape of a raid of a metho-amphetamine distributor's factory by DEA agents in San Diego.

Back in Washington, Linder, assisted by Walton, worked on graphics for the show. One night in the editing room, the show got its final name. There was a copyright problem with "Most Wanted," since the title was owned by another production company. Without hesitation, the imaginative Linder punched up on the monitor the name that would become a household word within a year—"America's Most Wanted."

A toll-free number had to be inserted, just for demonstration purposes. Leslie Groves, Herwitz, Linder, and Walton spent hours going through the telephone prefixes available from ATT, then MCI. First there was "1-800-TO-ARREST," followed by "FOR-A-TIP," "CRIME-TIP," "HANDCUFF," "ALL-EYES," "ALL-EARS" until they stumbled on the now-famous number "1-800-CRIME-88." Confident the show would be a hit, even before the pilot was completed, they called to reserve the last four digits for five consecutive years (e.g., CRIME–89, etc.) and those for CRIME-TV.

Linder's partner in Tokyo, Michael Barton, who would later be the show's art director, was faxing graphics daily from the Orient. Walsh had come to Washington to film some in-studio introductions. Finally, by Labor Day Weekend, Linder and Walton were editing the final version of the 23-minute pilot (30 minutes with commercials for broadcast). They spent two full days from 7 A.M. to 2 A.M. editing at a local video house until they were "brain dead." At one point, Linder was so tired that he went outside and lay down in the middle of the parking lot on his back. Walton continued to edit, then went out and woke up his boss, who went back and resumed his work.

There were two more days of 9 A.M. to 6 A.M. sessions, laying down Walsh's voice at an audio facility. Walsh was untrained at such sessions, but patient and eager to learn. There also weren't the talent ego problems sometimes encountered by producers with major TV or film stars. Walsh was there to do the job, though it took longer than normal.

The team pulled another all-nighter, then was back in the editing room at 10 A.M., for another 25 hours straight. This time they could see the end in sight. Herwitz stopped by to lend his support—beers and pizzas at midnight, followed by breakfast at 7 A.M.

By mid-morning of Labor Day, the pilot was sweetened and ready.

Herwitz, Linder, and Walton walked out of the editing house proud that they had just completed a solid pilot. It might even catch a fugitive and make TV history, they joked.

Then reality hit again.

Both Linder's and Walton's cars had been broken into during the night. The thieves had drilled through the trunk lock of Linder's car and stolen his new luggage.

It was a random act—nobody had staked them out. But everyone realized that now they were taking on the bad guys.

The next day, the office was packed up. Linder was off to Los Angeles to meet with Chao. They would show the pilot to Diller and the Fox executives, who would decide on its future. Walton went back home to South Carolina, wondering if he would have a job the next month. Herwitz went back to his corporate routine at WTTG. Over the next week, they would all wait and hope.

David James Roberts, meanwhile, was out there somewhere, unaware that a tape with his name on it was in Linder's new carry-on bag. It would catch up with him.

5

Will We
Catch Somebody?

The decision in Los Angeles didn't take long.
Everyone agreed that the project should go ahead,
and be prepared for a premiere on the seven O&O's,
probably in December.

Though the creators were satisfied with the pilot
project, Barry Diller and others thought it needed
some refinement. It showed promise, but it was still
a work in progress at this point. In fact, some would
later admit, it wasn't very good yet. The idea came
through, but not a lot. It was clear that people were
supposed to call in to help catch these fugitives, but
the urgency wasn't there. The segments were too
fast, too jammed together, and there was serious
doubt whether viewers could distinguish between
four fugitives. As for the filmmaking, Linder had
done well, but the show's style wasn't established
yet.

Linder called Walton in South Carolina less
than a week after they had finished the pilot.

"The good news is the show is on," he said. "The
bad news is, go home, get lots of sleep because you're
going to need it. Be in Washington on October 19."

Walton did just what the boss told him. He also

got weekly postcards from the Orient assuring him the project was still a go.

Linder headed back to Tokyo to clean up his affairs there. The idea of doing this show full time was incredibly exciting. He took Diller's criticisms well and would work out the rough spots. The only thing he really worried about was getting enough fugitive cases for three segments a week. He wasn't even worried about catching them.

On a trip to Bangkok, Linder discussed the show extensively with Michael Barton, his partner. Both being devoted students of film, they came up with several ideas for the filmmaking style of the pieces. Barton would also design the set, which would go through several changes throughout the show's history. Linder was interested in drawing from the avant-guarde films of the 1940s. He was also intrigued by the techniques employed in making contemporary music videos. These people could make very compelling films on a moderate scale. Their films could touch people and still be artistically interesting on their own merits.

They were going to pursue a commercial style that was very hot, gritty, sort of new realism. Barton suggested that the show should be multi-media, namely a combination of film, videotape, video recording, 8-millimeter film, and any other medium that could be recorded on. After all, police used so many different media in their work—nightscopes, infrared, video surveillance cameras, audio recordings, wiretaps, and more. The show had to be broad enough to countenance any kind of video or audio recording and still win its own artistic integrity.

The show would be a crafts-oriented program, a creative dream for any producer, cameraman, or musician scoring pieces. The people creating the segments should have full creative range. Every segment of "America's Most Wanted" would be a little movie unto its own. It would have its own creative style, its own theme, own scoring, so that no two would be alike. That would also work into the nature of the show, since no two crimes or no two fugitives are alike.

In a video bar in Bali one night during the trip, Linder saw a video that absolutely blew him away. It was called "Bizarre Love Triangle" by the group New Order. He was dazzled by the video editing style of the video and knew that this was the essence of what he wanted the title sequence to look like.

Back in Washington, Linder started assembling a permanent staff. One of his first calls was to Warner Bros. Records to track down the video's creator, Michael H. Schamberg. Schamberg and his team produced the opening and title music in a studio in Newark, New Jersey, using police footage shot in the area. The human eye which opens every episode of "America's Most Wanted" belongs to Schamberg himself.

Herwitz had continued to meet with the federal law enforcement agencies. The cases were still limited to ones centered around the seven O&O markets. Having the finished pilot helped show the agency heads exactly what "America's Most Wanted" was all about. And having John Walsh as the host— a well-respected friend of law enforcement throughout the country—didn't hurt either.

Down at the FBI, the internal battles had been resolved and the agency was willing to cooperate within certain boundaries. Wanted posters in the post office and running photos for a few seconds on news shows weren't catching many of the 10,000 fugitives being sought by the Bureau, much less the Top Ten. The American public is a visual audience and this show could catch their attention. This was also a way to focus on the criminal act, which would be an important way to educate society to the reality of crime. These segments would also describe the individual's habits, his characteristics, his modus operandi, as well as his description. It would be much more enlightening than a wanted poster.

The FBI did not want or ask for editorial or content control. If they thought the show was going overboard in the dramatizations or putting on excessive graphic violence, they would voice their objections. The show promised to maintain a responsible approach with a factual presentation of the information provided. It was just as concerned as the FBI was about the rights of the individual to a fair trial. The FBI was interested in informing, not entertaining the public. The show was interested in doing both.

As far as the daily relationship with the show, a member of the Public Affairs division would serve as a liaison between "America's Most Wanted" and the FBI. The liaison would consult with the Criminal Investigation Division to suggest possible cases, then bring these to the show. The PA office would also teletype the field offices, periodically asking them to submit possible cases which might benefit from the show. There were other cases which the show might learn about through the media, and the FBI would lend assistance if it was involved. In general, the Bureau was looking for cases of dangerous fugitives who could be caught by creating public interest in their cases.

Once cases were selected for filming, the liaison would put the segment producer in touch with the case agent assigned to that fugitive investigation. The agent would serve as an advisor for the filming, providing any information—posters, photographs, public records—which would aid the production and create local interest in the filming. The agent would not do anything to jeopardize an undercover operation, discuss any unusual ongoing investigative techniques, provide witnesses for interviews without prior approval or show evidence that might prejudice a fair trial later on. On the night of the broadcast, the agent would come to the show to follow up on viewer tips.

At BATF, the agents were impressed at the Minnick segment and had plenty more cases to suggest. They were just anxious for the show to get on the air and catch their gun fanatic before he killed someone. The only cases BATF was cautious about were those concerning causes. The Bureau is constantly involved with bombers destroying property for a cause, such as the abortion clinic bombings, or donors providing weapons to groups overseas, such as the IRA or PLO. One man's terrorist is another man's freedomfighter, so if the show was looking for someone affiliated with a particular political or religious cause, some viewers might call up to argue the cause rather than help catch the fugitive.

At the Drug Enforcement Administration, Herwitz had met with Anthony Wilson and Larry Gillina in the Congressional and Public Affairs Office. The DEA had given the show footage of a San Diego drug raid which was featured in the pilot. But it was the first time the show encountered a problem which would pop up sometimes—the fugitives were caught before the segment could be aired. That's great for law enforcement and public safety, but can cause headaches for producers, especially when the show is nearly on the air.

Similar to the FBI, the DEA would query their 19 field offices around the country to compile a list of drug traffickers, who are fugitives and could still be in the United States. The agency will also coordinate its efforts with the U.S. Attorneys and the U.S. Marshals in cases involving several jurisdictions.

Like other law enforcement agencies, the DEA was concerned with being careful not to prejudice the fugitive's rights for a fair trial. Some of the fugitive cases brought in by the DEA would prove to be some of the most violent shows on "America's Most Wanted." There is normally a tremendous amount of violence in drug trafficking today, officials point out. These are not street gangs or bank robbers, but individuals prone to major homicides without hesitation. In some DEA fugitive cases later broadcast on the program, the field agents would privately and politely tell the producers that AMW, in toning down the violence, did not represent how violent the individual really was.

At the U.S. Customs Service, Commissioner Nicholas Van Raab was an early supporter of "America's Most Wanted." Customs agents are concerned with only 30 fugitive cases a year, as compared with the FBI with more than 10,000 and the Marshals with over 14,000. But AMW would later help the Customs Service in a crucial fugitive case that involved one of its own gone bad, namely Charles Jordan, former head of its Miami operation.

Across the river in Arlington, Herwitz had met with Howard Safir, Associate Director of Operations of the U.S. Marshals Service, early in the summer before the pilot was completed and Walsh was on board as host. The initial reaction, as Safir would later joke, was "our usual instinct with the entertainment media, namely to tell them to go away." But as Safir, a 24-year veteran, would explain later, any law enforcement agency is naturally hesitant to cooperate when first approached by the media until they are sure what's being asked. It's just a natural instinct of any law enforcement to be cautious—"before you get into anything, make sure there is no downside," he added.

But once the Marshals saw Linder's finished pilot they realized that the show was a serious effort to catch criminals. They had also worked with Walsh on setting up the National Center for Missing and Exploited Children in Washington, so the new AMW host was given "a great deal of respect" with the Marshals. Safir immediately directed his staff to give AMW its full cooperation, and the Marshals would become one of the show's greatest allies in the law enforcement community. Together, they would catch dozens of fugitives and celebrate the Bicentennial of the U.S. Marshals Service with a special broadcast from Old Tucson, Arizona.

As liaison to AMW, Safir appointed his right-hand man, Robert "Big Buck" Leschorn, Chief of Domestic Operations, Enforcement Division. Leschorn quickly became the most ambitious of any liaison officer, constantly offering cases, advice, and criticism. If his size wasn't enough to frighten a would-be felon, one would only have to listen to his stories from 15 years in major case investigations. Among his elaborate stings to catch fugitives was the Washington scam where invitations to a Redskins Super Bowl party were sent out to more than 200 wanted fugitives in the area. Some 150 unsuspecting fugitive/fans showed up only to be arrested before the game started.

Every year the U.S. Marshals Service is involved with more than 21,000 cases of fugitives who have fled warrants to avoid prosecution, and has its own list of 15 Most Wanted fugitives. Of those 21,000, nearly 14,000 are tracked down and arrested in a given year. Leschorn knew that AMW would only help increase that number.

Before the show was ever developed, he would use the media to his advantage to apprehend a fugitive. In "pushing a fugitive," he would concentrate on a particular city, then get to the local media for them to print or broadcast the man's photograph in the newspaper or on television. A fugitive who had reestablished himself in "middle America" using a new name and identity is very difficult to apprehend. The fugitive knows that as long as he sits in a house and doesn't move, it's hard for a task force of eight to ten Marshals to find him. But you put him on television and the neighbor next door, or even the unsuspecting girlfriend living with the fugitive, will call the cops.

For example, the Marshals used the "pushing" technique in 1987 to catch Bernard Walsh, one of the most famous burglars in U.S. history. Walsh was alleged to have stolen $17 million in assets, including the moon medals of an American astronaut right from his home. Having run out of leads, the Marshals got Walsh's photograph in nearly every newspaper and on nearly every TV station in the United States. He was caught as a direct result of the power of the media and the cooperation of the public.

The Marshals had employed this technique hundreds of other times on a local, smaller scale with great success. But budget and manpower cutbacks had severely hampered their efforts in recent years, just as many other agencies have suffered.

There were some cases that the Marshals would like on the air that didn't work for AMW. Certain aspects in particular nonviolent crimes, such as money laundering or fraud by wire, don't make interesting television. Even the most imaginative producer can't make a compelling segment filming thousands of telephone transactions.

Like other agencies, the Marshals would not jeopardize their operations by cooperating with AMW. They wouldn't give up source information, informants, or sophisticated techniques. The case files would be "sanitized" before being turned over to the show for development.

To Leschorn, this was a dream come true. It would not only help catch fugitives, but it also would help save taxpayers' money. In a two-year search for a particular fugitive, the Marshals could spend up to $100,000 and thousands of valuable deputy hours. One phone tip could nab a fugitive and save that money for another case. That's a major priority in these times of overstressed budgets.

"Can you imagine doing pushing a fugitive in every house in America?" Leschorn told his field agents in the Marshals 93 field offices, as he coaxed them to submit cases often.

Linder needed a staff of reporter-researcher to start gathering cases for the debut, which was now pushed back to the first Sunday in January. Walton was still working as a production assistant, handling most any crisis that came along. Within four days of being back in the office, Linder hired Burke Stone, a veteran print reporter, first as a PA with Walton, then as the show's first full-time reporter.

The show also needed a secretary. Linder called Walton into the office and introduced him to Michelle "Mickey" McKenzie, also a native of Columbia, South Carolina. She was working as a secretary for a Washington law firm when she saw the AMW ad in a newspaper. Having worked in a Columbia TV station on an editing machine, master control, and been a production coordinator, she was an incredible asset to the new show. She quickly left her secretary desk to become a production manager, supervising all the location shoots. In later days, there would be up to seven teams in the field at once, and it was her job to reach them at a moment's notice.

The show's first newsroom was slowly growing in a WTTG conference room next to Linder's office down the hall from Herwitz. A fourth desk was added when Linder hired another veteran journalist then based in Los Angeles. She called him from roadside phone booths "every step of the way" as she drove east just to reassure her new boss that she was really coming to work. That was Nan Allendorfer, formerly of "Nightline" and several top-notch local TV news operations. Having already worked in Washington, she quickly called up some old contacts to get the AMW newsroom rolling.

Next came a hot young producer named Brian Gadinsky. Down in Miami, he had turned a boring talk show called "Montage" into the hit of the town in just a few months. Also helping in the early days was Mark Siegel, an intern from the University of Maryland.

The newsroom needed an experienced managing editor to keep track of the hundreds of cases which would later flow through the place in a week.

Call it destiny or a fluke, but at the same time Margaret Roberts had just quit her job at *Congressional Quarterly* to edit a book about lobbyists in Washington. But after four days, she realized the job wasn't what she'd hoped for.

A Washington, D.C., native, Roberts had started her career in journalism while in graduate school for her master's at the University of Chicago. She first worked as a coeditor on a feisty New Journalism neighborhood newspaper, then edited and wrote for *Chicago Lawyer*, an investigative weekly. Moving to

D.C., she was managing editor for the *National Journal,* an insider's magazine for Washington, before joining its rival *Congressional Quarterly*.

"There was a buzz around town about this new TV show that was being done here," Roberts would recall. "So I called up the studio and got Brian Gadinsky on the phone. He quizzed me about my career as a print journalist and working for television.

"He asked me, 'Do you look down your nose at TV?'

"Of course not, I replied."

Roberts went down the next day to meet Gadinsky and Linder, having that strange feeling that she would be offered the job and she would take it immediately. They did and she did.

A self-confessed "crime junkie since day one," she found the concept "electrifying," a new direction for journalism, discussing the idea with Linder for nearly an hour. She quickly saw the strength of the producer's intelligence, his integrity, his news judgment, and his commitment to make this show called "America's Most Wanted" work.

In the coming months, Roberts and her news team would need all the energy and commitment they could muster. They had to get cases fast. The January debut had now been moved to February 7, but it was rapidly approaching. They would be a close-knit team, working "their butts off" seven days a week, 15 hours a day. They even partied together after hours, but in the office it was all business.

They made cold calls to police agencies all over the seven O&O markets. Most of the time they got caught in a lot of bureaucratic runarounds.

"America's Most Wanted what?" they heard at the other end.

There was a lot of scrutiny. This was a concept so new that most agencies were very skeptical. They sent out dozens of tapes of the pilot and made daily follow-up calls. A few agencies volunteered cases, but often they were ones that an AMW reporter had already uncovered in the media. And in some of those, the police involved were not willing to cooperate. No police, no case.

The FBI and the Marshals provided dozens of files, but outside of Washington, nobody knew about the show. But that would soon change. Some of the police who had turned them down would come running back in a few short weeks.

Leschorn brought in the first case to be produced after the pilot. Linder hired Dallas producer Michael Cerny to film a segment in Pennsylvania about Robert Nauss, a convicted murderer who had escaped from prison hiding in a large wooden cabinet. Nauss was an Eagle Scout turned hard-core biker since age 19, who became vice-president of the Warlocks gang. In 1971, he had strangled his girlfriend, made love to her after she recovered, then beat and hanged her. Nauss was convicted of her murder, even though her body was never recovered, and sentenced to life in prison. Having escaped in 1983, Nauss had probably blended into everyday society with an average, clean-cut look.

While Cerny was out in the field, there were mountains of other tasks which needed to be completed before the debut.

Part of being a good attorney is knowing when to ask for advice. Herwitz had probably covered every legal angle about the show himself, but he wanted other opinions.

He contacted Fox's Washington attorneys from the firm of Williams and Connelly. After sending over the pilot and briefing them, Herwitz sat down with William McDaniels, David Kendall, and Kevin

Baine to get their opinions about the legal dangers of the show. Herwitz wanted to assure that the show would not be counterproductive. They wanted to assist in the apprehension of fugitives, not generate defenses or interfere with arrests.

First, the attorneys advised that AMW look for cases were there had been some form of judicial process where somebody had been indicted or been issued an arrest warrant. It should be a case where "somebody had said 'Bring this person in.'" The show should stay away from cases where a suspect was only wanted for questioning.

In the area of trial evidence, if a fugitive was portrayed on AMW, would that give any grounds for the fugitive, if captured by the show, to suppress evidence at the ensuing trial. No, said the attorneys. The show was simply depicting the crime and that would in no way taint the case or make inadmissible any evidence the prosecution had. Simply portraying the crime or an escape would not erect any barriers to prosecuting. The show wouldn't supply any evidence; the state would have to convict on what it had.

Linder and Herwitz were concerned whether portraying a fugitive would give any grounds for dismissal of a case. Would all this national publicity mean that you couldn't prosecute the fugitive after he's arrested? The attorneys pointed out a number of remedies for publicity short of dismissal, which itself was not a remedy. It was unlikely as long as the reconstructions were based on facts and done accurately. The fact that you let the country know that somebody is wanted for murder may be offensive to the person, but it's fact.

Change of venue from the locality was a possible remedy or the defense can take longer to examine the jurors. Even in small communities, it was amazing that despite a saturation of publicity on a case, twelve people could be found who had never heard of it. If a prospective juror is tainted by what they've heard outside the courtroom, they can be excluded from the case.

Another area of concern was whether a person arrested as a result of the show could claim an illegal arrest, such as a vigilante-type citizen's arrest. The attorneys reassured Herwitz that even if a person is kidnapped and brought into custody, if the charges were valid, the law does not inquire into how you were brought there. The show should always take great pains to ask viewers not to take the law in their own hands, not to apprehend the person themselves, but to call the information into law enforcement officials.

AMW was walking into a tricky legal environment. But if it safeguarded the rights of the victims, and produced accurate portrayals of the fugitives, it would not be counterproductive to the criminal justice system.

Now what about the telephone system? Setting up was one thing, but what about training the hotline operators? Without the right people and procedures valuable tips and time would be lost after the profiles.

Through his collegues with Fox's KTTV-TV in Los Angeles, Herwitz called a Sacramento telephone hotline consultant named Ann Stargardter. Over the past seven years, she had helped set up 26 news tip hotlines and consumer "Troubleshooter" programs for TV stations in 26 different cities across the country, including KTTV.

Stargardter had plenty of experience with writing manuals and training telephone volunteers for news and consumer hotlines, but she hadn't worked with law enforcement before. After some preliminary discussions with Herwitz and Linder over the phone from Sacramento, she called the five federal agencies currently working with the show. She wanted to know their priorities in getting the most information from the viewer tips by telephone. Next, she contacted various emergency hotline services, such as runaways, missing children, rape crisis, even the U.S. Customs Service at the Mexican border. They provided valuable advice on how they trained their operators.

The AMW hotline operators would have to illicit the most information out of a person in a relatively short period of time. They would also have to determine what kind of person was calling, how did they sound, what kind of noises were in the background, and did they really have the right person in mind.

With Herwitz's help, Stargardter visited the five federal agencies in Washington to discuss the hotline operations. She had already spoken to the liaisons so frequently that it was almost like meeting old friends. The reaction from the agencies were mixed. Some were so enthusiastic about her training manuals that they asked to incorporate it into their own training manuals. Others, such as the FBI, wanted their own experts to study the manuals before giving them their stamp of approval. But they finally did. From her consultations with the agencies, she also developed a working tip sheet for the operators to ask questions from, though the form would be revised several times in the coming months.

At the show office, she started familiarizing the staff with the 150-page manual she had written for the person training the hotline operators. That would be Grace Vista, a friend of Walton's from the University of Maryland, just hired as a production assistant to handle the hotline operations. The manual included extensive details on how to recruit operators, what to look for in potential candidates. Some people just didn't have the patience or the willingness to gather the information. AMW would also have to be careful about the people applying. Some might be enamored of the idea of being on television (since the operators would appear on camera) or have hidden ambitions of being a police officer.

Stargardter then put the staff to work, rehearsing for the operators. She set up role-playing situations in which one staffer would be the caller, the other the operator. Quickly, everyone realized how serious and difficult manning the phones could be, especially with a line of calls waiting. It is not just a matter of picking up the phone and asking a lot of questions. It demands certain skills—how to listen, communicate, interpret words, feelings, how to get the most information. What about the speed of the person's voice, the loudness, softness, speed, tone, hesitations, the umh's and the ah's. Certain words, inflections, and speeds mean definite things, which would mean the difference between getting the right details on a valid tip or losing it.

The questions had to be precise. What fugitive did you see? Where did you see him? What was he doing at the time? How do you know it was him? Did you notice anything else significant about him?

The callers would not have to give their names. It would be totally anonymous. The operators, not the law enforcement officers, would answer the phones and take the information. If the caller wished to speak to an officer, or the tip seemed very solid, the operator would hold up a card flag marked with the fugitive case name and the case agent would respond.

Before AMW would take a case, they would make sure that the law enforcement officers from all the agencies involved would come to the studio on the night of the broadcast, take the tip sheets, and follow up. Without their cooperation and investigation of the leads, it would be pointless to profile that fugitive.

Armed with plenty of advice, Vista began recruiting operators. She first contacted local colleges and universities, such as the University of Maryland, American University, and Catholic University. She spoke to career advisors and placement counselors, sending them posters for the bulletin boards.

The response was encouraging, though some applicants were confused about their responsibilities. At first, most journalism and TV majors applied, some thinking that it would be a chance to break into production. Instead, AMW needed good hotline operators who were interested in the criminal justice aspect, not being on camera. Vista had gone after the college crowd because of the unusual hours—Sundays from 2 P.M. to midnight (after the calls stopped coming from Los Angeles where the show was broadcast three hours after the East Coast).

For the first night, the show would need eight operators and back-ups trained and ready. It was now mid-January and the debut was rapidly approaching. MCI had provided the toll-free number, while Bell Atlantic provided the line. Another consulting firm, Jarvis in Virginia, was setting up the computer and answering system, called an Automated Call Distributor (ACD). Keeping the calls in "queue," it would ensure that callers would not get a busy signal and hang up. Instead, they would hear a message from John Walsh asking them to hold on, their call would be answered promptly in the order it was received. Meanwhile, an on-line computer would keep track of each operator's status (busy, finishing up, free), the number of calls waiting, and the total number of calls that come in that night for each case (the operator would punch a code after answering).

Out in Los Angeles, Chao was going through some mixed emotions about his brainchild. He was also getting set to film a pilot for an adult game show called "King of the Mountain," based on a popular Japanese competition show for adult participants.

He was thrilled that the pilot had gone so well and the project was set for launch. With three weeks to go, things were falling into place slowly, though the staff was putting in 15-hour days, seven days a week. Morale was excellent.

During the past six months, Chao constantly worried that someone else would put a similar show on the air before "America's Most Wanted" could premiere. A syndicated show called "Crimewatch" had been featured at NATPE that month, and it closely resembled AMW's approach.

The pilot had been shot very economically, coming in at $75,000. Suppose Roberts was caught before the show aired? He was the center of the first show. They would blow a third of the pilot budget and have to replace him quickly. He had been out there a year and a half now, and there were rumors he was out of the seven O&O market areas.

This had started as a "small, tacky idea," which everyone hoped would grow into something legitimate. Yet nobody was sure it would work. Suppose they went nine weeks without a capture? The show would have to quietly pack its bags, and disappear an embarrassed flop, which the TV critics and the competition would laugh about for years.

The foundation of American television is localism, Chao thought. This show doesn't serve localism; it serves nationalism. At the heart of any major network, despite the network organism itself, is localism. The local stations must have the ability to do its own news, sell its own advertising spots, do its own promotion—local everything. That's the way that the first TV stations started in the early 1950s, and that's the way it will always be in American television.

Maybe the best strategy was to develop a "Most Wanted" show in each Fox market. Perhaps 25 percent of the country would be enough to test the concept. If it worked, Fox would allow the show to go national, so Chao had hoped since August.

He had been allowed to set the debut date, but there were many factors converging at once, so he didn't have a lot of choices. It couldn't debut in the fourth quarter of 1987. That was a good advertising time, but the spots were already sold. From a programming standpoint, it was not a good time to premiere a new show. The other networks were putting on mid-season replacements and audience levels would be low in the holiday season.

January might be too fast, since Linder didn't have his staff in place for a premiere then. In February, he would be premiering during a ratings sweep period (when Nielsen audience ratings books are done for all markets to set advertising rates). It would be better to debut in January, then have a foothold going into sweeps, but the show wasn't ready. Okay, go for February, he decided.

The response from the O&O stations where the show would debut was mixed. Since they were owned-and-operated by Fox, they did not have the option to accept or refuse programming as other network affiliates.

It had been decided to put the show on from 6:30 to 7 P.M. on Sunday evenings. That would get it close to "Sixty Minutes" and attract some news junkies.

The FBC Sunday night lineup started at 7 P.M., so the station group would have control over the 6:30 P.M. slot.

Some people at the O&O's were excited about the prospect of innovative original programming. Others resented being told what to put on the air. They complained that original programming would cost more than putting on syndicated, local news, or reruns in the time slot. The stations would have to pick up a share of the show cost, depending on their market size and station rating-share average. For example, in the early days of AMW, a half-hour show would cost $120,000. New York would be charged $30,000, and so on down the line. That would be more than they would pay for a syndicated rerun. It would not be a major problem, but a minor economic strain until the show started turning an advertising profit.

Chao's programming laboratory had been set up to develop shows which would be tried out on the O&O's. "Dr. Science" stayed on for 13 weeks, costing the stations some money, but they had gone along. This was different, since the time slot was more lucrative.

From an advertising standpoint, AMW was not a completely "advertiser friendly" show. It was new, controversial, something some companies would shy away from. Local sales were not a problem, but national advertisers might be more conservative.

The negative sentiment was strictly in the minority. Several programmers at the O&O's welcomed the idea. Some, such as Dave Tillman at KTTV in Los Angeles, wasn't sure exactly what the audience mix would be, since a show like this had never been tried before. From experience, you would assume AMW would attract an adult audience. Would it be stronger among men or women, and what about the younger demographics? Who would be more interested in reconstructions of real crimes, fugitives' faces, and helping track them down? As it turned out, the show would attract a good audience mix, balanced across the board. He and others guessed that 6:30 P.M. would be the right time period, and they would be proven correct.

Others, such as Roz Brown of KRIV in Houston, realized the potential of a participatory show from the beginning. She didn't have to sell it to the other areas, since everyone felt it "had the ring of a good Houston show." It was innovative, and could break new ground in the expanding, "in" area being called "reality programming." Some viewers might complain about the crimes being reenacted, saying it wasn't their kind of entertainment. She and most others felt that the positive audience would outweigh the negative.

At the show, it was organized chaos. Barton was supervising the building of the set, while Walton and Vista were buying tables, chairs, and other props, mostly black to fit the motif. The bright, hi-tech look gave the feeling of being in a law enforcement situation room with monitors behind Walsh giving the sense of immediacy. He would sit on a high cushioned stool behind a table. Next to him would be law enforcement agents involved in the cases, who might be interviewed during the show. The set would modify several times during the show's history. (One TV critic knocked the original set, saying, "It looked like John Walsh was sitting on the bridge of the Starship *Enterprise*.") This "squad room" design would be expanded to include the phone operators and law enforcement on camera behind Walsh during the broadcast.

* * *

As for the fugitives on the premiere, Roberts and Minnick were a lock. Roberts was an FBI Ten Most Wanted and the most dangerous. Miller would be a strong candidate since he would give a balance to the show—a car thief, a bank robber, and a multiple-murderer/escapee.

Then Linder heard about a case of an unidentified Texas trucker who had abducted a mother and her daughter from their disabled car on Interstate 20 near Odessa. He had posed as a Good Samaritan, pretending to help them with their car problem, and offered to drive them to a service area. Instead, he kidnapped them and sexually abused them for hours. He then walked them into a field a few yards off the highway, shot each in the back of the head, and left them for dead. Miraculously, they survived. Their assailant was still at large and the leads were nil.

It was a compelling, breaking story. Because it had happened so recently, there might be a good chance of catching the man. The only identification available was an artist's composite drawing based on descriptions from the mother and daughter. This was a chance to show that AMW would be covering breaking news, current events happening that week, the most recent crime or atrocity, and track the fugitive while the trail was fresh. AMW would be viable and valid as a news program as well as an investigative magazine which covered older cases.

Linder hired Ron Zimmerman, a filmmaker based in Texas, to shoot the trucker segment on location where it happened. Both the mother and daughter asked to play themselves in the reenactment. Later they would say that it was a healing experience, making them feel as if they were doing something to help catch their assailant.

* * *

As the final premiere show was being put together, the other critical elements of getting a show on the air were in full force, including print advertising, on-air promotion, and publicity.

At WNYW in New York, on-air promotion producer Ron Scalera had been putting together some spots for the Fox stations to promote the first episode before the February 7 launch. Since the beginning of January, he had been discussing the project and his ideas with Linder and Herwitz, based on the pilot tape.

Scalera's approach was to get across to the viewer that this was a new kind of interactive television. You don't just watch passively. Instead, you can actually do something positive about the most threatening problem in American society, which is crime and fugitives at-large. The first step was to be informative. Tell the viewer that this is going to be a historic television show, an interactive show. Second, the promo would describe the fugitives being profiled without using any scare tactics. Give their descriptions, where there were last seen any telltale clues, and tell the viewer to watch the show Sunday at 6:30 P.M. on Fox.

For the premiere, Scalera used Roberts and Minnick, producing several versions of 10, 20, and 30 seconds in length to fit in various promotion spots the stations had available. He had to be creative, since the photographs of the fugitives were not up to the usual broadcast quality. These were people who weren't posing for a gallery photo session. The show had great dramatic footage to use, but the photos of the actual fugitive were blurry file shots. Using his experience, Scalera used various electronic devices not normally used in prime-time promotions. He moved the photos around the screen to enhance them, then superimpose the shot to make a more realistic image.

He would do an excellent job. One particular viewer would be very impressed by his work.

This would be a "bargain basement launch," as Chao would describe it later. The strategy was to rely heavily on the on-air promotions. There would be only print advertising ($100,000) and no radio buys. Walsh's seven-city publicity tour would be budgeted at $20,000.

Using images of Roberts from the FBI photos and stills from the documentary interview, the print advertising department put together an advertisement which was placed in *TV Guide* and newspaper supplements in the seven O&O markets.

When the first copies of *TV Guide* arrived at the studio, it was a solemn moment for the staff. Their show was really on the air and there was an ad with Roberts staring at them. "We're committed, we're really going to do this," Walton thought out loud. Everyone nodded in agreement and got back to work.

Walsh went out on an extensive publicity tour to all the seven markets over two weeks. Each stop was morning-to-night. They'd include early morning radio, midday talk shows, lunch print interviews, photo sessions, proclamations (Los Angeles declared John Walsh Day), sales cocktail parties, evening news, client dinners, more radio, and a few hours of sleep before he was up and off to the next city.

Walsh was an old pro at media interviews since the moment when a TV reporter shoved a microphone in front of his face and asked him how he felt about the death of his son. He was a passionate, driven man with intelligence, energy, and looks. The media loved him.

Over the past seven years, Walsh had testified

in front of legislatures in all but four states, and 17 times before Congressional committees. He and his wife, Reve, had been interviewed thousands of times on radio and television and had been featured in nearly every magazine and newspaper in America.

But this tour was different. He wasn't out there advocating for missing children or victims' rights, though he would mention these issues in every interview. Instead, he was promoting a new, controversial television show, which hadn't even been on the air yet. Critics questioned whether it would work and would it harm the rights of the individual, calling it vigilantism.

Even though he had committed to the show, Walsh still had a few lingering doubts before he left on the tour. It could be a way to get some justice for his son, Adam. Over the years, he had heard thousands of horrible stories from other victims of violent crime. There were so many criminals that had beaten the system. In all these legislative efforts he felt that he was changing things, but it wasn't directly related to catching people who had exploited the innocent, particularly women and children. It could be another tool in his arsenal.

It might also help police agencies work together, give them an extra resource. The "thin blue line" of police could only do so much with their resources and this could help.

Most marriages could never survive the agony that Reve and John Walsh had lived through. And this was something else to put a strain on them. Since Adam's death, they had two new children, who were the priority in Walsh's life. John talked it over with his wife once more. Her reply was simple and positive.

"We've sacrificed everything," she said. "You've

given up your job, our standard of living. You've tried to change things and help people.

"There are a lot of people worse off than we are. Look at what *Adam* and 'Street Smart' did, the power of the medium.

"Try it. If it doesn't work, if nobody watches, you can come home and go back to doing what you're doing. If it works and catches some criminals it would be wonderful. There will be less people to victimize our children and anybody else's children."

So off he went.

On the Friday before debut, the FBI gave the show as close to an official endorsement that it could. The Bureau now had a new director, William Sessions. As a former judge he was concerned about protecting the rights of the individual to a fair trial and the proper degree of publicity the FBI could make. After reviewing the established procedures and safeguards, he was willing to endorse it as a good work for law enforcement, but not as an entertainment, money-making venture. The FBI would endorse the citizen cooperation with law enforcement fostered by the show. There was a fine line between the commercial benefit for Fox and the benefit to the public, the Bureau had cautioned beforehand, but it would stress the public good.

AMW would be an extension of the FBI's fugitive publicity efforts. Later, Milt Ahlerich would admit that the Bureau and he personally did "go out on a limb a little bit," but it paid off. The bottom line was it could help catch dangerous fugitives.

Sessions appeared with Walsh and Linder at a press conference at the FBI Headquarters that afternoon. It was well attended by the 43 regular national correspondents from the electronic and print media which cover the FBI and the Justice Department.

After the conference, the three posed for photographs and video cameras in front of the AMW logo and a blow-up of the premiere show ad.

The word was getting out. Now it was time to do the show. Sunday, February 7 was almost too late.

6

He Wasn't the Only One Surprised

The promos were running on the O&O's, the ads had been placed in *TV Guide* and the appropriate newspapers. At the AMW offices, the final script was being finished, then refinished, over and over.

Friday and Saturday were long rehearsal days in the studio, nearly ten hours each day. The format had been pretty well nailed down in the past few weeks. The taped packages of Roberts and Minnick had been completed months ago. On Monday, Zimmerman had turned in a compelling piece on the unknown Texas Trucker.

The newest member of the AMW team was its show director Glenn Weiss, the news studio director at WTTG. He had been a "director of most everything" at WTTG for nearly eight years, and had heard about the new show in the building back in June. From what he heard this would be something radically different from anything produced there before. It would be taped just before broadcast—"live from Washington" to the nation. Sounded exciting, he thought.

There was some resentment about the new show among the veteran station employees. They didn't have any control over it and the entire staff had come from outside. But once the technical personnel started rehearsing with Walsh and Linder, the word spread that these guys weren't so bad after all. They might even make a little history.

Weiss offered his assistance to Linder during the summer, which the producer welcomed gratefully. Linder was unfamiliar with the DC production scene which Weiss had mastered since coming to town in 1979. A Long Island native, Weiss started his broadcast career with Cable News Network while still studying TV at the University of Maryland. He did everything from edit to direct, including audio and camera for six years before coming to WTTG. At Channel Five, he had directed local news, sports, specials, and a talk show called "Panorama." For a year or so, he had considered leaving to find a talk or entertainment directing job, then along came "America's Most Wanted." But even though he'd belong to AMW on weekends, he'd still be a full-timer at the station, directing the news and whatever else he was assigned.

Weiss had heard that the show's host, John Walsh, didn't have much television experience. Considering some of the news "talent" he had run across over the years, that wouldn't be a problem. The show wasn't that "studio-involved" anyway, since Walsh would only be introing pieces and throwing it to tape.

When Walsh first stepped in front of the camera on Friday, he was nervous. Though he hadn't gone to "anchorman school," he had considerable public speaking experience, but this was different. He was the host, the master of ceremonies.

"I didn't know anything about floor directors, countdowns, or technical stuff, so I looked at it as a challenge," Walsh would remember later about that first show. "I'd forced myself to be able to get up and talk in front of ten thousand people, to address committees, to address whole legislatures. That's a stressful, pressure situation in itself and this was another challenge.

"I just told myself that I am going to do the best I can and that's all I can do and approach it in a very businesslike and professional manner."

He would ask "lots of questions" and ask people to show him what to do when he didn't know. Don't wing it like some news guys he had seen. This had to be timed to the tenth of a second.

"But the first Sunday," he remembered later. "It was rough."

Linder and staff had run through the script with Walsh several times Friday and Saturday. They had walked through the show several times on the set.

Late Saturday night, Linder, Walton, and Ms. Roberts sat at the phone desk in the deserted studio, wondering what would happen there less than 24 hours later.

"I can't believe it," Linder said. "It's really going to happen."

"And what's gonna happen when it hits the air?" Ms. Roberts wondered.

"Aren't you excited, Margaret?" Linder asked.

"I'm still sweating details," she sighed.

Linder laughed. "That's what we pay you for. Keep sweating details."

Sunday morning the final rehearsal before taping began at 10 o'clock sharp in Studio Two. In the control room, Linder sat next to Weiss along with the technical staff, while Herwitz climbed up on a stool behind them. Chao couldn't make the christening since he was busy editing "King of the Mountain" back in Los Angeles. But he would be "bugging" them by phone every ten minutes or so.

Down on the set below, Walsh was dressed in a business suit, seated uncomfortably on a high stool behind a table on a big orange hi-tech set. Behind him were several live monitors laid into the set wall. He always had a lot of nervous energy and couldn't sit still normally for a minute. Now he was just squirming there in front of the camera, feeling like a news anchor. Maybe the next show he could talk them into letting him walk around or something.

He could see Linder and Weiss on the second floor through the huge control room window high on the other side of the studio above a two-foot clock. He could also hear them through an earpiece that never seemed to keep quiet. As the afternoon sped by, he would watch that clock ticking closer and closer to 6:30—H-Hour!

"John, could we just slow that down a little? You're going just a wee bit too fast. Could you punch that word a little more? Don't move until you get the cue. No, that's not the cue. Don't watch me, watch the floor manager."

For dress rehearsal, Walsh got his first make-up job and hairstyling from Penny Ross. She was so pleasant and friendly like everyone else, Walsh would remember, that he relaxed a bit, though he had already sweated through three blue oxfords. Several times during the runthroughs, Linder would stop the show to sit Walsh down and talk to him a bit. He was extremely patient, Walsh would remember, telling the host that he was trying a bit too hard in places.

To his right behind the set this time he could see the eight phone operators and the staffers—Walton, Vista, Roberts, Stone, McKenzie, Allendorfer, Siegel, and others—sitting at the desks, ready to take calls once the real show was on the air. That is, if anyone called.

Linder and Chao had been working on this for more than nine months. Hundreds of people, many he hadn't even met, had worked on this show for weeks. There were forty or more people running around the studio, doing something or other.

By one o'clock, Linder decided it was time to start taping. They would need every minute.

On the earpiece, Walsh would hear the opening start, as everyone in the studio did. It opened with a human eye, then a phone ringing. . . . "America's Most Wanted."

The floor manager counted down with his fingers. . . . five, four, three, two, one. He pointed at Walsh to begin. The host looked into the camera lens through the teleprompter and read the script rolling by.

"I'm John Walsh. Welcome to the premiere of 'America's Most Wanted,' a nationwide criminal manhunt, a partnership with law enforcement agencies across the country.

"Using actors, we will re-create crimes of dangerous fugitives, often at the location where they took place. We'll brief you on how the outlaws think and behave and where they may be hiding.

"Here in our studios, researchers are waiting for your calls on our toll-free hotlines. If you know something about these cases you're going to see, call us at 1-800-CRIME-88. You don't have to tell us your name.

"Some of the crimes you're about to see are tough. Parental discretion is advised, but we believe these stories demand telling."

Weiss cued the David James Roberts segment— after more than a dozen takes, that is. It had to be perfect, and Walsh was determined to make it that way.

Once the taped segment was finished, Walsh

would come back on camera to give a description of the fugitive as his photograph was on the screen with his age (44), height (6'3"), weight (218), eye color (brown), and hair color (black). Underneath was the show's toll-free hotline number. There were three other black-and-white mug shots shown, along with twelve seconds of the NBC documentary interview from prison. Walsh continued.

"Roberts sometimes wears wire-rimmed glasses, sometimes a mustache. He's a convincing talker who appears well educated and could be looking for work in the trucking industry. He has an eight-inch scar on his back near his shoulder blade and a scar on his right lip. Call now 1-800-CRIME-88."

A few more takes, then onto Ray Allen Minnick, wanted for multiple bank robberies and attempted murder. The man who said he won't be taken alive. The taped piece ran, then back to Walsh, with the photo and description. To commercial.

Time was speeding by, but the pace was slow. Camera positions were changed, the operators were moved closer, floor marks for Walsh were switched, the script was revised once more.

Back on camera, Walsh was now sitting with copy in his hand, looking like a news anchor. Seated next to him were two stern-looking police officers. The host introduced the tape segment on the unknown Texas trucker.

"This man is between six-feet-one and six-feet-three, he weighs between two hundred and two hundred and thirty pounds. He has a beard, black hair, and wears half-slippers. He is absolutely ruthless and he told his victims he did it before and he would do it again."

Walsh interviewed the officers, Captain Gene Kloss and Lieutenant Jerry Davis from the Ector County Sheriff's Office in Odessa, Texas. They gave the latest update on the case and asked for people with clues to call in.

Walsh turned back to the camera to wrap up the show.

"I became a victim of crime when my young son, Adam, was kidnapped and murdered. I decided not to be victimized by fear or revenge. But each of us can help, and must help stop crime. And you can make a difference.

"Remember the people you've seen on our program tonight. . . ." Walsh continued as he ran through the three fugitives' descriptions.

"They're out there. Maybe you know where or something, anything that could help. If so call your toll-free number 1-800-CRIME-88.

"Next week, you're going to meet Robert Nauss, a killer. He's an outlaw biker, convicted of murder in Pennsylvania. Now he's escaped from prison.

"I'm John Walsh. Remember, you can make a difference."

The credits finished rolling at 6:28 P.M., Eastern Standard Time. Two minutes to get it on the satellite to the six stations and to WTTG's master control. As someone would recall later, it was "very *Broadcast News*."

In the one-inch editing room down the hall from the studio, videotape editor David Shapiro had put some final touches on the master tape. The second he finished, an assistant pulled the reel off and raced out the door to the satellite feed room. A technician slammed it into the machine, cued it up, and the signal went up to the "bird." The monitor went to black for a tense moment. Up came "the eye" and the phone ringing. "America's Most Wanted" was on the air in Boston, New York, Chicago, Dallas, and Houston.

Another production assistant had dashed upstairs to WTTG's master control room with another
tape. The control switched the machine on and the
tape started rolling for Washington. (Three hours
later it would be shown in Los Angeles.)

Downstairs in Studio Two, the mood was a mix-
ture of excitement, relief, and nervousness, as the
show played on the monitors. The law enforcement
officers assigned to the three cases stood by the
phone operators ready to write with piles of pens
and 3-carbon tip sheets on the desk. The staff held
their collective breath. Would anyone call? Or would
they have a hundred lawsuits at their door on Monday morning?

Suddenly, the power of television erupted before
their eyes. Eight lines rang at once the first time
Roberts's photo appeared on the screen, and eight
operators picked up their receivers. By the end of
the first commercial, the ACD had ten calls waiting
on queue.

One caller, then another, from New York City
said they knew a man who looked just like the one
on television.

His name was Bob Lord.

Project Hospitality is located in the basement of
the Brighton Reformed Church on the corner of St.
Mark's Place and Court in a quiet rundown residential section of Staten Island, a borough of New York
City, south of Manhattan and west of Brooklyn. This
interfaith ministry for the homeless is on a hill, just
a few blocks from the Staten Island Ferry terminal
to Manhattan and the Federal Building, which has
a five-agent office of the FBI as one of its tenants.

Bob Lord had arrived at the church on a chilly
fall afternoon in November 1986. He had taken the
ferry over the day before, answering an ad for an

inexpensive room at the Richmond Hotel, where he could rent by the week. Down on his luck, he was nearly out of money. Coming out of the hotel, Lord started walking up the street to look for possible work. As he stepped off a curb in front of a church, he twisted his ankle and fell to the pavement.

The ankle hurt, but Lord could tell it wasn't broken. He just needed a few minutes to rub out the pain, so he sat on the steps of the white clapboard church to rest. A sign said it was the Brighton Heights Reformed Church. While sitting there on the cold brick steps, Lord noticed some men were coming from the other side of the church with coffee and sandwiches in their hands.

"Are they having some kind of function in there?" Lord asked one of the men.

A man in filthy, tattered clothes ignored Lord as he gobbled his food and hurried down the sidewalk. Maybe he could get a meal or something here, Lord thought, since he hadn't eaten since the afternoon before. Limping around the other side of the church, Lord saw a green sign saying this was "Project Hospitality." He went downstairs, got a sandwich and coffee, and left. The people were extremely friendly, and asked no questions.

At first, Lord thought Project Hospitality was a low-income referral agency, so Lord decided to see if they could help him find a job and housing. His hotel room cost $25 a night, too expensive for an unemployed man with $50 left in his pocket. The volunteers at the center gave some ideas for work, but he couldn't stay in one of its shelters until he was out of money. The next day he would qualify.

They didn't have a bed available in any shelter, but he could get a meal there. With no place else to go, Lord wandered the streets for the next several weeks. By day, he'd look for a job, then by night, he would sleep in the streets, in the terminal, or ride the ferry all night—it cost only a quarter.

Winter was coming and Lord was getting desperate. He was too proud for welfare. Though he was chronically ill with a lung problem, he was still capable of standing on his own two feet. Finally in December the Carpenter Shelter, a 15-bed facility in the basement of the old convent at Immaculate Conception Roman Catholic Church, had an open bed and a grateful Lord took it.

He quickly started helping out by cleaning up around the shelter when he wasn't looking for a job. People at the shelter were impressed with Lord. He had run out of money, but he wasn't crippled or paralyzed like so many other homeless men who wandered in there. He had a real sense of himself, was ambitious, concerned for others, and full of energy. The floors never shined so bright, and the usually foul air had a fresh, clean scent to it.

Among those Lord impressed was Terry Troia, the executive director of Project Hospitality for the past three years. He told her that he had most recently come from Chicago, though he had been born in New Jersey. He said that his family was Jewish, and he had a son, whom he missed, but didn't mention where the boy lived.

While a guest at the shelter, Lord found a job driving a van at a construction site in Manhattan, and became an unpaid intern at the shelter. He built a stage for the Christmas play, and even played one of the three wise men in the pageant. One morning in April, Lord had trouble with an unruly shelter guest and was late for his driving job. He came back early that afternoon to the shelter. He had been fired from his job.

Troia called up Lord's boss, since everyone at

the shelter felt terrible. The man wouldn't listen, Lord was history.

By coincidence, an opening for a supervisor at the shelter had opened up. The former shelter supervisor had married and moved to Atlanta. Lord applied for the job, but there was stiff competition from several other applicants. His experience and commitment won out and Troia appointed him the new supervisor in April at an annual salary of $18,000.

Lord was a tireless workaholic. In addition to his supervisor duties, he was an outreach worker at the Brighton Reformed Church, of which he was now a very active, devout Christian member. Saving his money, he had bought a beat-up used car and rented a two-room apartment in a two-story frame house at 295 Gordon Street, three blocks from the shelter. For a while, he had a girlfriend.

Lord's day started at 5:30 A.M., when he arrived at the shelter to get the 15 guests up, showered, and dressed. He then supervised morning gymnastics, followed by cooking and cleaning detail. Later, he would pick up some of the elder volunteers and drive them to the shelter. He also referred guests to alcohol and drug treatment centers, having earned training certificates from Columbia University's Community Services. Lights were out at 11 P.M., but Lord would often be called in to help resolve a problem.

The shelter was run like a boot camp, and the new supervisor was loved and admired for his sense of discipline and incredible energy. He made people feel wanted, loved, and important.

Lord helped open a second shelter for women nearby, and expanded the Carpenter shelter to 22 beds. He got some women from a local Lutheran church to make 100 quilts. Cutting through city bu-

reaucracy like an old pro, Lord negotiated a grant
from the Human Resources Administration for a new
boiler and heating system. He installed most of it
himself, along with three new showers.

The only time Troia would reprove her star supervisor was to take some time for himself. One night
she tried to get him to leave the shelter for a few
hours to go to the movies to see *Cry Freedom.* She
wound up going by herself, and Lord caught the 10
o'clock show by himself.

More than once she had to scold him for giving
away his own money to the guests. But Lord had
been there himself, and knew that with a little help
some of these men could get back on their feet. He'd
let them "borrow" $5 or $10, though he was worried
that the money sometimes went for drugs or alcohol.
The shelter was located just a few hundred yards
from the largest crack-dealing park on Staten Island.

During the summer, Lord did take a night off.
Troia, Lord, and the other shelter workers and volunteers went over to Gracie Mansion in Manhattan.
Mayor Ed Koch was hosting his annual celebration
for people working in volunteer shelters. The ami-
able Lord shook hands with the mayor and posed for
a photograph taken by one of the Carpenter volunteers.

The winter was the busiest time for the shelter,
and Lord put in 18 to 20 hours a day. The only time
he would sleep was to take cat naps in a back room.
His coworkers would sometimes have to force him
to eat. That's something that impressed Laura
Bruno, a reporter for the *Staten Island Advance,* who
wrote a story in December 1987, on the incredible
man running the Carpenter Shelter. More than one
client praised Lord as a hero in the story.

"That's basically what I see in Project Hospitality—people who care," said a shelter guest. "When

people like Bob Lord ride me hard, it took a while for me to realize that he was doing that to help me."

In late January, a young couple asked Lord if he could help them move to a new apartment. Lord said he would bring over three men from the shelter, as long as the couple would pay the men a few bucks. Lord would be the fourth, being a strong man himself at a stocky six-foot-three.

The group drove over to the house in the shelter van, having taken out the seats to load the furniture. They finished the job in an hour, and the only thing left was an old refrigerator. It would be a tough job getting it down the stairs, since there was a sharp right turn. They had to stand the heavy load straight up and push it along the railing. Lord felt a stab of sharp pain in his chest as something popped inside. He passed it off as a pulled muscle and they finished the job.

The next day, Lord started coughing up a little blood. That had happened before with his sinus condition. Monday, Tuesday, Wednesday—Lord was coughing up more blood at frequent intervals. He mentioned it in passing to Troia, who immediately made him go to Bayley Seton Hospital on Wednesday afternoon.

Lord took along a friend whose girlfriend had just kicked him out and drove the few miles to the hospital. The busy supervisor thought the problem would just require an X-ray and he'd be back to work in an hour or so. Instead, the examining doctor, Dr. Tarantola, head of the pulmonary laboratory, wouldn't let Lord step out the door. He needed tests right away.

Giving his car keys to the friend, Lord told him he could stay in his apartment and use the car as long as he did some volunteer work at the shelter. He called Troia, worried that the shelter couldn't run without him. She assured him that everything would be fine and his main priority right now was his health. He was sure he would be back there by Friday.

Thursday, Lord went through a battery of tests. Looking at the results, the doctor wanted to do a biopsy. He also wanted to do a CAT scan, and another test which required putting a tube in Lord's left lung. But the physician was concerned that some medication given the patient could cause him to regurgitate, forcing the contents of his stomach into the right lung. The test couldn't be conducted until Monday, so Lord would have to remain in his bed in semiprivate room #206 over the weekend.

Troia finally got over to see Lord on Friday evening, and found him extremely depressed. Though he had had some visitors from the shelter—Reverend Ratmeyer and a few friends like Doris Whiteman and Alma Hamersly—Lord was lonely. He had even brought along some paperwork, such as the volunteer schedule for the following week. Troia tried to cheer him up, saying that everyone at the shelter was concerned about him and wanted to visit.

"No, I'm okay, don't have them bother," he said. "I'm all right. By the time they come over, I'll be out."

On Saturday, Lord passed most of the day watching television, making phone calls, reading his Bible, and chatting with his roommate and his roommate's wife. Lord and he got into several deep conversations. He was impressed when he overheard Lord on the telephone counseling a woman whose daughter had been busted for crack. Because he had multiple sclerosis, the man couldn't write, so Lord wrote out a Valentine's Day card for him to give to the nurses.

Troia went back over to the hospital Saturday night. The shelter supervisor was still restless and depressed lying in bed all day and night. They watched some television, read Scripture, and prayed together. Troia left Lord's room about 9:30 P.M., and promised to come back the next afternoon.

Sunday morning, February 7, was a special day for Terry Troia. She was being ordained an elder of the church at Brighton Heights. But after the ceremony, a shock would take away her joy.

Reverend Lee MacCallum, pastor of Olivet Presbyterian Church, a member of Project Hospitality, handed her a copy of the current *TV Guide*. There was an advertisement for a new show on Channel 5 called "America's Most Wanted." In the middle of the page was a photograph that looked a lot like someone she knew very well—her shelter supervisor, fellow Christian, and good friend—Bob Lord. Only the ad called him David James Roberts and said he was wanted by the FBI, having been convicted of murder, rape, and arson.

"Please help catch this criminal before he kills again..." the ad said. "His crimes are unspeakable and he's still at large. Tonight, see the crime, see the man...then call 1-800 CRIME-88 if you can help ...Sundays 6:30 P.M."

Reverend MacCallum, Troia, and a few others from the church sat down and talked it over.

"Maybe this is an innocent man."

"We don't know for sure."

"Maybe it's not Bob."

The group made its decision. At three o'clock Sunday afternoon, Reverend MacCallum picked up the telephone and called the FBI.

The automatic call distributor was telling Grace Vista that she had more than 30 calls waiting to be answered. Later, she'd find out that they were missing dozens of other calls, since the tape machine with

Walsh's voice saying "Please hold on . . ." was taking only one call at a time. Only eight operators had showed up and they were getting tired quickly. Within fifteen minutes of the end of the broadcast, she had to ask the staff, Ms. Roberts, Walton, Burke, and Allendorfer to help out on the extra phones.

They balked at first, not realizing how the calls were piling up. But within a few seconds, the excitement took hold.

There was a pattern of calls developing on Roberts. Stargardter's rehearsals had paid off, they were getting the right information quickly. Allendorfer would later remember a caller who was hesitant about calling, but she was very concerned.

"She said, 'I don't want to be narcing or ratting on somebody who might be a good person, but he looks just too much like the person who's directing our project for the homeless,'" Allendorfer said, not really having time to analyze whether the tip was valid. That was up to the FBI. The woman was nervous, but she was very literate and intelligent.

Answering the phone and talking to someone who said they saw someone you had been obsessed with for seven months sent a chill down Walton's spine. A lot of people would say they saw the man, but just because the viewer was convinced, the squad cars weren't going to roll. Stargardter had said that if you got an address, it was a hot call, and these people were. Some were just calling to see if the number really worked and someone would answer. Others would want more information on the show and would be given the post office box number. But people were calling, so at least they had watched and AMW just might work, he thought.

As an attorney, Herwitz was probably among the most skeptical—and worried. Would they have the FBI chasing after someone who's a dead ringer for this guy, while he's out in Oklahoma someplace? But when he saw the agents huddling in the corner and picking up the outside phone lines, he knew something was definitely brewing. More than one operator had scribbled down the name "Bob Lord." Nobody was calling about him from Chicago, Houston, Dallas, or Boston—just New York, and some from the same block.

The operators weren't sure what was a good call, so when a caller said they had seen one of the fugitives, up went the hand with a card marked either "Roberts," "Minnick," or "Trucker." Several times all eight arms were raised with different cards, and Vista couldn't transfer all the calls to the agents. Finally, the agents just started jumping into the operator's seat.

The phones "stayed hot" for nearly three hours. Just as the weary, hand-cramped operators and staff were starting to break, the show was airing in Los Angeles. The lines lit up again. (As the operators would find out over the coming weeks, the most unusual calls would come after the West Coast broadcast when the number of psychics calling increased radically.) They wouldn't stop until after midnight.

There were some solid leads on Minnick, but nothing that the BATF agents were running after right away.

A lot of the Trucker tips were just people who had seen a truck like the assailant drove. By the next morning, the Odessa Sheriff's Department would have lots of tip sheets to take home, but few valuable clues without a known fugitive and a good photo of him. Linder would learn a lesson to stick to the known suspects, and leave the mysteries for other shows to solve.

And the producer would learn another lesson— you never know where a fugitive will be.

* * *

The FBI agents at the show were pinpointing
the locations that the New York area Roberts tips
came from. There had been about 75 from the New
York metropolitan area, which included the five city
boroughs, Long Island, Westchester County (New
York), and two counties in northern New Jersey.

The map pins of "good info" started forming a
circle. One call from Long Island, one call from Yon-
kers (N.Y.), four from Manhattan, one from Queens,
one from Jersey City, one from Union (N.J.), three
from Newark, six from Perth Amboy (N.J.). There
were twelve from Staten Island, clustered around
the northern portion of the island and the ferry terminal.

Terry Troia wasn't at the Carpenter Shelter
when five FBI agents walked in there at 10 o'clock
Sunday night. A homeless man had hanged himself
that night. The man survived and Troia was at the
hospital until 3 A.M. with the man. She found out
that Bob Lord had checked himself out against medical advice early Sunday morning.

The agents started questioning the staff members one by one. They were polite, yet methodical,
wanting to know about Bob Lord. The staff was
shocked. The news had spread fast that someone
looking like Lord had been profiled on this new show
on Channel 5 that was supposed to catch criminals.
What was most confusing to everyone was that the
show said this man was a brutal killer of children
and rapist of women. The man had escaped from
prison and was one of the FBI's Ten Most Wanted
fugitives. Bob Lord had never shown any sign of
impatience, much less violence. He had the greatest
respect for women, and loved to hold little babies in
his arms. He could never hurt anyone.

Other agents had come over from Manhattan

and were checking out addresses given by viewers who had called AMW in Washington just a few hours before. Getting the names and addresses of staff members and volunteers from the shelter, they started knocking on doors and asking more questions far into the night and morning. Others would be over in New Jersey asking questions and following leads. Monday morning six agents raided Roberts's Gordon Street apartment. He wasn't home.

They were a little puzzled though. Roberts wasn't that different from hundreds of unlawful flight subjects they were looking for at that moment. He was a smooth talker, very convincing. But a convicted murderer-kidnapper-rapist running a homeless shelter? They weren't sure that he could get anyone to support him, much less like him.

He had been last seen taking a westbound train out of Hammond and had made a statement to his captives that we was going to get a plane out of Chicago and maybe leave the country. Shortly after his conviction in 1977, his mother, a younger brother, and two sisters moved to the Middle East and joined a black Hebrew group. Roberts's younger brother, Frank, had been given a life sentence in 1975 for robbing a church in Gary, Indiana, and shooting a member during a worship service.

The FBI followed leads all over the country—Illinois, Tennessee, Ohio, New Jersey (his home state), and all over Indiana. They went anywhere they could find "lead material"—friends, relatives, associates, past inmates, old girlfriends. His family "was not very cooperative," according to case agent Tom Allison in Indianapolis.

They even checked out some in foreign countries, since he might have fled to Canada, North Africa, or Israel. They felt that they had had at least one positive lead about four months before when he was

positively identified at a truck stop along the New
Jersey Turnpike. Roberts probably demonstrated
more intelligence than the average fugitive they
were tracking. He had the ability to talk his way out
of things, convincing people that he was something
other than what he really was.

Monday morning in Washington, the AMW
staff was gearing up for next Sunday's broadcast—
Bobby Nauss, Peter Miller, and updates on Minnick,
Roberts, and the Trucker. Ms. Roberts arrived at
9 A.M., thinking she could concentrate on editing
and fact-checking the upcoming show's scripts. The
hotline was laid to rest until next Sunday. Or so
she thought.

Walton hadn't even poured a cup of coffee when
the phone started ringing. The hotline number had
been rolled over to the office phone. Viewers were
calling with tips from last night's show. Police officers from cities and towns in the seven markets were
calling to inquire about getting cases on this new
crimefighting show.

They couldn't cut the phone off—the one call
they missed could be the one to nail a fugitive. Walton took a turn on the phone, then Stone, then Allendorfer. It was clogging up the newsroom and
taking people away from the pile of work they had
to tackle before Sunday afternoon. Finally, Vista
called in two operators to answer the phones from
the studio phone bank. There were still "good calls"
coming in, especially from New York on Roberts. But
there were others from Maryland, another from
Houston, that also sounded "so good." The staff felt
like "rookie cops," unable to think of anything else
but those calls. Maybe it really is him.

The FBI weren't saying much about the hunt on
Staten Island. They did tell Linder on Monday that

they "believed the validity of the information they were receiving, and had launched a massive search" in New York, particularly on the northern tip of Staten Island.

"We were incredulous," Linder would recall later. "There was no way to describe it. I'd worked on this project for ten months, and even in that amount of time there was no notion of catching anyone through interactive television. One of us knew whether this would work, and whether we'd get any phone calls."

But there had been nearly 500 calls on Roberts alone, 1,600 in all, by Tuesday afternoon.

"Hmm, this might lead to something," Linder mused to himself. He wasn't sure if the FBI was just being polite or whether they were really on to a case.

By Wednesday afternoon, Ms. Roberts had written several memos to update Linder on some of the more detailed calls. One woman, who described herself as "a social friend" of Lord said she had known him since last November. He has a "militaristic posture," but is "gentle, calm, easygoing, and giving." Though a "formidable man," he could assert power over people yet command respect. He never had time to socialize; he was always working with someone in trouble. The shelter director had been urging him to take a vacation, and he was thinking about seeing his son or taking a cruise, maybe to Jamaica. The woman's daughter had spoken to Lord on Sunday morning, and he told her that he couldn't stand the hospital anymore. She had bought him pajamas.

Every week, Lord sent money to his son, about 14 years old, she thought. He was "tearful" every time he spoke about the boy. But she wondered how he could go on vacation, since Lord rarely had more than a few dollars to his name.

Ms. Roberts ended the memo with, "So what do you think: Is Lord Roberts?"

In Los Angeles, Chao was calling Linder constantly, "acting like a couple of Valley Girls" about the Roberts hunt. The executive was still in the editing room with "King of the Mountain." The producer was leafing through the tip sheets and phone logs, pulling out promising ones and reading Chao the lead. Linder sent him copies of the best ones by overnight delivery. They spent "an inordinate amount of time gossiping about the leads and what they meant," Chao would remember.

Chao still figured that the odds were slim of catching someone who had been on the run for a year and a half with a show that was only being shown in 25 percent of the country. He was probably in Pittsburgh or Kansas City, and one of his fellow cons would send him a copy of the *TV Guide* ad for a good laugh. Within three months, they'd be lucky if they caught anybody, Chao worried.

Meanwhile, looking toward the coming Sunday's show, the executive had some tough, but constructive criticisms for Walsh, particularly about him moving from side to side as he sat and spoke. The host took the advice seriously, not offended in the least. He and Linder talked over some ways they could smooth out his delivery. And he didn't want to sit behind a desk. There had to be some way to use that nervous energy to pump up the show. And could he also lose the suit jacket, loosen his tie, and roll up his shirt-sleeves?

Lord had checked himself out of the hospital against medical advice. Late Saturday night his roommate was asleep, and the shelter supervisor was still too restless and depressed to doze off himself. He decided to watch some TV around midnight. He flipped through several New York channels until he found a movie he had seen before and liked.

On came a commercial. There on the TV screen above his bed Lord saw his photograph. Or it looked a hell of a lot like him. At first, he thought it was an in-house hospital closed circuit video of the patients or something. Then the announcer on the TV said, "Watch, Sunday night, 'America's Most Wanted.'"

"Oh my goodness," Lord gasped. "'America's Most Wanted'—what is this?"

It took Lord more than an hour to check himself out. The nurses had to track down his doctor, who warned Lord that he was a very sick man and should stay in the hospital. He told them there had been an accident in his family and asked them to watch his things. By one o'clock Sunday morning, Lord had signed himself out of the hospital and was looking for a man he had heard about a few months before.

By mid-morning, he thought he could get his car and some things from his apartment. He had two suitcases already packed in the trunk. Calling the church to talk to Terry, he got Reverend Ratmeyer instead.

"Where are you at, Bob?" the minister asked gently.

"I just want to talk to Terry."

"People are looking for you. Why don't you tell me where you're at?"

"That's all right," Lord replied and hung up.

They were already on his trail. How far, he didn't know. The car and apartment were out. There was a guy who lived on Pine Street whom he knew from the shelter. The man was a telecommunications expert that Lord had helped get back on his feet. Maybe he could borrow his car and get off Staten Island.

Lord had lent him his own on several occasions. Time to call in the favor.

When Lord called the man, he was "quite busy," having a girlfriend over.

"I'm in a rush now, I've got somebody at home," he told Lord.

"Let me use your car."

"No, not right now, man."

Lord didn't want to take the man's car and leave it somewhere out of state like a thief in the night.

"Never mind," he said. "I'll see you later."

Well, he'd steal a car if he had to. Then he remembered another person on Pine Street who he had also helped. He hurried over there, though it was difficult for him to walk. His wind was still short and he had to rest frequently. All he needed was to start coughing up blood and attract attention.

He knocked on the door at 12 Pine Street, and asked his friend if he could "lay low there for a few days." She didn't ask any questions, the woman was just glad to have the company. The young mother and her four-year-old son liked Lord; he had helped her with some personal and housing problems.

For three days, Lord frantically tried to contact a man who could help him get out of New York. He knew that the FBI would be covering the bridges and the ferry terminal. Public transportation and taxis were out too. If he had seen this thing on television, chances were that a lot of other people had too. This guy could help him get some more money, and maybe a passport. He was over in Brooklyn though and his phone number was in Lord's address book—back in his apartment. There was someone else who might know the number, but he couldn't trust him at that point. He'd give the phone number from his Pine Street hideout to the FBI and they'd find him in five minutes. Wednesday night, Troia would recall, Lord called a Project Hospitality board member to say "he was sorry for hurting" them.

On Thursday afternoon, February 11, the agents found a man who gave them the address they needed. Six agents surrounded the tiny house at 12 Pine Street and snuck into the hallway, hoping for a surprise. Other than force his 220 pounds against the apartment door, the man inside didn't resist them. At 4 P.M., David James Roberts was in custody. He had his hat and coat on, just stepping out before the FBI stepped in.

Margaret Roberts was sitting in Tom Herwitz's office, hammering out some script changes. Herwitz was a tough legal expert and Roberts was a precise editor. Suddenly, Leslie Groves buzzed Herwitz, saying Wiley Thompson from the FBI was on line one.

Herwitz put the call on the speaker phone, since Thompson was probably calling about a case they had suggested for production next week. He had different news.

"Congratulations," Thompson said. "We just got Roberts in Staten Island."

For a moment, they just sat and stared—incredible! Ms. Roberts dashed across the hall. There was Linder seated at a desk and typing a letter.

"For a flash of a moment there was Michael leaning over typing, borrowing someone else's typewriter," she would later recall. "I saw him for that moment and knew that his life would never be the same."

"Michael," she said.

Linder got up and came across the room.

"David James Roberts has been captured."

Linder knew that Lord was Roberts but was afraid that the on-air promos had flushed him out and the FBI had lost him. He just smiled.

"Incredible," he said.

The news had already raced through the office like a fire storm. In the newsroom, Walton let out a rebel yell. In Los Angeles, Chao was dancing around the editing room. This thing just might work.

Within an hour of his arrest, Roberts had been brought over to FBI headquarters at 26 Federal Plaza in Manhattan. He was booked on federal escape charges, and "walked tall," as one observer said, as he walked out of the headquarters toward a waiting car. Politely, he refused comment to the mob of media that had congregated outside in the plaza. Spending the night in the nearby Metropolitan Correctional Center, he was scheduled for arraignment in federal court in Brooklyn on Friday morning. The woman who let him "lay low" for four days would not be charged, since she was still convinced he was Bob Lord, not an FBI Ten Most Wanted fugitive.

Back at Carpenter Shelter, it was like a horrible nightmare that they wished they could wake up from. They couldn't believe that the gentle, giving man they called Bob Lord was really a prison escapee, sentenced to six life terms for four murders, arson, two kidnappings, and a rape. Troia took the staff out to dinner so they could spend some time together, talking and praying about it. They had already decided to lend their support by going over to Brooklyn for the hearing. Others were talking about a Bob Lord Defense Fund. Reverend MacCallum was already calling a friend of his, Steve Hudspeth, to defend Lord. Maybe they could fight the extradition back to Indiana.

There were several people who had other reactions to Roberts's capture. Down in North Carolina, Patsy Patrick, Bill's sister, had offered a $2,500 reward for tips leading to Roberts's arrest. She had adopted Bill and Ann's surviving daughter, Anna Marie, now a senior in high school. She feared that the fugitive would take revenge on her family in Indiana. They were afraid for her safety since she was talking to the media about Roberts, even saying she would "meet him face-to-face." Patsy never told Anna Marie that Roberts had escaped from prison—until he was back in custody.

In Indiana, "Helen" had also feared retaliation from the escapee. She had married, divorced, and remarried. She wanted to forget about it, even though some of the local press were trying to track her down. Her sister was afraid to let her children out of the house, and had contacted the major networks after the escape. She was terrified, Lieutenant Quackenbush remembered, and so obsessed that she couldn't be consoled. Now, she could be.

Back at AMW, the celebration was brief. Allendorfer and Ms. Roberts were busy arranging coverage in New York to produce a four-minute "capture report" on Roberts. They had less than 48 hours to pull it off. A film crew from Channel 5 would provide some video footage of Roberts walking outside the FBI headquarters, reported by Steve Dunlop (later of Fox's newsmagazine show "The Reporters"). The AMW team managed to visit the shelter and get interviews with staffers and guests.

"I don't believe how one man could be two different people," said one volunteer. "(He was) just like a regular person going to work. Polite and got along with the homeless very well."

"Nice guy, sweet guy," added a guest. "He would do anything to help homeless people or anybody in trouble. He would never want to see anybody go hungry. It's hard to imagine, but unfortunately it's true."

They also interviewed the Reverend Paul Egen-steiner from Project Hospitality.

"I can't explain the evil that he did," he said. "I don't want to ignore it and yet my perspective is that he is God's child and he acted like God's child while with Project Hospitality."

Also appearing on the show Sunday would be Milt Ahlerich from the FBI and Patsy Patrick, representing the victims of Roberts's crimes, now "ecstatic" over his capture. Ahlerich would explain that 12 agents had followed leads in 13 locations around the clock, interviewing more than 100 people.

"Really candidly I would have to admit that we had no good leads other than he was in the New York area," Ahlerich said on the show.

Roberts was ready to fight his extradition back to Indiana with everything he could find. Hudspeth, a partner with Coudert Bros., a major international firm headquartered on Park Avenue in Manhattan, had agreed to take his case on a pro-bono basis. He had lived on Staten Island for 16 years before moving to Connecticut the year before. Their first task was to raise $2,000 for a polygraph test. Roberts not only wanted to prove his innocence for Indiana, but he also wanted to reassure his supporters on Staten Island.

With help from the defense fund and the clergy on Staten Island, they got the money for the test. Indiana officials were accusing them of using the tests to slow up the extradition proceedings. It took six trips back to the presiding judge before the tests were allowed. Meanwhile, he was fighting extradition, claiming that he was put in prison wrongfully.

The polygraphs wouldn't serve any legal purpose. New York State does not permit them to be used in court for any reason. Indiana allows them with the consent of both sides. There are a lot of mixed feelings among experts about how reliable polygraph tests can be. After this one, Hudspeth wasn't too sure either.

The first test—on the kidnap-rape-murder— came back positive. The one on the triple-murder/ arson was "questionable," Hudspeth would admit later.

"I think that on the kidnap-rape-murder, he was asked some very precisely focused questions tied to the evidence," the attorney explained. "On the triple murder that's a lot harder because it's such a circumstantial case, so you work around it and try to ask questions. It's not going to be the same, it's more loosely focused in terms of framing questions."

In other words, the polygraph did not help Roberts's case.

The extradition dragged on for several weeks, with Roberts getting moral support from his Staten Island friends who came to court. But the order was signed and he was on his way back to Indiana in late April. He would later plead guilty to escape charges and get an additional 30 years tacked on his life sentences. On May 11, the prison's disciplinary tribunal sentenced him to six years in solitary confinement.

Though Roberts is back in prison, he and Hudspeth are trying to reopen the case. The efforts have already gotten some attention.

For example, two major New York City publications have featured extensive investigations to Roberts's claims of innocence in both cases.

Reporter Laura Bruno, who had written about Bob Lord, the shelter supervisor in the *Staten Island*

Advance, got an exclusive interview with him at the Brooklyn Detention Center where he was being held. He was later transferred to Riker's Island. After writing an extensive follow-up on Roberts in jail, Bruno spent seven days in Indiana investigating Roberts's case, which was featured in an eight-part series in March 1988. It included an exclusive interview with Roberts's wife, Connie, who would not be photographed because she still fears harassment from Indiana officials, a charge they deny. Each part of the series included the caption, "The jury said 'Guilty!,' but did he kill?"

Journalist Aimee Lee Ball wrote a lengthy investigative feature for *New York* magazine entitled "Is David Roberts a Killer or Saint? Night and Day." Ball also tracked down the principals in Indiana, including the prosecutors, defense attorneys, and detectives, as well as Roberts in Michigan City.

At the Carpenter Shelter, people still refer to Roberts as Bob Lord, since that's what they knew him as. On the kitchen wall and elsewhere there are still some index-card notes about plumbing or heating procedures written in Roberts's neat handwriting. Several friends have traveled out to Michigan City to visit and write to him regularly. Many still insist that he is innocent.

Roberts still does also.

In a five-hour interview for this book, Roberts elaborated in detail on more than 25 points from both trials and investigations that he claims will prove his innocence. Hudspeth is looking to hire a private investigator to check into these points and perhaps win his client's freedom.

Among Roberts's claims are:

- There was no official cause of the homicides in the cases of Ann and Bill Patrick. How could he be convicted of a murder if there is still no explanation how it was done?
- Roberts says he was the victim of racial discrimination by the Indiana criminal justice system, particularly in Johnson County by the Ku Klux Klan. His attorney in the Patrick case, Tom Jones, was harassed by local police, Roberts says, which Jones confirmed in the *New York* article.
- He points out that the victim in the Indianapolis case was at first considered a suspect in her son's death, which police confirm as normal procedure. He also demands investigations into alleged family problems in the Patrick clan at the time of the murders.
- Witness George Jessup, the service station attendant who identified Roberts as the man who came in that night, wrote a letter in 1977 to Roberts in prison. Roberts claims that the letter shows Jessup's confusion about his testimony. In the letter, Jessup admits "ambiguities" in his testimony, but did not lie, as Roberts charged in a letter to him. He was "alarmed" that his testimony was "the corroboration necessary to convict you (Roberts) or any other man or woman." Roberts also challenges the difference in Jessup's height description of the assailant and himself. Jessup answered, "As I stated in court, I could be mistaken. To the best of my ability I am certainly not lying. . . . But if you are innocent, I hope you are exonerated. I would help all I could."
- Roberts stresses that he was forced to rely on public defense counsel and was denied proper investigative funds. Two public defenders were assigned to the Indianapolis case. One of them, Michael Riley, wound up marrying one of the op-

posing prosecutors, Patricia Woodward, after the trial. Roberts claimed he was never told by Riley about the relationship during the trial. In the *New York* magazine piece, Riley denied the charge, saying that he and cocounsel, Richard Sallee, informed their client of the romance and Roberts wanted Riley to stay on as his attorney.

• He also challenges the identifications in New Whiteland of himself and his car and the gas can evidence as circumstantial. As Hudspeth points out, Roberts is acknowledged to be an intelligent man, so how would he wander into an all-white area, ask for directions to his victims' home, then leave a gas can that could be traced? They also challenge the line-up procedures and the victim's description in the Indianapolis case as not properly linking him to the crimes.

• Roberts's wife still maintains that he was home the entire time that the Indianapolis crimes occurred. He says she has been harassed by the FBI and Indianapolis police. Though he has insisted that she divorce him and get on with her life, she has refused. The FBI states that the divorce filings are evidence that Roberts has lived a double life before. Quackenbush pointed out that Roberts dated one of his female probation officers after being released from Pendleton. The couple even vacationed together in the Bahamas, and she was fired afterward. Roberts never mentions the relationship.

• Roberts maintains that he was the focus of deliberate negative publicity by the Indianapolis media, particularly the *Star* and *News*. He says that despite the intense coverage of his arrest, crimes, and trials, neither newspaper has ever attempted to interview him. *Star* reporter Mark Nichols "left several messages" for Roberts at the jail after his

New York arrest, but they were not returned. The paper's current managing editor, Lawrence Connor, has no interest in a feature or investigative story about the Roberts case.

• The most compelling piece of exculpatory evidence would be the semen sample from the Indianapolis rape. Roberts says that the sample was not tested for the case. When his attorneys and he requested it, the police answered that it had not been properly preserved for testing. He later learned that blood-type tests could have been done to prove his innocence. Roberts says he hired a private investigator to go to the Indianapolis P.D. property and get the sample. He states that the investigator called Detective Larkins to inquire and when he arrived, Larkins said he had destroyed the sample "since it was taking up too much room." Larkins denies such a claim, saying the action would have been against the law. He also points out that the sample and all evidence would have been confiscated by the court and disposed of after the defendant had exhausted all appeals. "That's an old game that all your life-convicted felons are playing," Larkins adds. Roberts also claims that "an Indiana law requires evidence in criminal murder cases involving the death penalty must be kept for 100 years." Inquiries to several sources in state and city government in Indiana determined that such a law does not exist and never has.

When you talk to David James Roberts in prison, it's hard to believe that this charming, intelligent man has been convicted of four murders, four kidnappings, rape, arson, and escape. He is smooth, articulate, and explains his case with the expertise of a trial lawyer. But even sitting with him for a few minutes, one can see his ability to change his facial expressions, and thus his appearance, almost at will.

In his interview for this book, Roberts would not explain on the record how he escaped from prison. But he did narrate how he got to Project Hospitality.

In 1986, the parole board wouldn't even open up his packet. He tried to continue his federal suit by suing for representation and "got two kids who look like they should still be in high school."

A lot of officers in the prison sympathized with him, saying he had been framed, Roberts says.

At the Hammond train station, Roberts thought about taking a train west to Chicago. He had saved money from his income tax work in years past. Instead, he made a phone call. His wife would tell the *Staten Island Advance* that she came home from work that day and her son said, "Mom, Dad called and said to tell you good-bye."

Deciding to hitchhike instead to stay away from crowds of people, Roberts got a ride to Chicago with a trucker. He got off at the 87th Exit and took a train downtown.

"It was night and I was nervous as hell," Roberts remembered, thinking his prison garb would make him stand out.

As it turned out, his blue jeans and sweatshirts fit right into the folks around him. He stopped in a drugstore to buy shaving cream and a razor to shave off his mustache. Staying in a cheap hotel that night, the next morning Roberts bought some new clothes and a traveling valise, then took an airport limo to Midway Airport. There, over the loudspeaker he heard the name "Bob Lord" and decided it could work. His last name was Roberts and people often called him "Bob." He bought his ticket and boarded a plane for Newark, New Jersey, about 15 miles from New York City.

"I wanted to go to New York and eight million people," he remembers. "And I knew I'd feel more comfortable in the East than anyplace else in the United States."

From the airport, he took a bus to Port Authority. The first thing he wanted to do was have a seafood dinner, "something good after 13 years in this institution."

For days he just wanted to see the city, take in the sights. Getting rather bold, he walked into Manhattan's main post office to look at his FBI Wanted Poster. He found it and laughed—the picture was too old, no one would recognize him. Later, Roberts would visit the local police precinct in Staten Island with some homeless clients. No one suspected that the man at the front desk was pictured on a bulletin board somewhere in the building on the FBI's Ten Most Wanted List. After all, the fugitive knew that he probably wouldn't be caught if he did not behave in a criminal manner to warrant his arrest. Or at least he thought so.

Roberts didn't realize that he was still a very sick man. For his first month in New York, he couldn't do much of anything. In three weeks, he had gone through more than $1,200. His money was getting dangerously low.

In one of the newspapers, he saw a listing for some inexpensive single room hotels over in Staten Island. He boarded the ferry and checked in at the Richmond Hotel. The next day he wandered up the hill to look for work.

The rest is a story that the folks at Project Hospitality will never forget. Some still don't believe it. Why did Roberts, a fugitive, devote most of his freedom to helping others, when he could have fled from the country?

"Having been in prison, I could relate to the homeless people," he says. "But one thing was different there, I could call my own shots from beginning to end. I could start something and complete it. And after ten years or so of not being able to do that, I was quite taken by this. And I felt good about being able to help somebody.

"Terry Troia used to tell me that what we were doing was a form of ministry. I never thought of it that way. I was just doing it because it was something I liked to do.

"It didn't dawn on me until I looked up one day and realized that I was taking the very money that I was saving to get away with. As I found in escape, you never felt that you've gone far enough or ran far enough."

He didn't.

7

Going National

On Friday afternoon, February 13, Walsh, Lin-
der, and Herwitz found themselves back in the same
room they had been in a week before. Not Studio
Two, not the audio studio downtown, but the press
room of the Federal Bureau of Investigation at the
Hoover Building headquarters.

Director Sessions was holding another press
conference with the "America's Most Wanted" team
just a week after endorsing the show's crime-fighting
efforts. He was announcing the capture of a Top Ten
fugitive, thanks to a direct result of viewer tips to
the AMW hotline. The director of the FBI was calling
in the country's major media and saying "this
works." It would send a clear message to law enforcement.

"The production of 'America's Most Wanted' is
providing a very special and exceptional service to
communities across the country," Sessions said in
his statement at the press conference. "About a
third of all 'Top Ten' fugitives are apprehended as a
result of citizen cooperation. The program allows
millions of Americans to learn about fugitives and
to aid in their capture."

The show was making news, instead of covering it. To the amazement of all, AMW was getting national press coverage after only one broadcast on seven stations. The Roberts capture was all over the New York City papers and competing TV news broadcasts. It also ran on the wire services, giving AMW widespread coverage in the markets where it wasn't even available yet. *The New York Times* devoted a half-page feature to the show in its prestigious Sunday Arts and Leisure section, as a reporter followed along on the Nauss profile in Pennsylvania. In the article it was clear that the show was winning support, but had its enemies as well, and not just fugitives.

This was something that couldn't have been staged or even dreamed about last week. Except for one thing, that is, the show had worked. Roberts was only one fugitive, however, and AMW would have a long road ahead—with the critics, the network, and the viewers—before it would win widespread credibility and acceptance. The next few captures wouldn't be that easy.

AMW crews were already preparing to film profile segments on three other FBI Ten Most Wanted fugitives. In Boston, AMW was profiling Ted Jeffrey Otsuki, wanted for the murder of Boston police officer Roy Sergei on October 2, 1987. In New York City, a segment was being filmed on the case of Pedro "Pistolo" Estrada, 25, a former professional middleweight boxer allegedly turned contract hit man, now wanted for five murders. Down at the Louisiana State Prison in Angola, Louisiana, Mike Cerny was filming the reenactment of the escape of Danny Michael Weeks, who had been previously convicted of murder.

Linder and Roberts had initiated a weekly story

meeting with the reporters to let them "pitch" cases they had found in the media or been called about by police or victims. They had reviewed dozens of FBI fugitive files, but couldn't come up with many possible profiles. With the capture of Roberts announced on the second broadcast, February 14, the show had earned some acceptance in the law enforcement community outside Washington. Police from agencies in the seven O&O markets and elsewhere who had turned the show down before, were now coming back.

Some wondered if Roberts was just a "lucky break." Others, like Linder, were concerned that running ads and on-air promos of the fugitives with their faces would be counterproductive, that is put them on the run before the show aired. Roberts had already admitted to the media and the court that he had seen himself on a Channel 5 promo and fled. The FBI assured Linder that the ads and promos were helping the show and the subsequent capture of the fugitive. Even though AMW had contacted all the principals in the Roberts case over eight months in researching and filming the segment, the news obviously hadn't gotten to Roberts until the night before.

The ads and promos would not only increase audience saturation for the broadcast, it would also alert those who might not be able to watch the Sunday telecast, yet knew where the fugitive was. The promos might put the fugitive on the run, taking him out of his normal pattern. He would need a new support system, such as cars, money, food, friends, which would force him to contact new people.

"Putting a rabbit on the run, as it were, gives law enforcement an easier way to catch the fugitive than if he's hiding in his lair," Linder would point out later.

That would be the exact case with the show's second capture, which would take place nearly a month after Roberts.

On November 14, 1987, convicted rapist and armed robber Donald Adams, 30, walked out of Norfolk State Prison, a medium-security facility, only five days after he had been sentenced 12 to 15 years for raping a 25-year-old Everett woman, during which time he had been on parole for armed robbery.

According to an official report, Adams had been transferred from Cedar Junction State Prison, Walpole, to Norfolk on October 16, two days after pleading guilty to charges stemming from the rape. A Corrections Department worker discovered that Adams was scheduled to finish his armed robbery sentence on November 15, not November 25, as indicated on his discharge papers.

Instead of reviewing all the case papers filed on Adams, the worker only changed the release date. If the worker had reviewed the papers, he would have realized that Adams would have pleaded guilty and slated for sentencing on November 9. Also, the official paper committing him to prison had arrived at Walpole on November 13.

The paper was not opened and reviewed, despite procedures. Adams was released, by mistake, on November 15. The envelope with his "mittimus" lay unopened until November 16, the day after his unauthorized release was discovered.

A massive manhunt was launched, since police knew he would strike again. Adams reportedly saw himself promoed and on the March 13 show, the sixth AMW broadcast. Having been "flushed out," Adams was exposed to the eyes of thousands of viewers who had also seen the show. He was apprehended at 4:50 P.M., March 16, at a relative's home in East Boston, three days after his profile.

After Adams's capture, his victim told the *Boston Globe*, "I am so happy. We sent out for Chinese food. This will be my first night's sleep without nightmares."

The Adams profile had been produced by filmmaker Lorenda Pfaff, a married mother of two, based in the Berkshires of Massachusetts. She had previously produced a segment on Leroy Chasson, a convicted murderer, who had escaped from Massachusetts correctional officers. Chasson stabbed himself in his prison cell, while his wife, Kathleen, was waiting at the nearby hospital he would be taken to. Once her husband arrived for treatment, Mrs. Chasson, disguised as a nurse, pulled a gun on the officers and medical staff treating him. He grabbed the gun, and the two fled in her car.

With the flood of new cases pouring in every day, Linder and Roberts had developed an unofficial criteria for considering a fugitive for a profile. Soon it would become dogma, as the reporters would sometimes get up to a dozen calls a day from various places and people about fugitives in their areas. The newsroom had to provide material for three cases a week. Back-ups were also needed in case a fugitive was captured between the time his segment was filmed on location and broadcast on the show.

Geography was still the major consideration. The cases had to be linked somehow to the seven markets.

Some stories were coming from the newspapers and regional magazines in the seven markets that the reporters were monitoring. If a case sounded like a possibility, the reporter would first have to contact the police agency with jurisdiction to see if they were interested in working with AMW to apprehend the fugitive. Without their cooperation and follow-up on the tips, the show would waste valuable air time that could be used for another case. The police participation would also include access to files and technical advice for the filming. Photographs were also a major factor. There had to be clear, recent photographs, film, or tape of the fugitive.

Before a case was even presented in a story meeting, Roberts would have already developed the case with the reporter. In some, they could find what was lacking to make it a strong contender; others would have to be rejected for various reasons.

Among the factors that evolved for consideration were:

• A repeat offender with a history of violent crime, who is likely to strike again. He would have to be considered a "clear and present danger" by the agency looking for him, a top priority in the eyes of the law.
• Any case brought to the show by the victim of that crime would get first priority. Some of the show's most dramatic cases and satisfying captures would later come as a result of victims, or survivors of victims, coming forward with fugitives.
• The next priority would be individual police officers, who are passionate about a single fugitive case and need AMW's help. Hundreds of police officers and investigators would come to the show out of desperation. Usually, especially in large metropolitan areas, unless there's a significant break in a case in 30 days, a case would go into

the deep files. Detectives are so chronically over-
worked that they can keep track of only so many
cases, and some, especially those with a lot of media coverage, simply take priority over others. Yet
there would always be those unsolved cases that a
detective still would lose sleep over, even after it
was taken off the hot list. There would be
hundreds of law enforcement officers across the
country who would sleep better after help from
AMW.

• The availability of photographic evidence is critical. There would be some exceptions to the rule,
where aged forensic busts would be used for the
broadcast—with incredible results. AMW's experience would prove that what captures fugitives are
the images on the television screen. The more images, the better, and the more varied would be
even better. With more images, the fugitive's face
could remain on the screen longer than a single
shot, and along with different shots would help
leave an indelible impression on the viewers.

• Television is a powerful, visual medium. AMW is
a meeting of interests between law enforcement
agencies and millions of viewers watching the
show every Sunday. The show needs cases that
can be made into compelling television, and that is
the art of the program. It would tell the story of a
fugitive and his/her alleged crimes, which are
often extremely violent and brutal. But AMW has
a responsibility to portray these fugitives and
crimes without doing violence to the viewers themselves, without doing damage to them, and without crossing the lines of decency and sensibility. In
many cases, the actual profile would show much
less violence than many police officers, who work
in blood and death, see everyday, especially in
metropolitan areas and the drug war.

Some crimes would make more compelling television than others. For example, in a single bank office, an armed robbery by a vicious gunman can be more compelling a story than the loan officer who is quietly embezzling millions from behind a desk for a decade. Both are serious crimes against society, punishable by severe sentences, but one makes more dramatic and entertaining television than the other.

Every case is considered on an individual basis, its merits carefully weighed by those factors above. On some occasions, AMW has "bent over backwards," as Ms. Roberts would say, to bring a case to air that is lacking in one of these crucial areas. Someone, especially a victim of that crime or a police officer investigating it, would make such an "incredibly powerful case for the need or the virtue of broadcasting it," that AMW would profile the fugitive in hopes that the case would prove past experience wrong.

Other times, despite the passionate plea, the show just couldn't help out. In the months to come, Ms. Roberts and others would also feel humbled by these pleas, realizing the power that television has over people's lives, and the hope that a show like AMW offers them.

For example, Ms. Roberts would later relate an incident that was "very humbling, and unique, but representative of the personal commitment of many, many phone calls received from police and other federal agents, dozens every week."

On a July 1989, Sunday afternoon after the AMW crew had returned from one of the show's on-location specials (this one in Jacksonville, Illinois), Ms. Roberts was sitting at her desk in the newsroom wrapping up some details from the trip. From another office, she could hear a reporter talking to a young police officer. As the discussion continued, she realized that they were rehashing the values of a Florida case that had been presented in a story meeting a few months before. So she beckoned the officer and the reporter into her office, and the three of them discussed the case.

"I'm desperate at this point," pleaded the officer, who was from a small town in Florida. He had made a pilgrimage to Washington on his vacation with his wife and baby, who were waiting in the next room, just to make his pitch to "America's Most Wanted."

"I would do anything, extra work without pay, anything. I would love to see this case on the air because this guy needs to be caught and I don't know what to do. The case is dead in the water, and I don't know how we'll catch him otherwise."

Ms. Roberts politely pointed out the problems she saw in getting the case to air. The man was only suspected of committing a murder in Florida, and there was no warrant outstanding for his arrest. There was another part of this case that involved a crime in Cleveland, where the man was wanted for escape, having been convicted of theft. In Florida, he was suspected of fleecing his mother, then killing her.

Ms. Roberts made some suggestions on how they could shore up the case for consideration, but made no guarantees. The case had already been passed over for very good reasons, she stressed.

As the officer got up to leave, Ms. Roberts took his hand and said, "Again, I can't guarantee that the next time around, the decision won't be any different, but I'll give it a shot."

"That's all right, I understand," he replied. "I think in my career I'm probably going to be involved in another case that's this important or this major.

"I never even thought I would get this far and have a personal hearing with you about this case."

The officer left and went home knowing a few more things that he could suggest to the police in Cleveland to give the profile more of a plot line. And Ms. Roberts never forgot how that officer showed her in a very humbling way what a powerful tool the show had become for law enforcement, no matter where they were.

By March 22, two days after the seventh broadcast, AMW was credited for its third capture as a direct result of viewer tips as accused murderer Paul Steven Mack had been captured in Salt Lake City, where the show wasn't even being broadcast yet, on an anonymous tip from Ohio. Mack's arrest was also a preview about how bizarre some of AMW's captures would be—and the power of television helping the public cooperate with law enforcement.

A total of four fugitives who had been on the show were already in custody after less than two months on the air. Danny Michael Weeks, 34, one of the FBI's Ten Most Wanted, profiled on February 28, was apprehended in Seattle on March 20 as a result of an anonymous tip, but not directly from AMW. He had escaped from prison in Angola, LA, and had fled from custody twice before. For Weeks's capture report, AMW presented a television first—a videotape of an FBI Top Ten fugitive. The entire capture was videotaped by a man living across the street from the home of Weeks's female companion, since the woman's son had tipped off the FBI.

Mack, 39, was being sought for two separate murders of women in Sacramento, California, and Marion County, Ohio.

In April 1987, Sacramento police had issued a warrant for Mack's arrest for the murder of Karen Grace Winslett, a 21-year-old beauty queen and restaurant hostess. According to police, Mack lured her to his apartment for a photo session on February 19, and then killed her with a massive dose of a pain-killing drug he had put in her drink. Her badly decomposed body was later found in the rear of her hatchback car, which was parked in a Sacramento motel parking lot.

Six years earlier, in July 1981, the body of 19-year-old Annette Huddle of Harpster, a secretary at the Marion (Ohio) Country Club, was found in the Olentagy River. Mack was questioned in the case, but there was insufficient evidence to charge him. He was taken into custody on a probation violation discovered during the Huddle investigation, but released. Mack had previously served prison sentences for embezzlement, forgery, theft, and burglary, and had an arrest record back to age 14. Ohio officials were now hoping to use DNA printing on evidence to link Mack to the murder.

A viewer in Ohio's Marion County, watching the show on WFLD, Fox's Chicago station, recognized Paul Mack from when he was an employee of a country club there. The month before, she had received a call from an individual in Salt Lake City, Utah, asking for an employment reference for a "Sean Paul Lanier." She discovered there wasn't anyone by that name ever employed at the club.

The woman forgot about the call until she saw "America's Most Wanted" that night. On a hunch, she contacted the local sheriff's department. They relayed the information to Sacramento police, who then called Salt Lake City police. The Salt Lake police discovered that a man by that name lived in Murray, Utah, and had pawned something at a pawn shop. Fingerprints at the shop (mandatory by Utah law) were matched positively with Mack's prints. His Murray residence was put under surveillance, and he was arrested without resistance at 10:30 P.M., March 22, two days after his AMW profile.

Mack was working as a head chef at a popular local restaurant, and asked police to call his employer to say he wouldn't be coming in to work. Mack was later extradited to California to face the Sacramento murder charge.

Lieutenant Ray Biondi of the Sacramento County Sheriff's Department brought Mack's case to "America's Most Wanted." After Mack's arrest, Lieutenant Biondi told the *Los Angeles Times* (April 13, 1988, p. 12): "Television is a great medium for this kind of thing because it helps pique people's interest in wanting to help catch criminals. It is a great tool for law enforcement."

Just six days after Mack's capture, AMW helped encourage a fugitive to surrender to authorities, which would happen several times over the next two years.

Steven Kurt Baughman, 28, profiled on March 20 with Mack, walked into the Harris County Sheriff's Office, in Houston, at 2:45 in the afternoon of Monday, March 28, accompanied by his attorney. Baughman had allegedly shot the chief of campus police, an officer, and a janitor at the University of Houston-Downtown in late February. At the time, police were trying to arrest the first-semester freshman, just hours after he was released from the county jail on charges of assaulting an ex-roommate. He was also on parole after serving a two-year sentence for possession of a forged instrument and of a controlled substance.

According to police reports, Baughman grabbed a .357-Magnum from one of the officers. He aimed and fired four shots, wounding two of the officers and a janitor, who had rushed to help. The suspect then fled on foot.

Baughman made no statement at the time of his

arrest; however, sources later indicated that he was aware of his profile on AMW and it was a "significant factor" in his surrender.

In addition to helping to apprehend fugitives, AMW was capturing an impressive number of viewers in its early broadcasts. The debut had averaged a 7.7 rating and 13 share according to the A. C. Nielsen service in the seven O&O markets. (A rating point represented 1 percent of the nation's then 88.6 million TV households; the share is the percentage tuned in of sets in use at a given time.) By the fifth broadcast, the rating share would climb to a 9.1/16. By the eighth, it would have averaged an 8.76 rating and 16 share for the previous shows.

In several markets, the Fox stations were beating ABC's "Sunday Disney Movie," and giving strong competition to CBS, ABC, and other independents' offerings. In Washington, the show had debuted with a 12.4/21 to finish second in the 6:30 P.M. time slot behind "NBC Nightly News."

The show was getting stronger also. Walsh was getting more confident as the host, even though he wouldn't get the final script until a day before the show. With the captures, segments were often shortened or rescheduled and he would have to learn a new script overnight. He had made a 13-show commitment, but he already knew that if the show continued, he was ready to sign on for more.

Linder was getting more comfortable with the look of the show and the style he wanted from his segment producers. He was finding a group of young, hungry producers who should be making movies of their own. Soon he would boast that he was "raising a group of filmmakers who could make five minutes of quality prime-time television on $30,000." They could "mask the violence," he added, while not taking anything away from the drama or passion of the crimes.

Chao was trying to comprehend the early success of the show, but not getting overconfident yet.

"In 25 percent of the country, I figured there was no way we would catch these guys so soon," Chao remembered later.

"Then it clicked—the power of television. It's the only medium that can reach all those people at once—radio and newspapers can't. There's no medium like television."

Chao would admit later that they had "actually scared ourselves" with the early captures, especially how quickly the fugitives, such as Roberts, were arrested after their profiles. No one had ever "flexed the muscles of television" like this before. It shouldn't have happened that easily, he thought. Then it became clear to him that television was so widespread, even in seven major markets, that no one can ever live alone in America, and not be known by other people. People know you; you will be spotted. It was hard to hide from television, and you can't hide in American society. There was no place to go. And some fugitives would find that out—no matter how far away they thought they were from television—the hard way.

In mid-March, "America's Most Wanted" got a new team member, Dan Kavanaugh, who would join Gadinsky as co-producer. A friend of Linder's from their New York radio days some 13 years ago, Kavanaugh had produced a segment on fugitive Glenn Stewart Godwin for the March 27 broadcast (#8). Kavanaugh had been working as a partner in a small Los Angeles advertising agency when Linder convinced him to take a few weeks off and produce the

Godwin segment. Later, Kavanaugh would joke that Linder had promised him an L.A. segment, but the closest he could get was "the stinking desert."

Like Linder, Kavanaugh, also 40, had an extremely diverse media background to offer the show, especially in the commercial and marketing side. A native of Rochester, he had majored in music and liberal arts at Columbia University. After graduating, he worked as music director for a New York City station before starting his own radio syndication business. Nine months after beginning the venture, Kavanaugh was driving a New York cab.

But he gave up his hack medallion to be the on-road soundman for the Johnny Winter-Edgar Winter group in 1973, after which he got back into radio as a programming director at WQIV in New York, where he met Michael Linder, the morning news man. The station went off the air in 1975, and the two unemployed friends went separate ways, but kept in touch, hoping to work together again.

Kavanaugh went to Boston and after working for two stations there, he moved to Los Angeles. He formed a commercials-promotions company with now-film director Steven Lisberger (*Tron*), and branched into personnel management (singer Michael Sembello among his clients). In 1984, Kavanaugh switched back to advertising as a free-lance copywriter and TV commercial producer. The following year, he joined the firm of Broyles, Garamella and Kavanaugh. With a staff of thirty, the company did film, home video, and TV campaigns for a number of major studios.

By late 1987, Kavanaugh was growing tired of "the constant breakfasts, lunches, and dinners to smooze new business." He jumped at Linder's offer, and turned the Godwin segment into a "major spectacular." They shot in Rancho Mirage, blew up a truck in the desert, staged the escape in the American River next to Folsom Prison using a helicopter—"going kind of nuts and over budget."

Linder didn't worry about the overage. He wanted his friend to join the "America's Most Wanted" team immediately. It didn't take much convincing. He sold his part of the agency and came to Washington in time to work on show number eight. This would be a new challenge for Kavanaugh. He had done film, video, and audio, but not TV. But Linder seemed to prefer gathering a staff of people who had the aptitude, but not the specific experience. No one's experience was directly applicable. AMW was a hybrid format with elements from all areas of television and media. There wasn't anyone around who had done it before.

Kavanaugh's responsibilities would include the production details of the show, while Linder, as executive producer, would be the general overseer. Kavanaugh would be working on everything from field shoots to editing to music to scripts to posting the show (correcting mistakes after taping, if time). His cousin, John, meanwhile, would also join the show, first as an associate producer, then being promoted to a producer of segments on the road.

It was apparent that the O&O experiment was working. The ratings numbers proved that there was an audience building and the captures showed the concept could work.

Diller and his staff was noticing a "nice internal growth" in the show during its first several weeks. What was going on the air now in March bore no resemblance to the pilot they had seen in September. There was a balance to the show; the segments were beautifully made, like movies in themselves. But the show had to be careful of being too exploitive, steering away from extreme acts of violence.

The show was "interesting," as it was telling something about the criminal—his lifestyle, his habits, his family—not just showing a stabbing or shooting which viewers saw thousands of times before. It also showed police procedures, the criminal mind, prison escapes, and the effect of crime on its victims. No matter where the show went around the country, it was interviewing "camera friendly people," especially policemen.

Even Diller was shocked at the effectiveness of the show with the early captures. It might become a more important development in television than anyone involved with it would realize, since it showed the "interactiveness" of mass communications. "The program would link together several elements of modern communication to make the United States in a sense a town meeting," he would remark later. It would be both entertaining to watch, while effective in its effort to inform and tell a story.

Word about the success of "America's Most Wanted" was spreading quickly around the third floor of the Executive Building on the Fox Pico lot which housed the young Fox Broadcasting Company (FBC). Despite media reports of its financial losses and some show failures, the network was making headway with its Saturday and Sunday lineups. Even with only 115 affiliates against NBC (209), CBS (210), and ABC (214), covering 87 percent of the country, Fox was gaining credibility with advertisers and viewers. Many of its affiliates were UHF stations (the "upper dial" of channels 14 and above) going against powerful, more established VHF stations (13 and below), affiliated with the other networks. (As of December 1989, Fox had 127 affiliates for three nights of programming with two more nights slated for the next year.)

Fox was originally designed as a programming service to independent stations. In a year's time, it was already giving the affiliates some original programming instead of their usual slate of theatrical movies and syndicated prime-time hits. The Fox's new stars and shows were giving these stations a new look and a new identity in their markets. And they too were hearing about this new show that was catching criminals.

FBC's programming chief Garth Ancier would later admit that he didn't realize the full potential of "America's Most Wanted" in its idea stage. He was more concerned at the time with strong story lines for the Saturday and Sunday comedies and dramas. Jim McKay, FBC's Vice President of Development, encouraged Ancier to study the pilot, and predicted it would be a hit for the company.

"Conceptually, I did not think it would be an original show," said Ancier, now President of Network TV Production for Walt Disney Studios. "I thought it was a bit simplistic to just profile criminals and put up a number for people to call. But on the O&O's it became more complex and improved stylistically."

There were constant discussions about how real the re-creations should get, and some felt they were "too rough," Ancier remembers. Others complained that the re-creations were actually more conservative than the brutality of the actual crime.

Yet the show's success would lie with the American people.

"We're living in a time where people feel helpless with crime," Ancier would remark later. "This is a way for them to deal with crime, for society to get off their frustration. The issues of security and taking back your life are very vital issues and this show would help resolve them somewhat."

Ancier and the programming staff realized that "America's Most Wanted" could be a strong addition to the Sunday night lineup. FBC President Jamie Kellner was in favor of the show joining the lineup, but the problem was where.

(Syndication was never a viable option for "America's Most Wanted" since the format of the show demanded that it be shown in all markets on the same night. In the syndication marketplace, the stations are given a seven-day window and can play the show in any one of those days. Thus, the show could play in one market on Sunday, and by the time another market ran it on Friday, the fugitive might be caught already.)

The "bargain basement" launch, as Chao termed it, of the show on the O&O's provided a solid foundation for FBC to premiere the show. Diller's idea of creating a programming laboratory on the O&O's had its first successful experiment to put on the network, which was the whole purpose of Chao's lab.

One side of the FBC programmers favored the show to stay where it was at 6:30 P.M. Others, such as Ancier, favored it at 8 P.M., as a "good bridge" between two strong Fox shows, "21 Jump Street" and "Married . . . with Children." He argued that the affiliates wouldn't take the show at 6:30 P.M., as some of the O&O's had complained.

"Werewolf," a horror action-adventure series, had enjoyed the strongest debut of any Fox show when it debuted on Saturday night in July. But after being switched to Sunday at 8 P.M., it was having its problems. The rest of the Sunday lineup included "It's Garry Shandling's Show," "The Tracey Ullman Show", and "Duet."

Another factor favoring "America's Most

Wanted" was the Writers' Guild Strike, which had begun on March 7. The strike, which would run for 22 weeks until August 7, would have a serious effect on the launch of the fall TV season. It was already forcing daily talk shows into reruns.

"Werewolf" was put into "hiatus," while repeat episodes would be available to the affiliates to run in a different time slot.

"America's Most Wanted" was set to debut nationally on Sunday, April 10, 1988. Now, FBC would join the AMW team. Sales would sell national advertising spots. Affiliate Relations and Affiliate Promotions would get the stations psyched about the new crimefighting show coming to their neighborhoods. Advertising, publicity, and promotion, supervised by Senior Vice President Kevin Wendle, would get viewers to tune in.

They all had roughly two weeks to do their job.

It was a tough sell in the beginning for the FBC Sales force, led by Pat Mastandrea, now head of Sky Channel in Great Britain. They would soon be helped by two strong elements—ratings and publicity. The O&O ratings and national ratings would continue to climb as the summer went on. AMW was also getting substantial, prestigious media coverage, not only from its captures, but also on the show concept and its host, John Walsh.

"America's Most Wanted" was different from anything on the air. Usually a salesperson can make a new show pitch to an advertiser with "it's 'Cosby' or 'Wiseguy' or a news show." Selling the show as part of a package could be easier than selling it alone. Since most of the available Sunday inventory (available spots) were sold already for season, the sales staff was looking ahead to packaging it for the upfront (new season) sales meetings.

The show was having an impact on the television industry. It would make some advertisers nervous in the beginning with its subject matter, but it was unique, inactive, different television. The ratings made it desirable, which was hard for a client to argue with. It was also being seen as a public service with a very broad audience appeal.

On-air promotions and advertising had already set a successful pace with the early broadcasts. At least one fugitive, Roberts, had found Scalera's promo spots effective. For several weeks, the promo campaign would concentrate on getting viewers involved with the show—inactive television. It would also give a rundown on the fugitive, including strong visual elements, such as a scar, a tattoo, a weapon, or part of the crime or escape. If possible, the promo would include the specific geographic locations associated with the fugitive. Instead of a cold, flat picture, Scalera gave the viewers a three-dimensional portrait of the fugitive.

A second part of the promotion campaign would be to follow up on captures and thank the viewers for their help. The spots were not meant to sell any goods, but to encourage the American public to be aware of the show and its fugitives and help apprehend them. When the viewers did their part, the promos would come back and say, "Good job, America!"

The advertising campaign of using specific fugitives had also found success both as a sales and capture tool. For example, Roberts's friends on Staten Island first realized his Indiana past from the ad in *TV Guide* and subsequently called the FBI. The campaign would also feature Walsh as a prominent crimefighter and spokesman for victims' rights.

Later on, the ads would also take the fugitives' perspective, such as "If You're Wanted by the FBI . . . Hide!," "Watch Television . . . Catch Criminals," and "It's Not Everybody's Favorite Show . . ." with a man behind bars in the background.

The publicity staff already had some awareness to build on after the O&O campaign was handled by Rogers and Cowan Public Relations. The competition for Sunday newspaper TV supplements had lessened after the February sweeps period, usually dominated by star-loaded miniseries and movies-for-television. Two weeks wasn't much time to land stories in publications and syndicates with deadlines of a month and three weeks ahead. The campaign would have to rely on pitching feature stories to the TV critics and writers in the Top 50 markets, and hitting the lower markets through the wire services, listing services, and feature packages.

Walsh had already done a two-week tour to the seven O&O markets, which had resulted in some major "breaks." The captures were getting the show off the TV pages and onto the front pages of several major newspapers. Many TV critics were familiar with Walsh from the two NBC telefilms, *Adam* and *Adam: His Song Continues*, based on his son's murder and his quest for justice, as well as his HBO and PBS specials. He was an excellent, intelligent interview for both print and broadcast, such as "Today" shortly after the debut, with the FBI's Ahlerich. With his broadcast experience, Linder would also be an articulate spokesman for the show, which he would demonstrate on several occasions, such as on ABC's "Nightline" and "Good Morning America," both with Ahlerich.

As part of the national debut campaign, the publicity department produced a national satellite tele-press conference from the AMW set in Washington.

WTTG anchorman Morris Jones served as moderator for the panel of Walsh and Linder from AMW and the FBI's Milt Ahlerich and Floyd Clark, assistant director of the Criminal Investigation Division, representing the law enforcement point of view. The signal would be beamed from WTTG via satellite to the individual affiliates, where the promotion managers had invited the local press. More than 60 reporters called in questions during the hour-long conference from print, radio, and electronic outlets from all over the country.

A few changes were made in the set for the national debut with imput from FBC as expressed by Program Executive Marian Davis who visited the show staff for a week prior to the premiere. The phone operators would become a more visual part of the set with the law enforcement officers standing by. The set color would be toned down from orange to a slate gray, with added props (file cabinets, wanted posters, police patches) giving it more of a "squad room" look, designed by Dina Lipton. Walsh would stand, walk around, and sit on the corner of a desk alongside a large monitor showing the fugitive's photograph.

The cases were set for the national debut—three escaped murderers from West Virginia, Bobby Dean Stacey, David Williams, and Thomas Mollohan; accused murderer Patrick Menillo from Ft. Lauderdale, Florida; and William Fischer, wanted for the murder of his son in Southampton, New York.

"America's Most Wanted" was ready to go national. But would America be ready for it?

8

The Dragnet Widens

The pressure was also on in Washington for the national debut. But there were some lighter moments as well.

One afternoon in early April, Mike Walton was waiting for a prospective job candidate to show up for an interview. He was a friend of one of the staff, so the interview would be friendly and informal, Walton thought.

His intercom rang, so he picked up the receiver. "There's a David Roberts on his way back to see you," the receptionist told him.

Walton froze. Had Roberts escaped from prison in New York, hopped on the Metroliner? Now he was on his way to wipe out the entire AMW staff responsible for his capture. Shaking, he picked up the phone to call security, Linder, or somebody!

He looked up and a bright young man was standing in front of him.

"Hi, I'm David Roberts, Margaret's brother. How do you do?"

Shaking the young man's hand, Walton breathed a sigh of relief. Within the hour, the brother of the show's managing editor had joined the staff as a telephone operator.

During the tapings, Walsh was adapting to television, helped by constructive criticism from Linder and Weiss. He was learning to have the teleprompter operator write notes and cues for him on the script copy, so he wouldn't have to rely as much on the floor manager, now Karen Eidinger. During one episode's taping (May 1, 1988, #13), he would have to give a spontaneous "update," when during taping, the FBI agents in the studio informed the staff that Stephen and Melody Tripp had just been arrested in Bueyeros, New Mexico.

Walsh and his director were blending well, working out a system for rehearsals. Weiss noticed that Walsh was "a completely new man" after the initial captures, coming across as a natural speaker and good interviewer. The secret was to suit the situation to Walsh, not vice versa. They tried a lot of ways to work out his nervous energy. Rather than sitting like an anchorman, Walsh was walking around, becoming part of the set. He would do the profiles by the monitor, interview the police at a desk, and walk back to the phone operators at the end of the show. This was a good visual signal to the viewers, since the phones were a major part of the show, a symbol of interactive television. The show wasn't just putting a phone number on the screen, it was a two-way medium now, and this was the nerve center.

In the control booth, Weiss and his technical staff were also struggling with some rarely used equipment that was not accustomed to the strain and deadlines of a "live" weekly show. In later months, with some equipment failures and "other things not falling into place," the show would set some records for finishing closest to the actual broadcast. On one Sunday, the first half of the show was only done by 6:30 P.M., the deadline for starting the satellite feed to Los Angeles. The first half was taken off the tape machine and fed, while the second half was completed, then sent through space. On another occasion, the feed started at 7:10 P.M., during the broadcast of "21 Jump Street."

On the budget side, the show was a "bargain by network standards," according to Chao, since for the first few weeks it was coming in under $125,000. (By the second year, the cost would increase to $140,000 a show with about $30,000 more when it would broadcast live from location.)

As for the phone operations, Vista was zeroing in on the "perfect" candidates for operators. She needed more operators fast. With the national debut, the phone bank would expand to 16, then 26 incoming lines within two weeks. From the students who applied, she was looking for criminal justice, psychology, and sociology majors. More professional people were now applying, some from federal law enforcement, who were interested in part-time public service. They would call, saying, "I'm a big fan of the show, do you need any help?" These would prove to be the best.

The national debut made a good showing in the ratings with a 4.8 rating (4.3 million households) and 8 share, higher than a 3.9 rating two weeks before from "Werewolf." There must have been a lot of talking during coffee breaks the next morning because the following Sunday (April 17), the show soared to a 7.6 (6.7 million households) rating and 13 share, beating ABC in the time slot.

The media was taking note of the show's debut. Aljean Harmetz of the syndicated *New York*

Times News Service wrote, "Fox was delighted with the crime show's performance, although on NBC, CBS or ABC, a program with a similar audience share would be cancelled. Eventually, according to analysts, Fox must broaden its audience to keep and attract advertising revenues."

In the *Los Angeles Times*, John Voland noted, "America apparently likes law and order. Not satisfied with fictional cops and lawyers shows, audiences are watching programs like 'Most Wanted'— where viewers at home can call in with tips to help catch criminals. The size of the show's audience has grown by more than 2.5 million viewers (in one week)." (The Oscars won the ratings race that week with a 29.4/49, followed by a repeat of "The Cosby Show" at 22.2/38.)

The number of hotline calls had dramatically increased. The national debut broadcast attracted 2,700 telephone tips (487 hangups), compared with 499 calls the week before on the seven stations. There had been 120 calls on Fischer, 161 on Menillo, and 240 on the West Virginia prison escapees. For the second national broadcast, the total number of calls slipped to 2,591, but the percentage of actual tips increased to more than half the calls received.

Those viewer tips led to the show's fourth direct capture on April 9, the eve of the national debut. Murder suspect Carl "Fabulous" Dunstrom, 28, profiled with three other suspects on the March 10 broadcast, was arrested after about 30 heavily armed New York City police officers raided the basement of a Brooklyn apartment. Armed with a loaded .45-caliber semiautomatic at the time of his arrest, Dunstrom, a Jamaican immigrant, was wanted in five killings in Landover, Maryland, on January 22, and one in Brooklyn on November 26. The raid followed a three-week manhunt that began on an AMW viewer tip.

As profiled on the show, authorities called the murders "a massacre" that stemmed from a war between rival drug gangs in which four men and a woman were found shot to death, all Jamaican-born dealers.

The arresting detective on the case was quoted in *The New York Times* (April 11, 1988, p. B4), concerning the show's role in the arrest.

"Fantastic!" Detective John Herbert of the Brooklyn North Homicide squad, the officer who arrested Mr. Dunstrom, said of the television program's assistance in the case, "I wish we could have our own station. We could arrest a whole lot of bad guys."

Linder later noted the emotional impact that the filming of the segment at the actual Landover murder site had on the actors, who were accompanied by police advisors. There were still bloodstains on the floor and bullet holes in the walls. Even the wheelchair that one of the victims used was still there.

"There are even more impressive performances from our actors and directors who know they are actually walking through the last moments of a man's or woman's life where it actually happened," Linder would note later. "We've had some actors and actresses become hysterical and go through great emotional breakdowns at the shootings of these scenes."

"There's a psychic memory perhaps at some of these locations, and you start to reconstruct a murder where it happened not that long ago, there is an errie feeling about doing that. A strange sort of ritual that has tremendous emotional impact."

One actor, Thomas Bell, told *The Prince George's*

Journal (Maryland) (March 11, 1988, p. A4) that the sight "was a little disconcerting." Another, Angel Harper, playing the female victim, said that she was not only excited about playing a role, but also glad to have a chance to help solve the killings.

"You felt very afraid for how it must have been for anybody in that situation," Harper said.

That authenticity of the reenactment locations demonstrates the show's commitment to the facts and its integrity to put the crime on the air in an accurate way—"exacting reconstruction," which had developed as the show's standard.

Linder also pointed out that during that filming a piece of evidence overlooked by police was recovered by the crew, namely one of the fugitive's driver's license.

Five days later, AMW viewers' tips led to the arrests of Dunstrom's two alleged accomplices, murder suspects Steve McMillan, 24, and Kirk Bruce, 24, in New York City. They were also members of a Jamaican drug organization, police said. That was eight fugitives profiled in custody, six as a direct result of viewer tips in only two months on the air in only 25 percent of the country. But now the dragnet was nationwide.

With its impressive early captures and the news that AMW was going national, the number of inquiries from police across the country multiplied in weeks. Ms. Roberts added two more experienced journalists, Janet Tamaro (now a correspondent for "Inside Edition") and Tom Ramstack, to the newsroom staff before the national debut.

The Ohio-Utah-California connection in Mack's arrest dispelled the myth of the show being restrained by geography. Linder started approving profiles of fugitives in West Virginia, Connecticut,

Pennsylvania, and New Jersey, which were brought by agencies from those states.

Leschorn had also brought in stacks of cases for consideration, several of which would be broadcast with amazing, sometimes bizarre results. The Robert Nauss profile on the second broadcast had provided some strong leads, but he was still at large, probably living a quiet life in middle America far different from his outlaw biker days.

Most folks would consider the Marshals' next AMW fugitive as a kindly grandfather type they'd trust their children with. But as the marshals who tracked him would warn, don't trust 72-year-old William "Pops" Pegram. He had been a career criminal for 40 years, who spent most of his adult life in jail. On his "rap sheet," which measured more than a yard as it hung on the AMW set wall, included convictions for bank robbery, burglaries, grand larceny, aiding and abetting, illegal interstate transportation of stolen property, liquor, and firearms, prison escape, assault on a federal officer with a deadly weapon, and parole violation. Currently wanted on a warrant from Tennessee for his parole violation, Pegram had 3,636 days remaining to serve on his previous sentences. In addition to being a diabetic and having heart and prostate problems, Pegram (6'2", 200 pounds) had limited use of his right hand after being wounded in a shootout with a Tennessee police officer.

"This was a 75-year-old man who would say to your face, 'I've been an outlaw for 40 years, and I've shot cops, so I'll shoot you,'" Leschorn warned viewers in the Pegram profile. "He's a suspect already in a homicide committed since he fled. You wouldn't act scared when you see this man—until he pulled a gun."

The Marshals speculated that Pegram was on

AMERICA'S MOST WANTED ||| 185

the run somewhere in either Missouri, Arkansas, or Texas, joined by an escaped West Virginia convict Jack Dean.

Just before "Pops" was profiled, Marshal Stuart Earnest in Oklahoma City had submitted a candidate to Chief Louie McKinney, head of the Enforcement Division, for the Service's 15 Most Wanted List. Though not as old and established as Pegram, the 27-year-old fugitive had a 10-year record in four states. Using some 25 aliases, he had escaped from jail or custody six times, been convicted for 10 bank robberies (shot by a policeman during one of them), stolen cars, burglarized houses. He had a habit of befriending juveniles who looked up to him, especially pretty females. An obsessive fetish with keeping clean drove him to take up to several showers a day, even breaking into houses for them.

This young Jesse James loner would do anything to escape—cut through fences, jump over razor wire under fire, or con his way out by confusing a corrections officer. He loved the hunt and the chase. On more than one occasion after robbing a bank he sat in a nearby restaurant eating pizza and watched the police officers search for him.

One Marshal credited the escape artist with having "big brass testicles." He bragged that no jail can hold him and he had no qualms about shooting anyone, especially a federal officer, if he escapes again.

The Marshals had strong leads in Florida, but the fugitive could be in any warm weather state, since he passionately hates cold climates. He could be most anywhere in the southern United States.

Here was a dangerous repeat offender who would strike again, and probably was committing a crime as AMW was considering his profile. There were plenty of good photographs, a colorful story of television, and an army of Marshals to cooperate. Leschorn knew this was a perfect fugitive to test the national dragnet.

Every few weeks, AMW researcher-reporter Nan Allendorfer would go over to the Marshals' headquarters in Arlington, Virginia, to look over the stack of 15 or so case files that Leschorn would have waiting for her.

From her journalism background, which included a stint at "Nightline," she could scan through a file for the facts faster than most. From her film experience, which included a film degree from Penn State and associate producer jobs on several major TV projects ("Ripley's Believe It or Not," "Mysteries and Secrets," the miniseries "Amerika"), she had the eye for what would be a visually compelling piece.

One afternoon in early April, Leschorn had put a file out separate from the rest—a 15 Most Wanted that his bosses were especially anxious to catch. As she looked over the file, Allendorfer would immediately sense it was a perfect AMW case. The man had escaped from prison six times. Once he had smashed through a store's second-story plate glass window and jumped 15 feet with the police in pursuit. The photographs were excellent, and the Marshals even had some video footage of him in custody. And the rugged, six-foot fugitive with his wild red hair had "a cute, impish quality" to him, but that was only a disarming front, which he used well.

Back at the AMW office, Linder quickly gave the "green light" to a segment on a bank robber-escapee named Mark Austin Goodman. He hired New York City-based filmmaker Julie Harman to produce the segment. Allendorfer sent the producer the extensive packet of information on Goodman which the Marshals had provided. Meanwhile, Allendorfer pushed after leads from the files—people who knew Goodman, witnesses, family members, prison officials, police officers, even his accomplices. There was plenty to work with, but the pitch was the most crucial part of her work.

As a reporter, Allendorfer knew, as did all her AMW colleagues, that the first 30 seconds of a phone call to a potential lead was the most critical. The show wasn't still that well known and accepted yet.

"I knew that I had 30 seconds to convince this person that we were serious, professional, and concerned about catching this fugitive," Allendorfer would recall later. "I felt that I could be sensitive to people, especially the victims. But how could you call a rape victim and say, 'Would you like to talk to us on camera about your experience?'

"There were so many times that we got hung up on. But we had to be fair and call everyone to give them a chance to tell their side. We just hoped that our relationship with the U.S. Marshals would help. It did help us gain legitimacy, and we could have never achieved the level we did without them."

Allendorfer's main contact on the case was a task force of Marshals in Oklahoma City led by veteran lawman Bill Tsoodle. He and his deputy marshals would lead AMW through cases of files and evidence, including the door lock which Goodman had picked through in one of his more amazing escapes.

"Mark Austin Goodman is a white male, born on March 8, 1961, in Missoula, Montana," one file began. "He is being sought by the United States Marshal's office in the Western District of Oklahoma, on charges of escape from federal custody."

The files didn't have much about Goodman before he began his crime sprees in 1979. According to

Tsoodle, Goodman had been raised in Washington State and got into trouble early. He was a loner, didn't make many friends. Mark came from a broken home, which made him very bitter. His father was an airplane pilot for the forestry service, but was divorced from his mother. Mrs. Goodman was a nurse, responsible for raising two daughters and two sons, Mark being the oldest boy.

In his late teens, Goodman ventured out on his own. He had intended to marry a girlfriend in Washington when he reached age 18. It looked like he was going to start doing everything right until he started getting into burglarizing some homes.

By this time, Goodman had wandered down to Nevada. On August 28, 1979, Mark, now 18, got busted for the first time. Sheriff's deputies from Wascoe County in Reno caught him with a load of burglary tools, and linked him to local incidents. They would soon learn that they had a red-haired tiger by the tail.

In the morning, Goodman, using the name "Mark Austin Palmer," had been taken to the county courthouse to sign up for a public defender, supervised by Sergeant Robert Casey and Deputy Robert Sappington. At 10:49 A.M., Deputy Sappington was preparing to put handcuffs on the inmate as the group was being prepared to be taken back to jail. But inmate "Palmer" wasn't interested in going. Instead, he bolted from the line and smashed right through a lobby's plate glass door into the street.

Sappington and Casey chased out of the courthouse onto Virginia Street. Deputy John Handte joined Sappington as the inmate took them several blocks into a residential area of Reno. He ran down a street, paused, spotted his pursuers, and dashed down another. Finally, "Palmer" was cornered in a backyard on Sinclair Street.

"Shoot me! Shoot me!" the struggling inmate pleaded with the two deputies. He couldn't go back to jail, he begged. By now, some Reno police officers had joined the two deputies, and the inmate was behind bars by 11:30 A.M. The accused burglar wasn't kidding about his attitude toward jail. He attempted suicide on October 20.

The stolen property charge was dismissed and Goodman pleaded guilty to escape, for which he received a three-year suspended sentence. He was out by December 12, and headed north to Oregon.

By April, Goodman, now "Mark Green," and his burglary tools had gotten caught again, this time in Portland, Oregon. Down in Newport, Oregon, some latent fingerprints at a grocery store linked him to a March 2nd burglary there where the thief had bored through a roof. He was charged and convicted on both and sentenced to a term in the Oregon State Correctional facility at Salem. He arrived there on July 9, 1980. This was Goodman's first time in the "big house," at the tender age of 19. But not for long.

On the morning of December 8, 1981, inmate #9319-C crawled on his belly to the first perimeter fence in broad daylight. He cut through one fence, and slithered to the other. The tower guards spotted him and started firing at him. That didn't stop Goodman. He had already hacked through the second razor wire fence and was sprinting away down a gully.

Three days later, Goodman had made it back home into Washington State. Having stolen a car, he was driving down Highway 3 near Windy Point, right by a state trooper's car. Trooper Tom Arnold pulled him over; Goodman bolted out of the car and struggled with Arnold. Within seconds, Goodman had escaped from custody again and was off in the woods.

Police all over Washington and Oregon were hot

for Goodman now. He was becoming an embarrassment. On the morning of December 15, in Bremerton, Officers Jeffrey Kelly and Greg Steele spotted a red-haired man breaking into a Ford Pinto in a used car lot. Before they could stop him, Goodman hot-wired the car and was racing out into the early morning rush-hour traffic. Several vehicles were involved in the high-speed chase which ended when Goodman rammed the car into a police vehicle, then struck an innocent motorist, causing serious injuries. They didn't have him yet though. Goodman tried to run away, but he was quickly tackled by the officers, and several angry motorists.

Oregon wanted its prisoner back. First, Washington intended to teach young Mark a lesson. Apparently, he wasn't ready to listen. Jailers found him trying to hang himself in his cell. On January 20, 1982, Goodman was sentenced to 20 years for felony hit-and-run, burglary, auto theft, and escape and committed to the state prison in Shelton.

Goodman stayed in Washington only until November 18, however, when he was sent back to Oregon. This time the young con decided to stay put and prove to his keepers that he was getting it all back together. They were convinced, and paroled him on July 31, 1985, after two years, eight months, and 12 days of rehabilitation.

The prison stay didn't keep Goodman out of trouble for long. By December 7, Chelan County Sheriff's deputies in Wenatachee, Washington, were investigating burglary case #85-8171. They got their man—Mark Goodman. The court sent the prisoner to the Eastern State Hospital for a 15-day evaluation. The doctors didn't get a chance to finish their report because by January 31, Goodman was out the window and over the fence again.

Trooper Steve Mattson noticed a van spotted by

the side of a wooded highway outside of Ellensburg on the morning of February 2. This time, the police would catch Mark napping.

Mattson immediately knew the man sleeping in the van. When the trooper tried to take him into custody, Goodman turned into a wild man. He reached out the window and tried to fight Mattson off. He even tried to grab the trooper's sidearm. The struggle continued as Goodman rolled up the window on the trooper's arm as he reached in to subdue the suspect. With Mattson's arm in the window, Goodman tried to drive off, but the trooper got free as the van started away.

Still on the ground, Mattson fired at the fleeing van. He hit both the left front and left rear tires, but Goodman kept driving for several hundred yards. He then jumped out of the stolen van and fled into the forest.

Goodman had enough of the cold weather up north and decided to head southeast. For some reason, he wound up in Oklahoma by the spring, probably because he got a ride there with some friends. Later, Bill Tsoodle would joke that it was those friends whom Oklahoma had to thank for bringing them Mark Goodman and his dangerous games.

Goodman didn't have any friends in Oklahoma City, when he moved into the Cambridge Apartments. Out of prison, he could eat all the pizza and drink all the beer and Jack Daniels whiskey he wanted. He was spending a lot of time seeing movies and playing video games in arcades, where he would meet juveniles, the Marshals would learn. The teenagers would find Goodman "very charismatic" and looked up to him as a hero, especially the young girls.

Acting like a Peter Pan, "Mark Teufel" or "Howard Miller" would collect wayward boys, some eight to ten years younger than him. They were high school dropouts, substance abusers, failures already at age 16. He would even tell their parents that he was a contractor and would teach the wayward youths his trade. It was an answer to their prayers. The parents were very impressed as to how polite Mark was to them. Most of their children's friends wouldn't come inside to speak with them, but this one did. Only when the adults questioned him did he shy away and disassociate himself from them and become a recluse.

They would go over to Mark's apartment and eat pizza, and watch television all day, the teens would tell attorneys later. Goodman told the boys tales, many not so tall, about his criminal adventures, especially his escapes. He was going to teach them to rob banks. He would go inside and do the dirty work, while they would drive the getaway car. At least two boys decided to learn the trade.

On March 10, 1987, according to his later indictment from the U.S. District Court, Western District, Oklahoma, Goodman started his spree of bank robberies around Oklahoma that day. He hit the Capitol Hill State Bank on South Western Street, and made off with $6,000.

Seventeen days later, on March 27, he struck again, this time at the First Enterprise Bank on Northwest 122nd Street. Now, he brandished a "black metal firearm with a six-inch barrel." The job netted $7,319.

It wasn't a firearm, however. Goodman had drilled out the red plastic tip from a BB gun, making it look like a .45 or 9-mm semiautomatic pistol. It worked very well to scare even the most experienced tellers and bank officers on his next seven jobs:

• On April 7, the Local Federal Savings and Loan, Moore, taking $7,709, then assaulting a teller by shoving the gun in her ribs, pulling the action back, and threatening to kill her;

• On April 22, the Mutual Federal Savings and Loan, Oklahoma City, getting $4,537, and again threatening a female teller;

• On April 23, the Mutual Federal Savings and Loan, Moore, getting $3,796, and another female teller;

• On April 29, the Midwest National Bank, Midwest City, taking $22,622;

• On May 11, the Mutual Federal Savings and Loan, Edmond, taking $2,567, and assaulting a female teller;

• Again on May 11, the United Federal Savings and Loan, Oklahoma City, taking $4,839, and assaulting a male teller;

• On May 21, the Local Federal Savings and Loan, Oklahoma City, taking "a sum of money," and assaulting a female teller.

Goodman appeared to love "playing cat and mouse with the law," according to Assistant U.S. Attorney Teresa Black, who later prosecuted him. Goodman committed one robbery, using a bicycle for transportation. After hitting the bank, he rode around a while, then ate pizza at a restaurant near the bank and watched police search for him. At another bank, witnesses later said they thought they saw Goodman crouched in a culvert under the highway watching the converging crowd.

On one job, Goodman and his two teenage accomplices walked in the bank wearing paper painter outfits with velcro along the sides. Once inside, they would rip off the outfits and do their job. At the Midwest City Bank, one accomplice, Michael Le-

Claire helped Goodman scoop up $26,000, while another juvenile waited in the car. This time a bank officer with a gun came out firing at the fleeing pair. The bullets were hitting the sidewalk at their feet, LeClaire would later tell Ms. Black. They climbed over a wooden fence, and the bank officer got up on the fence and kept firing. After that, LeClaire had enough of the robbery game.

He and the rest of the boys were living the good life. One night they booked the best suite at a local motel and racked up a bill of $3,000 in room service. Their parents got suspicious when they brought home cars and stereos, and had thousands of dollars at their disposal. Mark was teaching them the building trade, and they were making good money, the boys told their parents. Goodman had also become involved with a pretty 16-year-old girl, who knew exactly how her older boyfriend got all the money he lavished on her. But the fun wouldn't last forever.

On May 26, Goodman strolled into the American Savings and Loan at 1330 North Bryant in Edmond, Oklahoma. He pulled out his gun, jumped over the counter, told the tellers to lie on the floor, and emptied a teller drawer. Before Goodman could make off with the $1,859 in his bag, an off-duty Oklahoma City police officer, working there as a security officer, had drawn his gun and ordered the robber to freeze.

Somehow thinking he could bluff a man pointing a loaded gun, Goodman whirled around and raised his gun at Officer Douglas Northup. The policeman fired twice, hitting the robber in the right chest area and right hand. He was taken to a local hospital for treatment, where he was identified as Mark Alan Teufel. A subsequent FBI check of his apartment at 8800 South Drexel revealed the gunman's true identity—Mark Austin Goodman, wanted in Washington.

First, Goodman had to face federal bank robbery charges in Oklahoma. Attorney Black was surprised to hear that the bank robber shot over in Edmond on Tuesday wanted to be arraigned only two days after being in surgery. The Public Defender's office questioned such a move, but apparently the suspect wanted to face his accusers. But the hearing was held in the room before U.S. Magistrate Doyle W. Argo.

"It was the first time I had ever done a hospital room arraignment," Ms. Black would recall later. "I had never seen a freshly shot person before. I remember him giving the FBI agents very hard looks.

"It didn't bother him. His chest was taped up over the bullet hole and his hand was in a sling. There he was lying in a hospital bed, all swollen, and somewhat anesthetized, but he wanted the hearing. There was really no question about how tough or how hard the guy really was."

Argo ordered Goodman held without bond.

When in court later, Goodman "was always looking around, always checking the exits," Ms. Black said.

"You could see his eyes roving around just looking for a way out," she said. "He was always trying to be friendly and disarming, like wave at the junior FBI agents, to try to get them to lighten up. He'd even pull his ears in fun. So he certainly knew how to try to work on you."

And Goodman did work on some folks in the Oklahoma County Jail in the next few weeks. He had learned the jail routine very well. At about 3 P.M., July 14, a recently hired aide in the hospital ward let him into the treatment room without a deputy to have his bandages changed. Some other inmates apparently had already left some civilian clothes in the room. He changed into the clothes, and put his inmate coveralls over them.

Once he was out in the hallway, some other inmates created a diversion. Goodman took off his coveralls and strolled to the jail visitor information desk. He handed a Bible to the desk clerk, saying he was leaving it for an inmate. The deputy assumed the man was a visitor, and let him out of the secured room with the other visitors. It took 24 hours to realize that the elusive Mark Goodman had escaped once again, this time on Bastille Day.

Having escaped from federal custody, Goodman now had the U.S. Marshals on his trail. A helicopter search by city and county officers had turned up nothing. A ground search uncovered that the escapee had slept in a lawn chair by a motel pool, then washed his hair in the public bathroom, had complimentary coffee and doughnuts, and left. Tsoodle and his men set up surveillance on some of Goodman's known associates. They also found records of a phone call, probably from the fugitive, coming from Austin, Texas.

From interviewing the teenagers who knew Goodman, the Marshals learned some of his habits. He had a fetish for keeping clean, sometimes taking three or four baths a day. He would always try to wear up-to-date clothing, many times stealing it from stores, though he had plenty of money from his bank jobs. A kleptomaniac by trade, he couldn't go into a store without even picking up a candy bar.

He also had a domestic side, they learned. He would often establish himself as a person who would like to have a wife or girlfriend and a place to call home.

On July 31, Marshals Bill Tsoodle, Phil Lakey, and Scott Rolstad, along with several deputies from Oklahoma County, followed a Goodman associate to a Holiday Inn in the northern area of Austin, Texas. He was arrested there "without incident." The officers also found he had stolen a motorcycle from Ardmore, Oklahoma, and had burglarized motel rooms on his way to Austin—to take baths.

On the way back to Oklahoma City, Tsoodle got to know the man he was tracking.

"For the first time in his life, this young man had realized that people had found out about him— the real Mark Goodman—and I think it really bothered him," Tsoodle would say later. "He asked the typical 'how did you catch me? I know you caught me on the telephone.' We told him we had done everything to catch him.

"All of his life he's been such a loner that nobody knew him until the Marshals' Service went in there and started their investigation. That bothered Mark because somebody had gotten into his head more than anybody else could."

During their conversation, Goodman wasn't a bit remorseful.

"I guess I can't go back to what I used to do, right?" he asked Tsoodle.

"That's what caught you, your burglary habits, you're gonna steal," the Marshal replied.

"Well, that's what I'm probably going back to when I'm released."

With a ten-count federal indictment for bank robbery facing him, escape from Washington, and parole violations from Oregon, that release probably wouldn't come for a long time. Goodman was arraigned in Austin, then transferred back to Oklahoma City for the escape charge, then the bank jobs. On August 6, he was sentenced to a period of observation and study by Judge David L. Russell in U.S. District Court, Western District of Oklahoma. The purpose of the study was to determine if the inmate was suffering from a mental disease or defect that rendered him mentally incompetent to understand the court proceedings and help defend himself. He went to the Medical Center for Federal Prisoners in Springfield, Missouri, where the study was completed. On September 16, being a high-risk inmate, he was transferred to the Federal Correctional Institution in El Reno, Oklahoma. According to standard procedure for inmates awaiting competency hearings, Goodman was held in a locked room in the prison hospital.

His keepers didn't notice that Goodman didn't intend to stay there long. Someone had slipped him something strong enough to saw through the wire of his bed springs, Tsoodle said later. Making a hook from the wire, Goodman prepared a special Halloween trick for prison officials.

In the early morning when all was quiet on the floor, he picked the heavy steel lock on the hospital room door. Outside, there was a raging thunderstorm passing through the area.

Out in the hall, he slipped past an attendant. Getting up the wall, he climbed up into an air duct in the ceiling that let him out by a skylight on the hospital roof. He scampered across the gravel-covered roof, then shimmied two stories down a drain pipe to the prison yard. Somehow knowing exactly what lay in front of him, Goodman had taken a blanket along, which he threw over the razor wire some ten feet above his head. The blanket was attached to some tape, which he used to fling it over. Though he had been shot twice only four months before, the athletic escapee climbed over the first fence, then the second. Once again, Mark Goodman, now 28, had escaped.

It was only at 8:30 A.M., after two bed checks,

that guards realized the dummy in the bed wasn't inmate Goodman. The alarm went out, and the Marshals were tracking him once more, nine hours behind the escapee.

The massive manhunt by five law enforcement agencies was concentrated in the Oklahoma City area. He had been spotted in rural areas around El Reno, where he apparently broke into a vacant house to shower and shave. A former friend positively identified Goodman riding a ten-speed bicycle along the North Canadian River in southwest Oklahoma City. A theater cashier said a man fitting his description had attended a movie with two other men on November 7. A sheriff's deputy working security there thought one of the men looked suspicious, but didn't get "a straight look at his face," according to a story in the *Daily Oklahoman* (November 4, 1986, p. 3). Officers covered the exits, but the men had already left.

Goodman had stolen a car and headed south to Norman and the University of Oklahoma. A student there reported his billfold stolen from a gym locker. Adams Chevrolet reported a Camaro stolen.

From interviewing Goodman's associates, Tsoodle and his task force, Harlon Woodbury, John Lassiter, and Paula Friedman, knew that Goodman had said he wanted to go south, perhaps Texas or Florida, where he wanted to sail on a boat. They sent Goodman's fingerprint card to state crime bureaus in the southeast region hoping to get a match.

They were right. Using the name from the stolen wallet, Trenton Jay Kirkpatrick, he had eluded police in Pensacola, Florida, and stolen a custom van off a car lot, where he abandoned the Camaro. Next, he drove east along the Florida panhandle, then south to Pinnellas County and Tampa, where he arrived in early January.

Going back to his old habits, as he had promised, Goodman looked for accomplices to help in his burglaries. In the early morning of January 30, 1988, he and Perry Jennings, his roommate of two months, hit an Ace Hardware store in Tarpon Springs, Florida. On the roof, they cut through a ventilation cover, then slid down a garden hose. They went on a shopping spree, taking all sorts of tools and supplies. The two then ran upstairs to the store office to crack the safe. Rather than set off an alarm by opening the office door, Goodman hacked through two dry walls to get inside the office.

Police, meanwhile, had gotten a call that two men were on the roof of the hardware store. They surprised the pair, now chiseling their way into the safe. The accomplice lay down on the floor and surrendered, but Goodman was running for a plate glass window across the room. He smashed through, and jumped down into the store, some 20 feet. With police and dogs in pursuit, he jumped over displays and counters until he got to the front window. With a crowbar, he smashed the window, dove through, and hit the sidewalk. He raced down the street into a swamp.

The police called in a helicopter from the Pinnellas County Sheriff's Office and the search lasted into the night. Once again, Goodman was playing his cat-and-mouse game with the law. A few hours later, he appeared in a van across from the hardware store and was arrested. Police speculated that he was probably watching the chase from the swamp for sometime before stealing the vehicle.

"Trenton J. Kirkpatrick," 25, was fingerprinted and booked. He was also suspected of some other similar local break-ins. Having burglarized three other stores that night, he was charged with 11 counts of burglary and grand theft, and held on $20,025 bond in the Pinnellas County Jail in Clearwater. As the court date approached, his public defender, Ron Eide, planned to suggest that his client plead no contest to some of the charges in exchange for probation. They didn't get the chance to chat.

At about 10 o'clock, Friday morning, March 4, the inmate had returned from a hearing. While waiting in a holding area, Goodman walked over to the discharge officer, who held all the inmates' property and clothing. Somehow the smooth talker convinced the man that he was scheduled for release that day. The man gave him his clothing and within a few minutes, Goodman marched out of the jail with the others being released after serving 62 days.

Pinnellas authorities contacted the FBI and the escapee's identity came back as Mark Austin Palmer, a prison escapee from Oregon and Washington. It wasn't long before befoe the Marshals in Oklahoma had an article about Palmer from *The Suncoast News* (March 5, 1988, p. 1) in Tarpon Springs. By March 20, they were down in Florida, hot on the trail of Mark Austin Goodman. Witnesses who knew "Kirkpatrick" confirmed enough details so they knew Goodman was back to his old habits. He had said he had contacted a girlfriend in Oklahoma, whom he planned to bring down to Florida. The whole episode confirmed what Tsoodle and his men had figured— using an alias, Goodman was probably in jail somewhere on burglary charges, getting ready to escape.

Headquarters in Arlington followed the recommendation from Oklahoma City that Goodman be placed on the USMS 15 Most Wanted List. Now, the pressure was really on to get him. That's when AMW got his file.

* * *

With Allendorfer's advice, producer Harman had begun writing a working script for the Goodman segment by late April. There was plenty of information to work with and the Marshals were very helpful. Allendorfer had already scouted by telephone several possible filming locations of Goodman's escapes in Washington, Oregon, Oklahoma, and Florida. The best location seemed to be Pinnellas County. The Marshals in Tampa were helping AMW get cooperation from the reluctant police there. From a dramatic filmmaking perspective, the hardware store break-in and escape had the best potential. They could also reenact his walk-out escape from the county jail. Filming the El Reno escape didn't seem possible.

With Tsoodle's assistance from Oklahoma City, Allendorfer tracked down plenty of news footage of Goodman from network affiliates there, and newspaper articles from Florida and Oklahoma. His family in Washington State and Guam had not seen him in three years. From the files, dating back to Goodman's arrest in Nevada, the researcher compiled an extensive profile, including the fugitive's quirks, such as his love for the sun and hate of the cold. He also calls girls "darlin'," likes Poison and Steppenwolf, and takes several showers a day. Goodman never exhibited any sign of violent behavior while on the run, except to police who tried to arrest him.

The first week in May, Harman and her crew arrived in Pinnellas County. Tsoodle and Woodbury had flown down from Oklahoma to act as advisors and be interviewed on camera. New York City actor Peter Bock would portray Goodman, based on the strong physical resemblance. With help from Detective Ed O'Brian of Pinnellas County, the producer interviewed Goodman's accomplice in the hardware break-in.

"I still think of him as Jay Kirkpatrick," the accomplice said in the interview, which would be used in the broadcast segment. A voice-over of his description of the burglary was used under the re-enactment filmed at the store where it happened.

"It was unbelievable and devastating to me," he continued. "He had picked up my son from school. He had cleaned up the apartment, in fact, I had even yelled at him real bad for not cleaning up my bathroom in the apartment that well and he's saying, 'I'm sorry, I'm sorry, I'll do a better job.'

"To think that he was one of the 15 most wanted men in America and I was yelling at him for not cleaning up very well. That was bad."

The crew also filmed some scenic shots of "Goodman" mingling with some teenagers along the beach. Completing the filming in four days, Harman headed to Washington to edit the final package. Kavanaugh and Tony Zanelotti, the associate producer, would sweeten the segment, while also mixing the music and Walsh's voice-overs.

For the final segment, Allendorfer had obtained a 10-second clip of Goodman walking into federal court in Oklahoma, and an aerial shot of the El Reno prison. The Marshals provided several good photographs which would be on the screen while Walsh read the fugitive's description.

The Goodman segment was scheduled as the second profile on May 15. Also being profiled was Marlin Chin and three other murder suspects from Washington, D.C., and William Walker, wanted for robbery and assault in Missouri. There would also be a capture report on prison escapee Thomas Lee Mollohan, who had been arrested in Cameron, West Virginia, on May 9.

* * *

In the AMW studio on Sunday afternoon, May 15, the taping was going smoothly. Up in the control booth, Weiss and Gadinsky were particularly pleased because they and several staff members had planned to go bowling after the show, their first night out in months. One act flowed into another—Chin, Goodman, Walker, and Mollohan. By 5:30 P.M., Walsh was back in the dressing room washing off his makeup and on his way home. The bowling group stopped for dinner down the street. There were few minor edits before the show was put on the satellite, so Linder, Kavanaugh, and Roberts left by 7 P.M.

Vista had given the phone operators their usual break until 7:30 P.M. At a nearby restaurant, Allendorfer was entertaining Tsoodle and Woodbury, while the other researchers were treating "their cops" from the Walker and Chin cases like royalty as well.

Everyone who needed to be back in the studio for the phone calls was in place by 8 P.M., when the show broadcast started on several monitors.

It was a quiet Sunday night at the Palm Beach County Stockade, a minimum-medium facility, in West Palm Beach, Florida. The inmates in K dorm were gathering around the TV for their favorite show, "America's Most Wanted" on local Fox affiliate WFLX, Channel 29. (The show has consistently been popular in the country's prisons.) Deputy Fred Merkle was observing the group while attending to his duties.

At about 8:25 P.M., by the end of the broadcast, a group of inmates walked over to Merkle. They told him that they knew one of the fugitives on television, Mark Austin Goodman. He was in the stockade under the name of James Ron Eide.

Merkle called the command center in the middle of the compound, and told Sergeant Thomas Holley, the shift supervisor, about the inmates' claim. Holley knew Eide. Now housed in dormitory unit G3, he had been there since March 3 on a 75-day sentence. The inmate had pleaded guilty to charges of burglary, grand theft, trespassing, and illegal lodging charges after his arrest for robbing a bookstore in Jupiter. Fairly well behaved, he was a trustee assigned to work the gas pumps, and was scheduled for release in four days.

Holley advised his supervisors, Lieutenant Kevin Bosman and Lieutenant James Holland, about the possibility that they had an "America's Most Wanted" fugitive in the stockade. All were well acquainted with the crime-fighting show and knew that federal fugitives were often found in custody under aliases. They picked up the telephone and called 1-800-CRIME-88.

The volume of calls coming into the studio had dramatically increased with the show's growing national popularity. Tsoodle and Woodbury had talked to several people in Florida who thought they knew Goodman. They had 247 leads, confirming he was in Florida somewhere. A few were coming from the Palm Beach area, which they suspected he had reached by now.

At 9:24 P.M., one of the operators got an unusual call. It was normal to get calls from police officers, but from a jail guard saying the fugitive was there under another name? She immediately raised her hand and called, "Anyone on Goodman?"

Tsoodle looked up from the stack of papers he was sorting. He walked over and took the receiver from the operator. A prison guard in West Palm Beach was telling him that they had an inmate named James R. Eide who strongly matched Goodman's description on the show. He went through the details of Eide's arrest. Tsoodle knew they were on to a hot one.

The stockade deputies put Tsoodle in touch with the fingerprint division. Allendorfer pulled Goodman's fingerprint chart from the file, and Lassiter read the classification codes to West Palm.

"19, 68, 14, 15, 11, DI, TT, 15, 17, 13."

They checked them again—a digit off on two fingers, but that was only a loop.

"Lock him down!" Tsoodle told the stockade supervisors. "We'll get back to you in a few minutes, but lock him down, please."

By 9:55 P.M., Sergeant Holley and two deputies were walking over to unit 63 to take Eide to a more secure location, namely the main county detention center about four miles away on Gun Club Road. When they arrived at the dorm, several inmates were still watching television, while others, like Eide, were lying on their bunks. Later, the inmates would say the Eide tried to switch the channel after AMW had been on a few moments, but he was shouted away from the set.

Sergeant Holley ordered Eide to stuff his property into a pillowcase and come with the officers. Eide obeyed and started toward the door. Deputies Jeff Maton and David Cook stayed behind in the dorm to collect the rest of the trustee's belongings. Holley handcuffed Eide's hands behind his back, and walked with the trustee over toward the command center.

Eide asked the sergeant why he was being taken out of the dorm.

"We'll talk about it when we get over there," he replied.

Walking just a few feet behind the prisoner, Holley couldn't see that Eide was slipping his deformed

David James Roberts was the first fugitive profiled and apprehended by "America's Most Wanted." Roberts was arrested by FBI agents in Staten Island, New York, on February 11, 1988, only four days after his segment aired. Though a Top Ten FBI fugitive, Roberts was running a homeless shelter in Staten Island, and was recognized by several friends and fellow workers. He had escaped from Indiana State Prison, where he was serving six life sentences for murder, arson, rape, and kidnapping. Roberts, who maintains he was framed by the Indiana criminal justice system, was interviewed by host John Walsh on the show's first anniversary broadcast, April 23, 1989.

Walsh and Sessions — AMW host John Walsh poses with FBI Director William Sessions at a press conference announcing the show's debut, held on February 5, 1988, at FBI Headquarters. The two are holding the show advertisement that several of Roberts' friends recognized in Staten Island, and led to his arrest four days after his profile. Seven days after this press conference, another was held in the same room to announce the capture.

Donald B. Adams, Jr., was the second suspect to be apprehended as a direct result of viewer tips on March 20, 1988, in East Boston, Massachusetts. Due to a bureaucratic foul-up, Adams had walked out of a Massachusetts prison, though slated to serve several more years for rape. Adams maintains that the show did not directly lead to his arrest, and he was falsely portrayed in his segment. He plans to seek a new trial.

On March 27, 1988, AMW broadcast an exclusive home video of the arrest of escaped murderer **Danny Michael Weeks**, one of the FBI's Top Ten Fugitives, by FBI agents in Seattle, Washington, one week earlier. The tape was the first known broadcast of an arrest of a Top Ten fugitive by an FBI SWAT team, and taken by a relative of Weeks' accomplice who had tipped off the FBI.

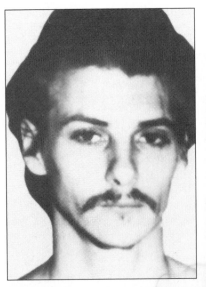

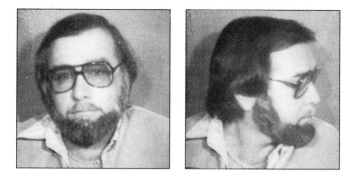

The fastest capture of an AMW fugitive directly from viewer tips was in El Centro, California, on July, 17, 1988, when the roommates of **Robert Wayne Fisher** recognized him from his AMW profile while he was sleeping in their motel room (see below). Fisher, wanted for the murder of his wife in Lake Charles, Louisiana, was working as a roughneck on a local geothermal well and using his real name and address. He was arrested by El Centro police only 33 minutes after the broadcast. Fisher was returned to Louisiana, where he was convicted of second degree murder and sentenced to life in prison without the possibility of parole, pardon, or commutation of sentence.

Credit: Jack Breslin

At age 72, **William "Pops" Pegram** was the oldest and one of the most notorious criminals ever profiled on AMW. His rap sheet, which includes prison terms for assault on a federal officer, bank burglaries, illegal interstate transport, grand larceny, and parole violations, stretches nearly a yard long. U.S. Marshals credit AMW for aiding in his arrest in Belize on September 11, 1988.

After being profiled on AMW, Massachusetts prison escapee **Stephen DeLorenzo** wrote to the show in July, 1988, and offered to surrender if officials agreed to his terms. The FBI confirmed that the letter was written by DeLorenzo, but he did not call into the hotline on July 24, as he had stated he would. He is still at large.

After being profiled twice on AMW, accused weapons smuggler **Edwin Maldonado** was arrested in Brooklyn, New York, in a joint drug enforcement sweep on August 23, 1988. He is currently being held in New York City where he faces charges of violating federal weapons and racketeering laws.

Sentenced to die in Philadelphia's electric chair, convicted murderer **Joseph Kindler** escaped from the city's jail to Canada, where he was arrested in Montreal on burglary charges. But Kindler also escaped from jail there, until a viewer watching AMW via satellite dish recognized him as a man working in a local repair shop in a remote area of St. John's, New Brunswick, Canada. The case was brought to AMW by Claire and Steven Berstein, sister-in-law and brother of the man Kindler murdered. (Captured: Sept. 6, 1988)

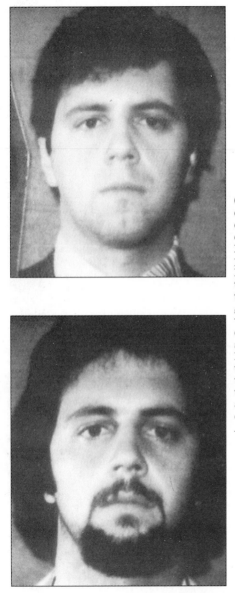

Outlaw biker and convicted murderer **Robert Nauss** escaped from a Pennsylvania prison in 1983, having been sentenced to life for the murder of his girlfriend. Nauss was profiled twice on AMW, but is still at large. U.S. Marshals suspect that Nauss has taken on an entirely new identity and slipped into everyday, middle American life.

Convict **Leroy Chasson** escaped from a Massachusetts prison with the help of his wife, Kathleen, when he stabbed himself in his cell, then had her meet him at the hospital with a gun. Chasson and his wife were profiled four times on AMW, and viewer tips led FBI agents to their house in Denver, where he was killed in a shoot-out on September 22, 1989.

Con man **Leroy Carter** was accused of swindling a retired Chicago woman out of her life savings. He was caught in Harlem, New York, on August 17, 1988, when a viewer recognized Carter from a promotion spot on Fox Channel Five, New York, for the upcoming Sunday's episode (Aug. 21). Carter was sentenced to 3.5 to 7 years in the New York prison system, and faces fraud charges in three other states.

Mark Goodman

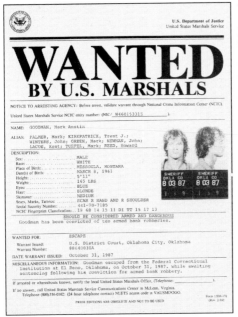

U.S. Marshals' 15 Most Wanted Poster, issued following his escape from the Federal Correctional Institute at El Reno, Oklahoma, on October 30, 1987.

Mug shot dated December 11, 1985, Chelan County Regional Jail, when Goodman was arrested by deputies for burglaries in Wenatachee, Washington State.

Small mug, taken when first admitted to the Medical Facility for Federal Prisoners, Springfield, Missouri, August 12, 1987, for study and observation before his bank robbery trial in Oklahoma.

WANTED

DENICE DELYLE STUMPNER
BEING SOUGHT BY THE GREEN BAY POLICE DEPARTMENT

Motorcycle gang member Denice "Bobber" Stumpner is accused of being an accomplice in the brutal 1983 murder of Margaret Anderson in Green Bay, Wisconsin. According to police, after quarreling with gang members, the victim was raped, beaten unconscious and dumped in a snowbank with her throat slit. Three other bikers were convicted in the murder, while Stumpner is still at large.

DOB: 10/15/53
Height: 5'6"
Weight: 200 pounds
Hair: Brown/Curly
Eyes: Blue
Race: White

Remarks: Long scar on stomach

Thanks to viewer tips, **Denice Delyle Stumpner** was arrested by FBI agents on a horse ranch in Golden, Colorado, on June 29, 1988, only ten days after his AMW profile. He was sentenced to fifty years for his part in the brutal murder of a Green Bay, Wisconsin, woman in 1983.

James Charles Stark, a three-time convicted sex offender wanted in California for murder and kidnapping, was captured by a 10-second promo spot a week before his scheduled profile on AMW. On April 24, 1988, viewers in Ann Arbor, Michigan, recognized Stark as a homeless car wash worker and he was apprehended at work the next day.

Frederick Merrill, nicknamed "The Peanut Butter Bandit" after his mother smuggled a gun into prison in a jar of homemade peanut butter to help him escape, was captured in an apple orchard in New Brunswick, Canada, on September 22, 1988. Having

WANTED

FREDERICK MERRILL
BEING SOUGHT BY THE CONNECTICUT STATE POLICE

Connecticut prison officials say career criminal/escape artist Frederick Merrill made his latest getaway last August by using hooks fashioned from bedsprings to scale two razor-topped fences. Previously convicted of burglaries, auto theft and escape, he was awaiting trial on charges that he beat and sexually assaulted a 55-year-old woman. Known as the "Peanut Butter Bandit," he has escaped three times from prison, once using a gun smuggled into him by his mother, who hid it in a jar of homemade peanut butter.

DOB: 11/8/46
Height: 6' 1"
Weight: 165 pounds.
Hair: Brown with Grey
Eyes: Blue

Remarks: Tattoo on left shoulder-arm of a heart with "Mom", surgical scar on abdomen.

escaped from prison in Connecticut, Merrill had fled to Canada, but viewer tips helped link him to some Toronto burglaries. He later escaped from prison in Montreal, but was recaptured, and faces charges there before being returned to Connecticut to face charges of escape, rape, and burglary.

Charles Jordan, a former U.S. Customs supervisor in Florida, was wanted for conspiracy and narcotics when he was profiled on December 4, 1988. Jordan was captured on June 15, 1989 in Jackson, Wyoming and his trial is now pending.

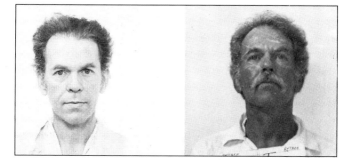

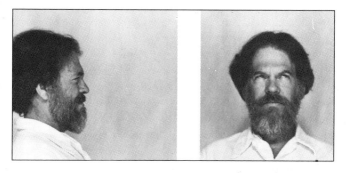

James Ray Renton was profiled on the show August 21, 1988. He had escaped from an Arkansas prison where he was serving a life sentence for the murder of a police officer. After a viewer called in a tip, Renton was captured in Austin, Texas, on September 6, 1988 and returned to the maximum security unit at Arkansas State Prison to serve his life sentence without parole and an additional four years for his escape.

Donald Bruce Parsons, a twice convicted sex offender, was being sought for child molestation when he was profiled on September 11, 1988. He was captured in Phoenix, Arizona, on October 21, 1988 and is now serving a 36-year sentence in Colorado State Prison.

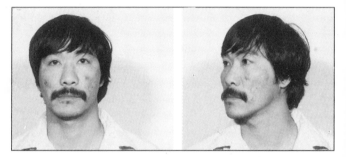

Hien Tat Chu, wanted for murder in Oregon, was to be profiled on December 11, 1988 but was captured four days earlier as a direct result of publicity for the upcoming segment of AMW. He is now serving a life sentence in Oregon State Prison.

Steven Ray Allen was profiled twice, on February 19, 1989 and again on July 2, 1989, before he was captured in Porcupine Springs, Idaho, on August 12, 1989. He was wanted for murder in Utah and is now awaiting trial in Moah, Utah.

Steven Randall Dye, now serving a ten-year sentence in New Jersey, was profiled on May 8, 1988. Dye was wanted on murder and attempted murder charges and surrendered on May 20, 1988 in San Diego, California. The state of Ohio has a murder case still pending.

Meeting in The Rose Garden — For the signing of the Missing Children's Act on October 12, 1982, President Reagan congratulates John and Reve Walsh, holding 3-month-old Meghan, on their work for missing children. *Credit: White House Photo*

Walsh and Travanti — Taken on the location set of "Adam" in Houston, Texas, during the filming of the NBC telefilm in July, 1983, John Walsh poses with Emmy-winning actor Daniel J. Travanti, who portrayed him. Travanti also played Walsh in the film's sequel, "Adam: His Song Continues," and is heavily involved in children's issues and charity work for the Adam Walsh Child Resource Centers. Both Travanti and JoBeth Williams, who played Reve Walsh, are close friends with the Walshes today. *Credit: Alan Landsburg Productions*

Greeting Reagan — Following a Cabinet-level meeting on children's issues on July 8, 1988, Walsh, now host of AMW, greets President Reagan, thanking him for his support on children's issues and victims' rights. One of four meetings Walsh had with Reagan in the Oval Office since 1982.

Meeting with the President — (From left) Reve and John Walsh meet with President Reagan, holding Meghan, age 2, as then-U.S. Senator Paula Hawkins (R-Florida) looks on. Hawkins responded to the Walsh's plea for help when Adam was missing and asked them to help lobby for Missing Children's legislation. This meeting was on May 13, 1984, shortly after the National Center for Missing and Exploited Children was funded, with Walsh as an advisor. *Credit: White House Photo*

With the other fathers — In 1985, Walsh was chosen in the "Everyman's Father" category by the National Father's Day Committee. Here he poses with four of the other seven honored fathers (from left) actor Ben Vereen, New York Governor Mario Cuomo, athlete-sportscaster Bruce Jenner, and baseball catcher Gary Carter.

Michael Linder, executive producer, huddles with co-producers **Brian Gadinsky** (2nd left) and **Dan Kavanaugh** (middle, glasses), and director **Glenn Weiss** (right).

right wrist out of the handcuff. As they reached the medical building, about halfway in their 50-yard walk to the command center, Eide smashed his shoulder into the unsuspecting officer. Before Holley could recover, Eide was running behind the medical building toward the fence. As he reached the gas pumps, Eide leapt up on a 55-gallon drum sitting next to the fence. In a second, he was over the 10-foot barbed wire fence, and on the ground on the other side.

Sergeant Holley reached the fence as Eide took off behind a large dirt mound in the Riker Compound, a gravel facility next to the compound. Without a hand radio unit, Holley ran to the command center. He was yelling there had been an escape. The supervisors called in all available guards and immediately set up a perimeter around the stockade. Several deputies climbed over the fence or took off in patrol units to apprehend the fleeing Eide.

About 30 minutes had passed since Tsoodle last talked to West Palm. An operator came over, saying the stockade supervisors were on the telephone again.

"You probably won't believe this," said the deputy down in Florida.

"Try me," said Tsoodle, who by this point was ready to pull his hair out with all the leads that were tumbling into the studio.

"He's escaped."

"Are you pulling my leg?"

"No, he escaped. This guy named James Eide, he's gone."

"Holy shit!"

By 11 o'clock, it was clear that Eide had made it across a small creek by the stockade onto the highway, probably heading north. Back at the stockade, the deputies were verifying names and addresses in the belongings Eide had left behind. No leads there, most of them were false.

Some 20 deputies were being spread out farther and farther from the stockade. There were dogs, helicopters, and road units combing the area, especially the swamp near the stockade. About two hours after the escape, there was a sighting about a mile from the stockade, but when officers arrived Eide was long gone.

The search dragged on with no sign of Eide. Finally, at 4:15 A.M., with the bloodhounds exhausted and off-the-scent, the search was called off until daybreak.

Back in Washington, Tsoodle had called Randall Slack of the Marshal's Enforcement Division out of headquarters. He began dispatching marshals from Miami to help the Palm Beach Sheriff's Office in the search. They had sent a photograph of Eide to Oklahoma already, and it matched. Eide was Goodman.

Here goes another nine months on the road, Tsoodle thought.

Allendorfer had been desperately calling TV news desks in the Palm Beach area, trying to get someone to cover the breaking story. But at 10:45 P.M., they were racing to get the 11 o'clock news on the air, and didn't have time for someone calling from this "America's Most Wanted" show from Washington about some escape. Finally, she convinced an assignment editor to send out a crew, which followed the search into the morning.

Gadinsky was called back from bowling, since he had excellent media contacts in the southern Florida area to help get footage for next week's show. When the party left the lanes, he and Weiss were locked in a frame-by-frame battle with a visiting Fox publicist.

At 7:45 A.M., Eide had been sighted at a gas station about five miles from the stockade. A female attendant told an investigator that a man matching the escapee's description had been a passenger in a white Maverick with a black male driving. They asked for a dollar's worth of gasoline so they could get to the Interstate, and left heading north on Military Road.

By now, the USMS Enforcement Division was pouring its resources into the Palm Beach area. One of their Most Wanted was running around somewhere in the county and they were determined to get him. At 11:30 A.M., Marshal Mel Hess and nine deputies arrived at the sheriff's office. They advised Sheriff Richard Wille and his staff that Eide was Goodman, a federal prison escapee wanted for ten armed bank robberies. The fingerprints and photos between Oklahoma and Florida had positively matched.

Sheriff Wille devoted as much manpower as he could to the search, while he had already launched an investigation into the incident at the stockade.

In Washington, Monday was usually a day off at AMW, but Linder and several staff members had come into the office to follow the chase.

The attorney, Herwitz, was a little less excited.

Great, now we have 15 captures and one escape, he thought. What did we do?

But he wouldn't have to worry long.

At four o'clock Monday afternoon, off-duty Deputy Robert Fiaschi was standing at the photo shop at the Concourse Plaza in Jupiter, Florida, about 15 miles from the stockade.

The deputy turned to see Eide, whom he recognized from the stockade. He was dressed in his brown trustee pants, a sleeveless white T-shirt and white tennis shoes. The trustee was strolling through the mall as if on a shopping trip. Fiaschi immediately called the Jupiter Police for backup, then walked cautiously up to Eide, now standing on a sidewalk at the other side of the plaza near Seagrape Square. He was chatting with a gentleman when the deputy came up and gently put his arm around the escapee's shoulders.

"How's your day going, buddy?" the deputy asked Eide, trying to keep things calm and friendly. "What are you doing out?"

He noticed a bulky gauze bandage, wrapped with silver duct tape on Eide's left wrist.

Two Jupiter units arrived on the scene. One of the officers asked the suspect for identification, and he gave the name of "Allan Dale Matzer." The officer asked him to spell his last name. He couldn't. How about the high school he attended? Nope.

The unresisting escapee was arrested and handcuffed. The officers removed the bandage from his wrist. A handcuff fell free, the other still locked to Goodman's left wrist. His seventh escape had ended just 18 hours after it had begun.

At the Jupiter Police Station, the suspect admitted being Mark Austin Goodman. On his person he had identification in the name of Matzer and $334.74 in cash, which was tagged and logged.

The seven marshals took custody of Goodman 45 minutes later, and he was taken to the Metropolitan Correctional Center in Dade County, south of Miami. He waived extradition and was back in Oklahoma City via the U.S. Marshal's airlift plane for a date in federal court there on May 26. Magistrate Ronald Howland set the trial date for June 20 on the escape and bank robbery charges.

As for Goodman's two Oklahoma accomplices, one, still a juvenile was not prosecuted, but the other, LeClaire, had turned eighteen and was prosecuted as an adult. He was sentenced to six years.

Goodman spent the summer at El Reno in an isolated cell area called "the box car." There was a four-man hold order on him, which meant that any time he was moved, four guards accompanied him. He could only walk with leg irons in a 20-by-60 foot area. The inmate was "sleeping a lot," exercising and catching up on his reading, but he could hardly make a fist with his right hand, which had atrophied with lack of physical therapy.

When he arrived in court in July, Goodman was facing a heavy sentence—up to 225 years behind bars. His public defender, William Earlin, advised him to plead guilty rather than go to trial. At 1:30 P.M. on August 3, Mark Austin Goodman was sentenced to 35 years for eight bank robberies and five more for escape. He could be paroled after 15 years, yet he faces outstanding warrants in Washington. Pinellas County and Pensacola could also prosecute him on charges in their jurisdictions.

Goodman was transferred to the federal prison in Leavenworth, Kansas, where he was soon listed on the "hot list" as a potential escapee. Twice, guards had found a rope and a dummy in his cell, so he faced administrative action by the Bureau of Prisons.

In September, Goodman was transferred to the federal prison in Lompoc, California, from which convicted spy Christopher Boyce ("The Falcon and the Snowman") had once escaped.

As the prisoner got on the U.S. Marshals' plane

out to California, an Oklahoma marshal who had worked on Goodman's case asked him if he would escape from Lompoc.

He just gave the marshal an impish grin.

As Tsoodle told AMW in an interview, "I think that when we catch him, I'll tell him because this is the second time we caught him, that it's over this time. And Mark will probably look at me and smile and say 'You'll look for me again.'"

Goodman declined several requests to be interviewed for this book. He did tell Tsoodle that he "didn't appreciate their show," namely "America's Most Wanted." He also denied that he bumped into Sergeant Holley while making his escape—he "just beat feet." As the trustee assigned to the gas pumps, he had placed three 55-gallon drums against the fence "in case things got a little hot." He was shocked to have been profiled on AMW, saying, "I don't believe that people would spend that money looking for me."

In an interview, Sergeant Holley said he would do a few things differently if he had the night over again. Instead of walking the trustee over alone, he would have put handcuffs and leg irons on him in the dorm. A patrol unit with two more guards would have been at the dorm door to drive him over to the command center. The inmates at the stockade still talk about that night, he said. Every Sunday night, everyone there watches AMW.

How could Palm Beach County and Pinellas County have a federal fugitive in their custody and not know it? It happens a lot all over the country, and often the jails find out the inmate's true identity only after he/she is released.

As Sheriff Wille explained in an interview, anyone arrested in the county is fingerprinted when booked, which is standard procedure in most jurisdictions in the United States. The prints are classified, then run through the county files for outstanding local warrants, especially under another name. The print cards are then mailed off to the Florida Department of Law Enforcement in Tallahassee.

In Tallahassee, the card usually arrives some two to three days after booking, according to Patrick J. Doyle, director of the Division of the Criminal Justice Information Systems, Florida DLE. Depending on the backlog (in November, 1989, there were 70,000 cards waiting), the card is put through a name search to determine outstanding warrants on that name, not aliases. If there's no "hit," the card goes off to the FBI in Washington.

The FBI gets the card within four working days, depending on the mail. The backlog with the FBI Fingerprint Division is usually 12 to 15 working days, according to Dan Greathouse, Section Chief of the FBI's Latent Fingerprints Division. It could take a month after booking before the card is run through the arrest file system to match it with a card already there.

Historically, Greathouse pointed out, until the advent of automation, the FBI had fingerprint technicians who would examine each card and put a classification on them—not an individual identifier, but a road map to a match in the file. There could be up to 2,000 matches in the system, which meant the difference between a few minutes or a few days to make the comparison.

With the AFIS (Automated Fingerprint Identification System), comparisons of minute identifying parts of the print are made in seconds. The suspect's correct name is not necessary to find an outstanding warrant. They are attached to the prints, and when a set matches, the agency holding the person is immediately notified. But by that time, sometimes a month or more, the person could have been released or bonded out.

Within the decade, Greathouse said, new technology would provide electronic fingerprinting. Instead of inking a person's finger and pressing it to a card, it would be placed on a scanner. The image would be recorded and the files automatically searched. Ideally, warrants could be checked within hours, but not all states would be able to afford getting into such a nationally automated system, Greathouse cautioned. If the "larger states," containing "80 to 90 percent" of the population could communicate with this technology, most of the country's law enforcement could exchange information in a matter of minutes, he said.

The current system is far from perfect, Greathouse explained. The FBI often receives fingerprint cards that are smudged or unclear for classification and file searching. The cards must be sent back for refingerprinting, if the suspect is still in custody. By no means does the FBI files cover 100 percent of everyone arrested in the country, Greathouse noted.

At the time of Goodman's arrest, the state of Florida was going through a lengthy transformation to the AFIS system, both Doyle and Greathouse stressed. The transformation was being done by a private firm in Anaheim, California. There were some 2.2 million criminal histories in the old Florida files, Doyle explained. The cards were crated and shipped to Anaheim in batches of 10,000, after being run through the Tallahassee system. Once the image-transfer process was completed in Anaheim, the cards and AFIS optical disks were shipped back to Florida. The cards were recrated and shipped to the FBI in Washington. During that conversion time, getting the card from the local Florida booking desk to the FBI computer could take up to five months, Doyle stated. (The AFIS is now operating in Tallahassee, and Palm Beach County has one on line as well.)

Once again, Goodman managed to find a lucky break in the system—for a while, anyway.

9

**Reaching Back
Through Time**

By the time "America's Most Wanted" celebrated
its first national anniversary, 75 of the 159 fugitives
profiled would be in custody, 45 of those captures
being a direct result of viewer tips to the toll-free
hotline. Seven fugitives had surrendered after being
profiled.

In that year more than 92,000 phone tips had
been received by the show, with a startling 65 percent of the callers insisting on leaving their names
and addresses in case investigators needed their further help. During the week of June 5, the hotline
fielded a record 5,010 calls, some of them leading to
two witnesses coming forward in a Maryland murder
case. On the average, the show now receives about
1,500 calls a week, with only 35 percent being hangups or information calls. (Viewers can also write to
the show, care of P.O. Box Crime-89, Washington,
DC 20016.)

The show's creators were right—people would call
in because they wanted to help fight crime. In a research study done with audience focus groups, Fox
asked the following question: "If you had information
on a fugitive profiled, would you call in with that

information?" Of those surveyed, 93 percent "strongly agreed," while 98 percent "agreed (to some degree)." The ability to call in with information was rated as the most appealing element of the show.

Since it began, "America's Most Wanted" had worked with some 100 local, state, and federal law enforcement agencies in 120 cities in the United States, Canada, and Mexico.

On a special anniversary broadcast, the show received congratulations from both the FBI and the Marshals.

"We have posters in post offices and spots on television, but the dramatizations of the actual crimes make an impact on the public, giving them a greater incentive to participate," said the FBI's Oliver "Buck" Revell.

FBI Director Sessions had appeared on the show during the previous May 29 (broadcast #17) to announce three additions to the FBI's Ten Most Wanted List. One of those fugitives announced, Jack Farmer, wanted for racketeering, was apprehended the next day in Lantana, Florida, thanks to viewer tips.

"We try to figure out creative ways which go beyond rounding up the citizens in a posse to deal with the national and international adversaries," said Marshals Director Stanley Morris. "These are new challenges and we have to look to new technologies like TV and 'America's Most Wanted,' which have helped us do that."

The anniversary show also featured an interview with David James Roberts, the first fugitive captured by AMW, coming from Indiana State Prison in Michigan City, Indiana. (For the full interview, see Appendix B.) Also interviewed were several victims of crime aided by the show's captures, which were reviewed in a highlight segment.

The show had also attracted a local audience following, which would impress advertisers in both rating/share numbers and demographics. The show had become a consistently strong competitor in the 8–8:30 P.M. time slot against other shows, beating some 60 programs in head-to-head battles. It was the first Fox series to defeat a regularly scheduled competitive show when it surpassed ABC's "Mission: Impossible" on November 27, 1988. In the 1988–89 season, it beat the ABC competition ("Spenser for Hire," "Supercarrier," and "MacGuyver") 37 times; NBC ("Family Ties") 22 times; and CBS ("Murder, She Wrote") once.

As for ratings, AMW arranged a 9.2 rating and 15 share for the 1988–89 season, a strong increase over its 6.8/13 average the season before. Its highest household rating was an 11.6 on February 5, the show's first anniversary on the O&O's, and its highest share was a 22 on July 23, the show's remote from Las Vegas, Nevada.

As for demographics, according to the Nielsen National Audience Demographic (NAD), "America's Most Wanted" has its strongest appeal in the Pacific regions, followed by the East Central and Northeast, performing better in larger counties than smaller. It demonstrates above average appeal in large households (4 or more residents), and is the strongest among broad audience base with a total household income below $40,000.

The show started out as a program appealing to the Fox target audience of young adults and teens (ages 18–34), but soon broadened to include everyone from children to adults over age 55. It consistently ranks number-one in its time period among adults ages 18–34, 18–49, and 25–54, and number-two among adults over age 55 and teens.

More than 20 top national advertisers continually buy out the program on a weekly basis.

While audiences increased, the most news-making aspect of "America's Most Wanted" was its captures. (See the chapter following for details on the most outstanding.) The most amazing was of a fugitive who almost never saw the air, having been turned down twice before.

Since December, 1971, the case of John Emil List had baffled New Jersey police. His very name sent a chill through residents of Westfield, New Jersey, who wished he had never lived there. Every policeman in the state cringed at the thought of a man escaping from brutally murdering his mother, wife, and three children—without a trace. The law enforcement agencies predominantly involved in the hunt for List—namely the FBI, the New Jersey State Police, the Union County Prosecutor's Office, and the Westfield Police—had never given up looking.

For seventeen years they had followed every lead that trickled in. They occasionally sent out flyers to the media with updated photos of what List might look like today. They would fly all over the country, even overseas, to quietly interview someone resembling the multiple murderer, who had probably slipped back into oblivion. He had probably remarried, maybe had more children, was working in insurance or accounting, and never had so much as a parking ticket. Despite his unspeakable act, List was most likely still a devout conservative Lutheran of the Missouri Synod, teaching Sunday school, and reading his Bible everyday.

The leading List investigators for most of the later 1980s were Captain Frank Marranca of the Union County Prosecutor's Office and Lieutenant Bernard "Bernie" Tracy of the Westfield P.D. The town's chief in 1971, James Moran, who led police through the List mansion on that horrible night the bodies were discovered, had retired in 1986, after 26 years on the force, but never let go of the case. Even after retiring, the former chief kept the FBI wanted poster of List in his jacket pocket.

In late 1987, Marranca and Tracy decided to pitch the two national crimefighting shows, "Unsolved Mysteries" and "America's Most Wanted" on the case. Maybe someone watching would have seen List, gone to church with him, or even live next door to him, they thought. It was a shot in the dark, but nothing else had worked.

With 22 years in law enforcement, Marranca had taken over the prosecutor's homicide squad early that year. He had been assigned to another unit when the murders took place and always thought "something more could be done on it." Over the past 17 years, the case was periodically reassigned to a different detective who might put a different perspective on the fugitive's whereabouts.

There was even a little joke in the office. When vacation season came, someone would always send a prank postcard, saying, "Having a lovely time, wish you were here. Regards, John List."

Bernie Tracy had become involved in the List case in 1980, when he joined the Westfield P.D.'s detective division. Any leads that came in, it was Tracy's job to track them down. Every year the press would pick up the story for an anniversary follow-up, and some tips would trickle in. Tracy would contact the local police departments, but 95 percent of the leads were dismissed "right off the bat" since the physical description would be way off. Some would go a little further. After one call came from Long Island about a real estate broker strongly resembling List, Tracy and some other officers went into the man's office, pretending to be perspective buyers. But when they sat down, the man was the wrong height, hair color, and eye color. Those were things that a person just can't change.

For years, on the List children's birthdays, List's wedding anniversary, and the date of the murders, Westfield's chief investigator, Robert Bell, and UC's Sergeant Jeffrey Hummel, would stake out the Westfield cemetery where the family was buried, in case List showed up to visit the graves.

When Marranca first took over homicide, he assigned Sergeant Edward Johnson to work with Tracy to compile a new flier. They concluded that if List was still alive, and had not killed himself over the murders, he was probably in the Midwest, married, Lutheran, and maintaining a low profile. He probably never even had gotten a parking ticket, much less attended a policemen's charity function. Using some computer and artist techniques, they had an aged photograph of what List should look like at age 62.

Since List was most likely still a devout churchgoer in a conservative Lutheran sect, they contacted the national hierarchy of the Lutheran Council in hopes that it would help circulate the flier among its more than 10,000 member churches. The elders answered that they felt that they were not in a position to help track down and apprehend List, Marranca would say later in an interview. The Associated Press did run the flier, and several supermarket tabloids picked up the story and aged photograph.

Marranca and Tracy made their pitch to the TV shows, by phone and by mail. But they were turned down by both—the case was too old, too gruesome. Most important, there were no recent photographs of List, which would make it difficult for viewers to properly identify him. They were sorry, but they couldn't help now, but maybe next year.

Having followed the case for nearly 18 years, Marranca wasn't going to give up.

With AMW's increasing popularity, speaking appearance requests for the host and the executive producer were flooding the Fox publicity department. Linder's weekly schedule was packed, his only day off being Monday. He could do telephone interviews, but taking a full day off for a speaking engagement required several weeks' notice.

Walsh continued his legislative lobbying and children/victims advocacy with the Adam Walsh Child Resource Centers. Dates were booked almost a year in advance. Once he testified to a committee of the Oregon legislature by a special telephone hookup during a break from AMW voice-overs. Sometimes he could combine a Fox request with an AMW Center appearance. Once a month or so, he squeezed in a Fox sales party or press day in a particular market that had been patiently waiting for months.

The law enforcement community was particularly anxious to honor the show and have someone speak at their conventions and meetings. In July, 1988, the Justice Department had honored Linder with the U.S. Attorney General's Distinguished Public Service Award. The U.S. Marshals named Walsh the 1988 Citizen of the Year at its "America's Star Dinner" on December 8 in Washington, celebrating the Marshals' Bicentennial.

In February, just after the show's O&O anniversary, Linder had agreed to speak at the Eastern Armed Robbery Conference in Wilmington, Delaware. The executive producer was looking forward to the event, especially since he enjoyed meeting law enforcement agents, who might have some new cases. Fox publicity had also scheduled some media interviews to help promote the show in that area.

Linder and Michael Barton drove up to Wilmington in the morning, and the producer delivered a 40-minute keynote speech to the group. He also included a video highlight reel, which summarized the show's conception, captures, and philosophy. His presentation was warmly received with nearly a half-hour of questions following.

After the questions, Linder started to leave the room when two men came up and shook his hand. They had a very concerned look in their eyes, he would remember later.

Marranca and Hummel had heard that Linder was going to be the keynote speaker at the conference. Maybe an in-person pitch might help, they thought. They loaded the files into a station wagon, and drove to Wilmington to meet the executive producer.

The two asked Linder "very politely" after the speech if he would come up to their hotel room and review this material on a "very compelling case." On the way up, they briefly described the List case, which Linder vaguely recalled turning down.

In the room were seven or eight bankers' boxes of the original case files. On the bed the investigators laid out dozens of 8″ x 10″ black-and-white glossies of the house and the discovery of the victims.

Linder found something very disturbing and very haunting about the case. The victims' bodies had begun to bloat, having been discovered a month after their murders. List had covered the faces of the women with rags, but not the boys'. In the photos, there were swab marks where List had mopped up the blood, so when each child returned from school, they would not think anything was wrong. He had laid out the bodies very neatly, at right angles to each other, except his mother, who was stuffed in an upstairs closet. And here was this big empty mansion, furnished in used office equipment, and the owner had vanished.

The "sticking point" Linder told the investigators was the image. There was no photograph taken of John List since 1971. But he would give the case careful consideration.

In AMW's second episode, the show had used a forensic bust of fugitive Robert Nauss, which was sculpted by Philadelphia artist–photographer Frank Bender. Nauss hadn't been caught, but the image provided a new vehicle. It was a three-dimensional sculpture which showed an infinite number of face planes when rotated in front of the camera. A police mug shot provided only a side and front profile. The bust could point out some oddities in List's features—the structure of his ear lobes, one ear sticking out further than the other, and a mastoid surgical scar.

Within two weeks of their meeting, Linder called the Union County Prosecutor's Office. He had a "shopping list" of four or five items. List had left behind several confessional letters, which detailed the crimes. If AMW couldn't use the actual language of the letters, at least they could tell the show what he said. Get the cooperation of the principals involved in the case, and help us find some of the people who had worked on the case in the past.

The investigators "were delighted" that AMW had agreed to do the case. Linder made no guarantees, since this was "strictly an experiment." He had decided previously that it wouldn't be fair to take a case more than eight years old, since the fugitive could be dead or in jail under an alias.

This was a definite long shot, but Linder couldn't ignore it. John List's victims cried out for justice.

* * *

Over the next few months, Marranca, Tracey, and others met with Ms. Roberts and the AMW researchers. They detailed every piece of John List's life and his crimes, all the way back to the beginning.

John Emil List was born on September 17, 1925, to John and Alma List in Bay City, Michigan, on the east coast of the state. His ancestors, staunch Lutherans, had immigrated from Germany in the late 1800s and settled in Frankenmuth, Michigan (according to a nine-part investigative series in *The Courier-Journal*, Plainfield, N.J., published in August 1989). In November 1924, List's father, John Frederick, 60, married his cousin, Alma List, 38, just a year after his first wife died of cancer. His adult son from that marriage, William, was the best man.

List spent his early years in Bay City, where life was conservative, traditional, and church-bound. German was spoken at church, at school, and at home. His father owned a local dry goods store in the tiny town of about 1,500, where many of the residents were related. He would be a lonely, only child, and fiercely overprotected by his mother. His childhood world was pathetically small, limited to a few blocks around his home. He was very studious and religious, but not at all athletic. His mother didn't allow him any friends.

Shortly after graduating from Central High School in 1943, List enlisted in the U.S. Army. The "class prophecy" in his high school year book simply stated, "John List is in the Quartermaster Corps." He returned on leave to Bay City for his father's funeral, who died on August 30, 1944. At the time, List, now 18, was a private, stationed in Louisiana and preparing for combat overseas. He would earn several medals in Europe and the southeast Pacific, not for combat bravery, but for service, sharpshooter, and good conduct.

Discharged in April 1946, List, 21, returned home to Bay City for a few months, before heading south to Ann Arbor in September to enroll at the University of Michigan to study business administration. A tall (6'1"), shy young man, List's college life was similar to his childhood; he concentrated on his studies and church activities. In his senior year, he pledged a professional business fraternity, Delta Sigma Pi, strictly for career development, not for social reasons. Occasionally, he dated Anne Hachtel, later mayor of Bay City. His mother, a registered nurse, visited her son at least once a month on campus.

List was a solid "B" student, and got his bachelor's degree in June 1950. At that time, veterans could apply their military service toward college credits, so List was awarded an MBA two months later. Having joined ROTC on campus, he was commissioned a second lieutenant upon graduation during the Korean War.

Helen Morris Taylor was John List's first love. The Army had shipped him to Fort Eustis, Virginia, where he met Helen at a bowling alley in nearby Newport News in October 1951. Her husband, whom she had married at age 16, had been killed in action in Korea six months before, leaving her a widow with a 9-year-old daughter, Brenda. He had only been buried a few days before Helen met John, now 26.

Premarital sex was strictly forbidden in List's religious beliefs, but Helen must have changed his mind. Fearing she was pregnant, the couple eloped to Baltimore on December 1, 1951, according to Helen's sister, Jean Syfert. List's bride was a Methodist, but converted to his faith before the wedding. They were "opposites," Ms. Syfert remembered, but List loved his new wife. He was willing to care for her, not just because it was expected. Yet a quick marriage wasn't consistent with List's character. He later legally adopted Brenda. They honeymooned in Washington, D.C., then left for San Francisco, where List would work as an Army accountant. They passed through Bay City, so List could introduce his bride to his mother.

About a year later, List left the Army, and moved his family to Detroit, where the bright, ambitious young businessman had found a junior accountant's job at a prestigious firm. Later, they moved across the state to Kalamazoo for a better position. The couple was very affectionate in the early years of their marriage, Ms. Syfert recalled. They were anxious to have children, but Helen had two miscarriages before their daughter, Patricia, was born in 1955. Two sons, John and Frederick, would be born within three years. Brenda also lived with them, soon playing mother to her half sister and brothers.

Something was brewing in the marriage. Helen didn't get involved with the church, while John drilled the children in religious questions. According to one Kalamazoo business associate, she even left a message at work that the baby had soiled his diaper, and he should come home and change it (*Courier-Journal*, August 14, 1989, p. A–6). Other folks said she drank too much, and lived above their means. Her mother-in-law also visited quite frequently. She also reminded her present husband that her first spouse had been a war hero, not a pencil-pusher.

In 1961, Brenda, 18, married and left home. The same year, the Lists moved to Rochester, New York, where he took a job with a growing new company called Xerox. Soon List was working 12-hour days and making strides within the corporation. Life at home was getting worse. He longed to spend more time with the children. Helen was drinking so much that he canceled liquor deliveries to the house (*Courier-Journal*, August 14, 1989, p. A–7). The children were becoming protective of their mother's problems, and they started looking away from their parents for good times.

For some unexplained reasons—perhaps for career or family—List moved them to Westfield, New Jersey, in November 1965. He bought a broken-down, three-story, 19-room mansion on a hill at 431 Hillside Avenue, which he intended to restore to its former splendor when built by millionaire John Wittke, some 75 years before. He took a job as vice president and controller at the First National Bank of New Jersey, his Xerox career on the slide.

Strictly upper-class, Westfield was a wealthy, beautiful New York City suburb, full of stately, well-maintained homes. John started teaching Sunday school at Redeemer Lutheran Church, and was co-leader of its Cub Scout pack, but had few friends. Neighbors remember the couple as boring and reclusive. He did enjoy playing a war board game that involved precise military strategy, and he'd usually win. Yet less than two years after his new job and new mansion, List's financial problems started to overwhelm him. Helen's health was also drastically going downhill, and she had become a nagging wife, still very extravagant. By May 1968, according to Ms. Syfert, she was bedridden, having been diagnosed as having brain atrophy and a tumor. Alma List had moved there from Michigan, and settled into a third-floor apartment in her son's home. She had even loaned him $10,000 to buy the mansion.

He was fired from his job with the bank, and was unemployed for nearly six months before finding an accountant's job with a firm in the city. The company decided to relocate, but he wouldn't move with it. He lied to his family, not even telling them that he was again unemployed, according to Westfield Police. Instead, he went to Westfield train station every weekday morning and read books all day. With the bills piling up, List eventually started selling insurance for the State Mutual Life Assurance Company, based in East Orange, N.J. He usually worked out of his home, but not very well. In the first ten months of 1971, List made only $5,000. At one point, he could have even qualified for welfare. The Hillside mansion, which he bought for $80,000, was mortgaged twice.

He had also become the house-husband, with Helen unable to do the simplest chores. They no longer shared a bedroom. The children, now teenagers, were becoming interested in more outside activities, such as athletics, drama, and the opposite sex. Their lifestyles sharply conflicted with their father's ultra-religious edicts. He was also deeply disturbed by the changing times with its drugs, free sex, and immorality.

In 1971, Patricia, now 16, was a junior in high school, loved being in plays, and was in a work-study program. She even had a boyfriend for a while. John, 15, also worked part-time and played soccer with the Roosevelt Junior High School team. Frederick, 13, was in the eighth grade in the same school as John.

Rick Baeder, a Westfield resident who used to play with the List boys, told AMW that their father "was a very quiet man, very reserved, very observant, very methodical person in the way he did things." He and the boys played games in the empty ballroom, as List could not afford to furnish the mansion. Baeder remembered that List would never be dressed casually and even wore dress slacks and a long-sleeved shirt to mow the lawn. People found him quiet, tightly wound, and not very friendly, quite the opposite traits for a would-be successful insurance salesman.

By the fall of 1971, John Emil List, 46, hit his breaking point. He applied for a gun permit at the Westfield Police station on October 14, but never picked it up. He had already purchased a .22-caliber revolver and a 9-mm pistol, though police never knew where he got them or when.

Having planned his solution for several months, List picked November 9, 1971 as Judgment Day for his family.

According to police investigations, this is what happened in the List mansion that autumn morning.

On that cloudy and cold morning, the three teenagers had left for school, followed by their part-time jobs. Helen, 46, was in the first-floor kitchen, still in her nightclothes since she rarely dressed. She was making coffee and reading the newspaper. Alma, List's mother, 85, was upstairs in her third-floor apartment fixing her breakfast and doing little chores.

List walked up behind his wife and shot her once in the head. She fell dead. He dragged her body to the ballroom, where only ten days before he allowed Patricia to hold a Halloween party for some 50 friends.

Next, List walked upstairs to the third floor. He walked into his mother's kitchen, looked at her, then shot her once in the back of the head. Rather than take her downstairs, he stuffed her body in a closet.

By ten o'clock, List was calling his employer to cancel a meeting, saying he was sick. The rest of the morning and afternoon he followed out his carefully planned list of details. He wrote letters dated that day to excuse the children from school with the excuse of a sick, out-of-town relative. He also wrote a four-page, detailed letter to his pastor, Reverend Eugene Rehwinkel, which most sources confirm was a letter of confession. He also called Patricia's drama teacher, Barbara Sheridan, to say that his daughter would be missing play practice for awhile.

List also cancelled the mail, milk, and newspaper deliveries. He drove down to his bank, Suburban Trust, and cashed about $2,100 in bonds. List returned home and waited.

Patricia came home earlier than usual, having felt ill at her part-time clerical job at a local insurance company. Her father was waiting behind the kitchen door, and shot her once in the back of the head. He dragged her into the ballroom, still with her coat on, and laid her at a right angle to her mother.

Frederick arrived home next. His father was waiting and shot him in the back of the head, then dragged his body into the ballroom, laying him next to his sister and mother.

Over at Roosevelt Junior High, the soccer coach had decided it was too cold to practice outdoors. John was among the players excused from practice, so he headed home and arrived there about 5 P.M. His father was waiting. The elder List must have had trouble killing his oldest son, or the boy showed signs of life after the first shot. Police found his body riddled with nine bullets in his back and head. His limp, bloody body was then dragged into the ballroom with the others.

List had put the bodies on sleeping bags, and covered the women's faces, not the boys', with rags. With more rags, he mopped up the blood in the kitchen and ballroom. He shoved the bloody rags into several brown shopping bags and left them near the bodies in the ballroom. Turning down the heat to slow the decomposition of the bodies, List put a funeral dirge on the record player, which was piped throughout the house.

Picking up the suitcase he had already packed, John List got into his 1963 Blue Chevrolet Impala and drove away.

The children's friends noticed they were gone from school, but their father had already excused them due to an illness in the family in North Carolina. By Thanksgiving, Helen's sister, Jean Syfert, hadn't gotten answers to two letters she had written. List missed his Sunday school classes, and the family, sans Helen, were not at services. The neighbors noticed that the lights were flickering out in the List home. On the night of December 7, 1971, they called the Westfield police.

Officers Charles Haller and George Zhelesnik arrived at the List home at 10:10 P.M. They found Patty's drama teacher, Ms. Sheridan, and Edward Illinano, head of the town's drama group, already there looking for Patricia.

The long driveway was muddy and rocky from the rain. They walked to the right side of the house and looked for an unlocked window. Finding one in the rear of the house, they opened it and climbed into the ballroom. Lying on the floor, on sleeping bags, were four bloated bodies. Haller checked Helen List for vital signs. He felt nothing but a hardened, cold arm. The police officers called headquarters over the radio for help.

The house was cold and there was funeral music playing. Blood stains made a path from the ballroom to the kitchen. Washed dishes remained on the kitchen sink. Halloween decorations were still in the ballroom, and fish were swimming in their tank. The stench of dead hung heavy in the rooms.

More police arrived within minutes, including

Chief Moran, who ordered an immediate search of the house for more bodies. In an upstairs closet, they found the body of Alma List. They would have to break the corpse's legs to remove it. Moran directed his men to drain a nearby cistern on the third floor in case more bodies were in it. There weren't.

In the next several hours, the entire house, garage, and property were searched inch-by-inch. Investigators from the Union County Prosecutor's Office arrived, along with the medical examiners. The five bodies were removed for autopsies. The police broke into a file cabinet, where they found the alleged murder weapons, a checkbook with a $7.94 balance, and several letters addressed to relatives and List's pastor, Reverend Rehwinkel. Police asked him to gently break the tragic news to the Syferts in Oklahoma, and other List relatives. Later, at the post office, police discovered that List had mailed a special delivery letter to himself with the file cabinet key. Otherwise, there was not a trace of John List, now wanted for five murders.

News of the murders shocked Westfield and the entire state of New Jersey. The curious were causing traffic jams on Hillside Avenue and surrounding streets as they strained for a look at the murder house.

Following services at Redeemer Lutheran, Helen List and her three children were buried in Fairview Cemetery on Saturday morning, December 11. The town was jammed with national media and unwelcomed visitors. Alma List was buried the next week in Bay City, Michigan.

Since List had probably left the state, the FBI was called in on the case. But the next clue indicated that List was by now out of the country. On December 9, his car was found parked at the long-term lot

at John F. Kennedy International Airport. The ticket
on the dashboard indicated it had been put there on
November 10. It was impossible to trace the passen-
gers who flew out of there on that day, and List was
probably using an alias.

The investigators checked the armed services,
obituaries, insurance companies, and arrest reports.
Over the years, the unsolved case became a sick joke.
The List mansion burned to the ground the following
summer by mysterious causes, some rumors saying
the accused murderer had returned to finish the job.
Today, a stately red-brick Georgian home stands on
the site.

That's what the investigators gave "America's
Most Wanted" in the spring of 1989. Linder turned
the file over to segment producer, Jim Coane, who
was not only a great filmmaker, but also a man with
"a big heart." He would need it with this story. This
was Coane's fourth case for AMW, and certainly his
most challenging.

Coane remembered later his first reaction when
he opened the List file and started reading it—"gruesome, five brutal murders, what an animal." He was
right across the river in New York City, but had
never heard of the John List case before. This would
be a "period piece," taking place in 1971, different
from most AMW cases which were present-day.

The problem Coane faced was making the profile
realistic, yet not totally gruesome. A man is accused
of murdering his wife, mother, and three children in
a seven-hour period. How do you do such murders
with a pistol tastefully?

The piece had been scheduled for the May 21
broadcast (#66), so Coane had about three weeks to
get it in the can. The Westfield police and UC Prosecutor's Office were ready to help with every pro-

duction detail. Through New York casting director, Kelly Case, Coane found a "terrific look-alike for List," actor Mark Zimmerman. His associate producer, Sandy Tait, scouted locations, and secured permits for shooting off the guns. They also needed period cars, such as a '65 Mustang and a hippie Volkswagon van, and clothing from that year. Coane wanted a church with a bit more "Americana" than the one List attended, who probably wouldn't have cooperated anyway. The town, in general, however, welcomed the AMW production. Those sensitive about how the image of Westfield would be portrayed, expressed a "sense of relief" to Coane and his crew.

Tracy, Marranca, and Newark FBI agent Barry Martino would serve as advisors, along with several other principals involved in the case over the years. On camera, they would interview Reverend Rehwinkel, now living elsewhere, Baeder, Tracy, and Haller. Tracy helped find a suitable house, and his youngest son's Sunday school class played "List's" class in the filming.

The producer decided to "telegraph" the violence to the viewer. They would use cooler tones, on the blue side, since the house was not heated. "List" would be shown mopping up the bloody floor. The camera would show the bags of bloody rags and the red-soaked mop. The actor would be shown pointing the gun, but the gun explosion would be heard over black.

The filming was not without its nightmares, however. On the first night, the murder scene was filmed with five of the actors covered with sheets and lying on the floor. They came back the next morning and told Coane that they had not slept at all that night, especially Zimmerman. They had nightmares about the incident, something that many AMW actors experience. There they were in this empty house, doing a crime that had happened so close to Halloween. It was a very goulish feeling.

Back in Washington, Coane had "very little editing" to do and the piece was ready for broadcast.

In Philadelphia, Frank Bender got the same file as Coane did. He had four weeks to research, design, and sculpt a forensic bust of how John List would have aged in 18 years. Originally a professional photographer, Bender had been doing skull facial reconstructions for 13 years, having gotten the idea during a tour of the city medical examiner's office. He had been doing fugitive busts for about four years, having made several, including Alphonse Persico and Hans Vorhauer, for the U.S. Marshals Service, who recommended him to AMW. List was his third bust for AMW, after Nauss and "the man with the broken nose" wanted for art theft.

With List, Bender had a particular problem, since he had to create a three-dimensional bust from a front view photograph. As a photographer, he was used to seeing objects in dimension, then putting them on a paper. This would be the reverse. He hired Dr. Richard Walter from the Michigan Department of Corrections to compile a psychological profile on List.

First, there was the black hair, now gray and probably progressively receding based on hereditary factors. As for glasses, List would wear heavier frames to give him a look of authority, so people wouldn't question his background. He would have put on some weight and have jowls, being a sedentary man, but not a smoker or drinker. He would have a pale, drawn look, not being out in the sun a lot. The man had worn dress clothes mowing the lawn, so Bender would put a coat and tie on him. The tie was a professional type, red with diagonal stripes, giving the in-control look. The coat was dark blue with a very conservative fit. List had a long mastoid scar behind his right ear to his collar line. The right ear was closer to his head, and slightly lower than the left.

Before bringing the bust to Washington, Bender brought it to the Westfield police, who showed it to some people who knew List well in 1971. Most gasped when they saw Bender's final product—it was John List.

Tracy and Martino drove down to Washington on Sunday morning, May 12. Marranca was attending a training school in Tennessee, but would be in contact by phone that night when the tips came in.

List was being profiled along with body builder John Riccardi, wanted by Los Angeles Police for the murder of his girlfriend in Venice, California. An unidentified Milwaukee rapist was also being featured, though the only images were from a surveillance camera at an automated teller machine. Host John Walsh also reported the capture of prison escapee and armed robber Michael Taylor, who had been captured in Rapid City, South Dakota, the day before. Taylor had seen his profile on April 9, and fled to get out of the view of American television. He didn't go far enough. A suspicious pawn broker tipped off Rapid City police when Taylor tried to fence his stolen jewels.

Tracy would recall later being nervous as he watched the broadcast on the studio monitors. Would anyone call? Would they just get a bunch of dead-end leads? Over the next few hours, they would get about 200 "decent" tips. Some sounded good, others seemed to be people who called every week. Even the bad leads were written down, just in case.

It would be difficult for Tracy to track down the leads out of state, so the FBI would have their field offices check them out. One sheriff in South Carolina said a new preacher had come to town recently and he strongly resembled List. The man overnighted a videotape of the preacher's TV show to Tracy. No good—he looked similar with the glasses and hairline, but the face wasn't right. Other people were sure they had seen List, but had the biography wrong—the man they knew was married 20 years or was too old or too young. Then at 9:10 P.M., there was this woman from Denver who claimed she knew the man and his wife. She even gave an address.

During the next week, FBI agents in 23 field offices would be checking out AMW leads on List in New Orleans, Phoenix, Alabama, and elsewhere.

On Thursday morning, June 1, in Richmond, Virginia, Agent Kevin August and three others had several leads to check out. A viewer calling "America's Most Wanted" 11 days before had given an address in Midlothian, a suburb about 25 miles southwest of the city, for a man who looked like a fugitive named John List.

They arrived at the home of Robert and Delores Clark to check out the lead. Only Mrs. Clark was home, her husband was at work at a Richmond accounting firm. Agent August showed the woman an FBI wanted poster of John List, wanted for five murders in 1971 in New Jersey.

Delores Clark's hands started to shake. She went into another room and brought out photographs from the couple's wedding in Denver four years before. The agent studied the photo carefully. The resemblance was too close not to have a chat with Mr. Clark at work.

The slender 48-year-old woman was very cooperative, but she just couldn't believe who the agents suspected her husband really was. She didn't know too much about his days before they met at a church picnic in Denver back in 1977. August left an agent with the woman, and headed back to Richmond.

By 11 A.M., the three agents arrived at the accounting firm of Maddrea, Joyner, Kirkham, and Woody in a two-story professional building across the street from a shopping mall. In the small office, they asked to see Robert P. Clark.

"Are you John List?"

"I know who I am. I'm Robert Clark."

Behind his ear, the agents found the mastoid scar, and the unusual right ear position. Clark didn't resist as the agents took him out of the office before his shocked coworkers. As they took him to the waiting car to escort him to the Richmond FBI office for fingerprinting, the man didn't even ask what he was accused of doing. He denied being the man they were seeking. He wasn't angry or upset. Only a single tear rolled down his cheek.

Clark was fingerprinted at the office, and his prints matched with those from List's military record. It was a match. The trial had ended. John List, now 63, had been caught. What had taken police nearly 18 years, television had done in 11 days.

By the time List was on his way to being arraigned in the afternoon before Magistrate Richard G. Lowe in federal court, the phone was ringing at the Tracy home in Westfield. The detective had left work ill that day, down with the flu. In 15 years with the force, he had missed only five days and this was one of them. His wife had brought home some med-icine, and Bernie was in bed.

"It was Barry Martino from the FBI," she said. "He said to call him back. He's got something to make you feel better."

Tracy called the agent in Newark.

"You're not going to believe it," he said. "We just caught John List."

Tracy was speechless. He remembered sorting through the tips in the living room. There was one that had a lot of information and an address in Rich-mond.

Within ten minutes, Tracy was on his way to Newark for a press conference at the FBI office in Newark.

Everybody would be there—the Westfield P.D., the FBI, the UC Prosecutor's Office—and they agreed that without AMW, John List would never have been caught.

Down in Washington, Linder and Coane were out in the suburbs filming a pilot Linder was devel-oping called "High School Confidential." At the show's office, Margaret Roberts got the FBI call and couldn't believe the incredible news. Nor could she believe it the next day when she saw herself quoted on the front page of *The New York Times* (June 2, 1989, p. 1).

At the high school where "High School" was film-ing, the phones didn't stop ringing in the classroom turned into a production office. The show had reached back in time and caught John List.

On Thursday afternoon, the story was strictly a New Jersey story with most of the media barrrage coming from New York City, New Jersey, and Phil-adelphia. By Friday morning, when the New York-based international media read the story in the newspapers, and saw it on the morning news shows, the capture of John List was a major story.

Reporters were swarming into Midlothian, interviewing the startled neighbors of the Clarks in a planned community called Brandermill. Living in a three-bedroom blue ranch house, the Clarks were quiet, churchgoing people, who kept to themselves and seemed very much in love. They had moved there last July, having come from Denver in February. There, the media were already trying to trace List's trail back to Westfield.

The story hit all four network newscasts on Friday, all featuring Bender's bust, which was credited as a major element in the capture. It also appeared in the weekly newsmagazines, tabloids, trades, and thousands of newspapers across the country and around the world.

As it turned out, the woman who called from Denver had once shown Delores Clark the aged picture of John List in a supermarket tabloid. The wife turned pale, and just muttered, "Oh my! Oh my!" The woman persisted, and Delores said, "That's not my husband." But she wouldn't show it to him.

A week after her husband's arrest, Delores Clark held a news conference, while he was being held under suicide watch at the Henrico County Jail.

She did not believe that her husband was John List, accused of five murders, despite two more positive fingerprint checks. He was a good husband, who had a deep faith in God. He had told her that his first wife had died of cancer before he came to Denver, and he had no children. The couple even regularly watched "America's Most Wanted," and he had even suggested it to neighbors.

"My husband is a gentle, loving, and protective man," she told the press. "I do not believe this is the same man." She would stand by him.

Despite the ten-fingerprint match, body scars, and relatives' identification, List's attorney in Virginia, David Baugh, said his client wasn't leaving the state. New Jersey had to prove his real identity.

In a surprise turnaround, the man accused of being John List waived extradition to New Jersey. However, he signed the document as Robert P. Clark.

On July 9, in Elizabeth, New Jersey, List pleaded innocent of the charges presented against him. His bail was set at $5 million, and his trial was scheduled to begin on December 4. As of October, that date has been postponed and his public defender, Elijah Miller, wouldn't comment on when he expected the trial to begin. All the attorney would say is that Mr. Clark had waived extradition and decided to meet the charges against him and has entered a plea of not guilty.

Many of the witnesses in the case have moved out of the state, but Marranca and his detectives have kept track of them. One in particular would like to talk to List. His former milkman claims he still owes $180, Marranca said.

Eleanor Clark of the UC Prosecutor's Office will be on the other side of the courtroom when List's trial finally begins. In October, she was awaiting motions by the defense, probably for closure (keep media out), change of venue (out of Union County), and to suppress (all the evidence found). She will have to file her answers to those motions and wait for a hearing. There is another major murder case set for trial in the county in February, and Ms. Clark didn't think List would be tried until that one was over. He will not be subject to the death penalty.

According to an officer at the Union County Jail, List is being held in the intake unit, isolated from the general population. He's not in a cell, but a glass room, so he can be under 24-hour observation and protective custody. He gets out for a daily shower and to make phone calls. Everyone else in the unit must be locked down when he is let out. The inmate reads his Bible, and gets frequent visits from a local pastor who stays about an hour each time. He gets his mail after it's checked for contraband, eats three square meals a day, but doesn't go for recreation because he is in isolation. The officer called List "an ideal inmate."

As for his trial from Westfield to Midlothian, UC investigators said they can account for every year, but won't comment specifically on the details. On his résumé, Clark did acknowledge graduating from the University of Michigan. Few employers ever check out résumés, the investigators said, or try to verify college degrees of someone that old. Two books are currently being written about List to be published after the trial.

According to *The Courier-Journal*'s series, written by Jill Vejnoska and Mary Romano, after two months of investigation in five states, List had a classmate in high school and another in college named Robert Clark. The eighth story traces how List got to where he was when arrested. List surfaced in the winter of 1973, as Robert Clark, when he was hired as a short-order cook in Golden, Colorado. He listed his birthdate as April 26, 1931, six years younger than List, and had an authentic social security number. He lived alone in a trailer park near the Holiday Inn where he worked.

The fugitive moved to Denver sometime in 1974, getting better jobs, and living an unassuming life. In 1977, at a singles' function at his Denver church, he met a divorcee named Delores H. Miller. They bought a two-bedroom condo together in 1981, but didn't get married until four years later. "Clark" was very religious, and was a member of the church council at St. Paul's in downtown Denver. (If the Lutheran Council had agreed to circulate the New Jersey wanted flier on List, imagine who might have opened the letter at St. Paul's.) He was also working as an accountant again at various firms in Denver.

In 1986, "Clark" was fired from his job at a packaging firm, and Delores complained to a friend about their financial woes. Their condo was foreclosed in December 1987, and he was desperately searching for a job. He found a $24,000-a-year position at a firm in Richmond, Virginia, and moved there by himself in February 1988. Delores joined him four months later, and they bought a $76,000 house in Midlothian. No one knew they were there, except a few friends and neighbors, until a year later, when the FBI stopped by one Thursday morning.

10

They Can Run, But They Can't Hide

Back in '87, the creators of "America's Most Wanted" just wanted to help capture a few fugitives—they didn't care how many, just as long as viewer tips could help nab a few in the first six weeks.

They never imagined that one would be caught only 33 minutes after the broadcast some 2,000 miles away from where he was wanted for murder. Or that another would be recognized by his fellow car wash workers by a 10-second promo for the next week's show. Or fugitives would be turned in by other inmates, by their tattoos, by their victims, or by fellow nature lovers.

Still more would surrender after seeing themselves profiled. Another would write to the show and offer to turn himself in under certain terms. Though viewer tips wouldn't help find any missing persons, the media hype generated by the AMW presence would pressure the local authorities to action. A parent would help arrest her son's molester after seeing an AMW profile on an accused child molester. Two would even try to shoot it out with the law when cornered.

The Fastest Ever

When Robert Wayne Fisher fled a murder charge in Lake Charles, Louisiana, in January 1988, he "thought there was but one chance in a million" that he would ever be profiled on "America's Most Wanted." Nor did he expect to make national news as the show's fastest capture to date.

On the humid, hot night of August 26, 1987, Fisher, 46, walked into the Lake Charles Police Department and turned himself in. He told the desk sergeant that he had just killed his wife, Tamara Lee, 29, at their Murray Street home after an argument. He had sat out in his car for a while in the parking lot of the station, while he decided whether to shoot the officers inside, officials said. He certainly could have, since police found several high-powered weapons and ammunition in Fisher's car after his arrest.

Police and medical personnel raced to the home, but they found Tammy, Fisher's third wife, dead on a bar stool near the north door. She had been shot three times at close range in the chest and abdomen. Tammy left two children, both of whom were in the house at the time of the shooting.

Fisher was booked into jail on second degree murder, but posted the $100,000 bail about an hour later, and was released. He was also charged with possession of a 9-mm Uzi Para semiautomatic, which had been converted to a machine gun. Later, based on police investigations, Fisher would also be charged with two counts of indecent behavior with juveniles, based on photographs of two nude minors.

According to police and the Calcasieu Parish Sheriff's Department, the couple was quarreling over Fisher's continued obsession with sex and pornography. Investigations revealed that Fisher had taken numerous pornographic photographs of several individuals. He worked as an oil rig supervisor for 22 years, making up to $50,000 a year. But when he was home his activities revolved around pornography. Being bisexual, he frequented "swingers' clubs," officials said, and often experimented with his club lifestyle. He even recorded his sexual activities in a handwritten ledger, which revealed that Tammy had prostituted for her husband.

She had one bad marriage already, and wanted to try to make this one work for the sake of her son, 9, and her daughter, 5. Their final argument was over some photos that Tammy had found of the children's baby-sitters, ages 12 and 13, nude in a hot tub, police said. After their mother's murder, Tammy's children were returned to their father in Florida.

The couple had split up months before the murder, but Fisher constantly visited Tammy, begging to return and promising to mend his ways. Despite her family's desperate pleas for seven months, she and the children returned to him.

Fisher was scheduled to appear in court on January 11, 1988. But sometime before that he decided to buy a motorcycle, a helmet, boots, gloves, camping gear, and a camera. When his court date arrived, Fisher was gone. A warrant was issued for his arrest, and the FBI called in.

Several weeks after Fisher's disappearance, Detective Ernie Childress's friends suggested that he call "America's Most Wanted" to help find the fugitive. An investigator in charge of warrants for the Calcasieu Parish Sheriff's Office, Childress had never seen the show himself, so he watched it "a few Sundays" before calling the toll-free hotline after a broadcast.

An operator promised that someone would get back to him, and the next morning Burke Stone was calling from Washington, D.C. They talked for a while that morning, and several other times, before Stone said that AMW had agreed to take the Fisher case.

Brian Gadinsky arrived in Lake Charles on June 21 for a four-day filming at various locations, including the Fisher home, nightclub, and an offshore oil rig. He also interviewed Tammy's mother, Margie Vaught, at her home. Local actors were used for the roles. The local Fox affiliate, KVHP-TV, Channel 29, produced a special "AMW in Lake Charles" segment for broadcast, and the filming was heavily covered in the Louisiana media.

The broadcast was set for July 17, and by coincidence, it was Childress's birthday.

The desert town of El Centro, California ("Where the Sun Meets the Winter"), is about 120 miles east of San Diego, and about 10 miles from the Mexican border. It's frequented by lots of itinerant workers looking for work on the geothermal plants there. On a Sunday night, there's not much to do but watch television.

On July 17, that's exactly what two riggers, Eugene Scott and Rick Tonget, intended to do in their room at the El Patio Motel on Adams Avenue. But they would be watching "America's Most Wanted" very carefully that night. During the week, they thought that they saw their roommate, Robert Fisher, promoted for the upcoming show.

They had been rooming with the stranger for about two weeks, and worked with him on a nearby geothermal well. When the show came on at 8 o'clock (Pacific time), he was sound asleep in the other room. So they closed the door, and nervously watched.

Sure enough it was Fisher. But they weren't the only ones who noticed. Out in the rental office, manager Shari Jones and her husband, Don, were also watching the show and recognized the man in #15. Don grabbed his registration card and the man had signed in as "Robert Fisher" with his last address listed as Lake Charles, Louisiana. They had not noticed anything unusual about the quiet man, who just came down to pay his weekly rent of about $100.

The couple called the hotline from the motel pay phone, even before the segment was over. But due to a malfunction in the hotline system, they got a recording saying the switchboard was closed and to call their local police. Out by the pay phone, they found Scott and Tonget, who had also called and gotten the same strange message. They decided to call the El Centro Police.

Already several other calls from geothermal workers were coming into the El Centro P.D. switchboard. Officer David Benavides was having a "pretty busy night with a lot of domestic fights" when the dispatcher called him over the radio. He knew about AMW, and at first, thought this could be a case of mistaken identity. But on his way over, the dispatcher informed him that there had been more calls, so he figured the suspect "could be the guy."

Benavides and Officer Dave Finbes arrived at the motel about the same time, 8:32 A.M. They were supposed to meet the clerk, but were intercepted by Fisher's roommates, nearly hysterical by this point. Though still sleeping, Fisher usually kept a gun under his mattress, they told the officers.

"I asked him three times, he was positive," Benavides remembered later. "I'm positive," he said. They showed him with a beard and I've seen him with one. It's him!"

By this time, Benavides was certain that the

man inside was the fugitive just profiled on the show. He called for two units to join him at the location. Sergeant Steve Nunn had just pulled up, and wanted to go to the post office to find a wanted poster of the suspect. But Benavides didn't think they had time, especially if Fisher woke up and found out he had just been on national television.

The police evacuated the two rooms on either side of #15. The roommates said Fisher had a gun under the mattress and more in his duffel bag. Nunn had one of the roommates check if Fisher was still asleep. He was.

Two officers covered the back door, while Benavides and Nunn rushed in the front. Benavides was the first inside with his gun drawn.

"I told him to freeze and he woke up," the officer recalled. "He looked at the window, then behind him, then he looked down. I remembered what the roommate said about the gun under the mattress. He looked like a caged animal, looking for a way out.

"I had to tell him three times to put his hands in the air. And then he just looked straight down to where we later found a gun. He just kept looking, like he was in a daze. Then he finally put his hands up."

The officers cuffed Fisher.

"Do you know what you're being arrested for?"

"I have a good idea."

"Are you Robert Wayne Fisher?"

"Yes, I am."

Fisher was taken down to the police station and put in a holding cell. Benavides remembered that the prisoner "paced back and forth, once it sunk in."

The dispatcher called Lake Charles for a description of Fisher, and it matched the man in custody. Ernie Childress got the best birthday present ever.

According to letters found in Fisher's belongings, he was very depressed. He intended never to be taken alive, and would shoot his way out with police.

Fisher fought extradition back to Louisiana, but was returned to Lake Charles on August 29, and was held without bond. On April 12, after a two-day trial, a jury convicted him of second-degree murder. Twelve days later, he was sentenced to serve the remainder of his life in prison without the benefit of pardon, parole, probation, or suspension of sentence.

County officials agreed to let Fisher meet with the media after his trial. But before the press conference could be arranged, he decided to make some more news. At about 7 A.M. on Saturday, May 13, Fisher and two other inmates grabbed a jailer from behind when he turned his back. They forced a deputy into a closet and took his keys. The trio unlocked the bars over a window, crawled down a pipe to the roof, and jumped onto a car, then onto the sidewalk.

Fisher was apprehended about 20 minutes after his escape a few blocks from the jail, as were the two other inmates. He was still wearing his bright orange jumpsuit with "CPSO" on the back. A short time later, he was transferred to the Louisiana State Prison at Angola.

In September, Fisher agreed to a telephone interview for this book.

AMW: You have mentioned to the Lake Charles media that you felt that you were misrepresented on "America's Most Wanted." Why is that?
Fisher: Well, on the way that the show portrayed me. About the only thing that was correct was my name. I had never told anybody what had happened. And they didn't know, so they made up a story.

AMW: At the trial, what did you say happened that night?

Fisher: It never came out. The truth is still not out.

AMW: What is the truth then?

Fisher: That would take a long time to go into. If we were face-to-face, it would take me a couple of hours or so to tell you, to go into it and I can't do it from here.

AMW: Perhaps I could arrange a visit sometime.

Fisher: That would be fine.

AMW: Meanwhile, could I ask you a few questions surrounding the incident. For example, were you planning on holding a press conference?

Fisher: I did. I tried to.

AMW: What were you going to discuss at that?

Fisher: What...the way I was done. And especially by the attorney that I had retained (Evelyn Oubre).

AMW: You felt that she didn't do a proper job?

Fisher: Anybody that would listen to the entire thing, can look at the transcript, it's pretty plain. Some other things, some information that I have in my possession. And with them, I can explain. A person can check on these, it's pretty obvious.

AMW: Where did you go after leaving Lake Charles?

Fisher: I went to California.

AMW: Why were you using your real name?

Fisher: It's pretty hard to get a job out there unless you have ID. And I didn't have any fake ID.

AMW: Where were you working?

Fisher: On a drilling rig, drilling for steam. A geothermal well, working on the rig as a roughneck.

AMW: Did you know about "America's Most Wanted" before that?
Fisher: I had seen it.
AMW: Were you aware of the possibility that you might be on?
Fisher: Ha, ha. I didn't think there was but a chance of one in a million.
AMW: What did you think when you awoke and found the police there?
Fisher: Naw, I didn't know how they'd found out I was there.
AMW: Any resentment toward your roommates or the other people who called?
Fisher: A little bit.
AMW: Why did you attempt to fight extradition and stay there in California?
Fisher: I intended to fight it.
AMW: Why?
Fisher: Let's not go any farther.

In addition to being the fastest capture ever, Fisher holds another distinction. He and Gene Wasson were the first to be captured from the same city, and were in Calcasieu Parish Jail at the same time.

Wasson was profiled on February 12, being wanted for the stabbing death of 18-year-old Harold James Morvant in Sulphur. Morvant's body was found in an industrial canal on June 16, 1984. Missing since May 27, the youth had been stabbed some 30 times, and his body was wrapped in a tarpulin, then weighted with pieces of metal. According to Calcasieu deputies, Wasson was the last person to see Morvant alive. He was upset, they believed, about a relationship between Morvant and his daughter.

At 7 A.M., the morning after his profile, Wasson, 42, was arrested by FBI agents and local police in Roselle Park, New Jersey, as he left for work at a

Union manufacturing plant. The night before, several tips were phoned into the show and Roselle police from neighbors and coworkers. One viewer even brought a videotape of the show to the police station as proof. The fugitive was using the alias "Dean Watson."

Upon his return to Lake Charles, Wasson entered a guilty plea to an amended charge of manslaughter, though he had claimed self-defense previously. He was sentenced to the maximum penalty, 21 years in prison, on June 12.

It Only Took 10 Seconds

For months before he ever heard of "America's Most Wanted," child advocate John Walsh carried a flier from the National Center for Missing and Exploited Children. It was a morgue photograph of an unidentified girl found shot dead in Banning, California, on May 1, 1987. He hoped that in his travels, he might find some sheriff, some social worker, or even a desperate parent who might help bring the girl's body home.

Little did Walsh realize that as host of "America's Most Wanted" he would do more than that. In ten seconds, he would help catch the girl's alleged killer, James Charles Stark.

Stark had served in the U.S. Army in Vietnam from 1968 to 1970. When he returned, he was a changed man. He had been a high school honor student, a 4-H Club member, and played flute in the Army Band. Then he served three prison terms for sexually assaulting young girls.

At 11:37 A.M., May 1, 1987, a man driving a copper Dodge "Coachman" van with a white camper top, pulled into the Chevron gas station, just off Interstate 10 on Highland Springs Road in Banning, California, a quiet town of about 15,000 nestled in the mountains 60 miles west of Los Angeles. Stopping at the full-service pump, he asked one attendant to fill the tank.

According to Banning police, the young woman riding with the man tried to open the right front door. As two attendants watched in horror, the man grabbed the screaming girl by the hair, and forced her head between his legs. Taking a revolver from beneath his seat, the man allegedly shot the girl in the back of the head. She stopped screaming and went limp. The van sped off, and an attendant called the police.

With a description of the van and the driver, police checked the Banning area, not knowing which direction the van headed after going north on Highland Springs. At the south end of the road, a van matching the description was found, but no one was in it. Searching the van, police found a California ID card in the name of James Charles Stark.

Realizing they probably had a homicide victim somewhere in the area, police searched for four hours with helicopters, canines, on horseback, and in patrol units. About eight feet off the road in a ravine, a mounted officer found the victim's body. She had been shot again in the back of her neck and dumped there. A later autopsy estimated she was between 14 and 16 years of age. Investigators could determine little except that she had been seen with Stark in the area that morning, and was probably hitchhiking when he picked her up. She was later buried in Riverside by strangers, namely a minister, social workers, and a funeral director.

Police said Stark forced a Banning resident, Dwight Ewing, 60, to drive at gunpoint out of the area toward Lancaster and the Mohave Desert. According to Ewing's account, they stopped for food, then Stark bought new sneakers, socks, and T-shirts, after washing the blood off his feet. Stark got out of Ewing's vehicle near Bakersfield, and let the man go.

The Chevron attendants, meanwhile, identified a photo of Stark which Banning police had obtained from the San Bernandino Sheriff's Office. A warrant was issued for his arrest on charges of kidnapping and murder, as a nationwide alert was issued. They also learned that Stark was a registered mentally disordered sex offender. He was paroled in November 1985.

"America's Most Wanted" had learned about the Banning case through media reports in early 1988. By then another twist had developed.

On February 24, 1988, police said Stark shows up at the home of his ex-wife's husband in nearby Hermet, saying that he's looking for his sons. The man tells Stark that they don't live there, and immediately calls police when he leaves. A search by police in two counties turns up nothing.

The next night, a man forces his way into the car of an East Hemet woman at gunpoint. He rapes her, then forces her to drive him to Bakersfield, before releasing her. The man had told the woman that he had murdered a girl in Banning. The victim later identified a photo of Stark as her assailant, police said.

Though wanted for murder and kidnapping, Stark had boldly returned to the area for a few days, allegedly committed another kidnapping and rape, then slipped away.

In early April, AMW segment producer Glenn Kirschbaum arrived in Banning to film a segment on Stark, interviewing the service station attendants, police, and other principals. The town was deeply shocked over the brutal murder, the most publicized homicide ever. Detective Dave Nunez had only had five homicides to investigate between 1986 and 1988.

The segment was slated for broadcast on May 1, a year to the day of the young girl's murder. Since the show's debut, Walsh had always previewed the fugitives for the next week's broadcast. So on April 24, he mentioned that viewers next week would see the case of James Charles Stark, a three-time convicted sex offender wanted for murder and other felony charges in California. The promo with Stark's photo lasted about 10 seconds.

Moments after the photo flashed on the screen, the switchboard lit up at the Ann Arbor Police Station in Michigan. By 8:31 P.M., police received the first of four tips identifying Stark as a street person named Jim Cherry, who frequented a homeless shelter. The Ann Arbor police immediately contacted the FBI and Banning police manning the phones in Washington. The call confirmed three other tips already received on the hotline from Ann Arbor. Another person called the Ann Arbor FBI office, and reported that Stark was working at the Big M Car Wash on Stadium Boulevard.

"The instant I saw the picture, I was positive. My heart started beating real fast," said the man who called the FBI, as reported in the *Ann Arbor News* (April 26, 1988, p. A4). "I never would have suspected. He seemed pretty innocent to me."

But by now police knew the homeless man working at the car wash might not be so innocent. That night and the next morning they looked for Stark at his usual stops, but he wasn't around. By 9:40 A.M., they found him at work at the car wash.

Lieutenant John Atkinson asked the man if he

was James Stark, and the suspect's "eyes bugged out." He started to back away from the officers and FBI agent Richard Heideman. Stark ran, but was quickly tackled and handcuffed.

After being positively identified by fingerprints as Stark, the suspect complained that his ribs hurt from the arrest struggle. Officers took him to a local hospital to be examined. On his way out of the hospital, Stark bolted away from the officers, ran down an embankment—still handcuffed to belly chains—onto the railroad tracks below. After a chase of about 300 yards down the tracks, which run next to the Huron River, the officers subdued Stark again. The arrest made the front page of *USA Today* (April 29, 1988, p. A1) with the headline "Fox fingers 11th fiend."

People in Ann Arbor called Stark "a diligent worker," "happy-go-lucky," "very friendly, very caring," "a very, very decent guy," and "an outstanding citizen," saying that during his year there he often helped out the less fortunate, even mediating disputes (*Ann Arbor News*, April 27, 1988, p. 1). Police later determined that he had returned to California via Greyhound bus in February, and rode back to Ann Arbor on motorcycle. In his apartment, police found two guns mounted on his motorcycle, showing he was ready to flee if necessary.

Stark challenged his extradition to California for nearly four months. His attorneys argued against the state of Michigan, which has no death penalty, sending him back to California where he could face execution. In early July, Stark was back in Riverside County with two separate trials facing him. As of December, no dates had been set in either.

On the May 1 broadcast (#13), AMW showed the morgue photograph of the unidentified girl in hopes of someone calling to claim her remains. More than 200 calls came in with physical descriptions that matched the girl's. Out of those, three families flew out to view the body, according to Nunez. The girl's mother was watching the show that night. The dental charts matched, and the family took her home. She was about 19 at the time of her death, having had some mental problems and living in halfway houses around the country, Nunez said.

Better than an "O. Henry" Ending

Fugitives have often seen themselves profiled, or heard they would be, and been flushed out of hiding. Sometimes, they run right into the arms of the police. But accused murderer Hien Tat Chu never expected to be nabbed by the woman who spotted him.

In 1980, Chu, a former seminary student and veteran of the South Vietnamese army, arrived in the United States as a refugee. He was sponsored by the Rich family as he settled into life in Portland, Oregon. They helped him enroll in an electronics program at a local community college in Eugene.

While at school, Chu complained that some other Vietnamese students were constantly harassing him. One, Tam Cong Do, had even assaulted him, Chu claimed, and was having an affair with his girlfriend. On June 4, 1982, Chu, 23, stabbed Do 18 times, while he slept, killing him in a mad, stressful rage. He surrendered to police. Chu was convicted on a reduced charge of manslaughter and was sentenced to ten years at the state prison in Salem. His attorney and friends had argued that Chu was a gentle man who had simply been relentlessly provoked by a bully.

While he was in prison, Chu became the subject

of several feature stories in the Oregon media. They described him as a studious, soft-spoken poet, trapped in a cruel lesson in American justice. He had escaped from torment in his homeland, only to be imprisoned in his adopted land.

Chu was paroled in May 1984, four years after his arrival in America. Soon after, he began a relationship with 18-year-old Bonnie Sue Rich, daughter of his host family. They had a daughter. When Bonnie became pregnant again by Chu, she left her husband and moved in with him. But it was far from paradise. Bonnie, now 23, had left Chu, 37, several times, only to return.

Then on the night of April 2, 1988, Chu exploded again. They had been arguing in their '76 Fiat as they approached the intersection of Northeast 33rd and Killingsworth Street. He accused her of seeing another man, which she denied. Their two children, a 9-month-old boy and a two-year-old girl were in the car witnessing the argument. Chu was getting more angry, and the children huddled near their mother. A friend, Doan Tran, whom they had just picked up, was sitting in the back seat with the little girl. Chu held their son on his lap, as Bonnie drove.

Bonnie stopped the car and started to get out. From under the baby, Chu pulled out an automatic pistol and fired twice at Bonnie. Wounded, she tried to flee, crying for her baby. Chu fired again, then chased Bonnie, and strangled her until she fell to the pavement. With their infant son still under his arm, Chu fled down the street, as Bonnie bled next to the car. She died from multiple gunshot wounds a short time later at a local hospital. Chu left the baby at a friend's apartment and left Portland.

Portland Police theorized that Chu went down the California coast, and spent time in San Francisco, Oakland, and San Jose. Sometime in the fall, he was bold enough to return to Portland, though a murder warrant had been issued on him. Chu was reading *The Oregonian* newspaper on November 11, and was obviously "spooked" when he saw an article (November 11, 1988, p. B6) saying that a crew from "America's Most Wanted" was in town filming his profile, said Detective Kent Perry. He fled again.

The family of the man whom Chu killed never forgot his crime, though he was paroled early from prison.

At Thanksgiving, Do's sister, Chun Lyen "Lynn" Thi-Do, was visiting friends in Portland, when she heard that Chu had killed again. She and her husband, Chi Nguyen Huy, were avid watchers of "America's Most Wanted," and thought the show could help catch him. They contacted both Linder and Detective Perry, who informed them AMW had already completed filming a profile on Chu, scheduled for December.

As she tells the story:

"We came back home (to Santa Rosa), and my husband and I were thinking about giving a reward or something. There's a big Vietnamese community in California, and maybe he's hiding somewhere among them. So maybe if we had some way of letting people know, it might work out that someone will see him. That's why we wrote to 'America's Most Wanted.'"

On Wednesday, December 7, Lynn had a dentist appointment down in San Jose, about 50 miles south of their home.

"We decided that we had a craving to go to one of the restaurants that we used to go to when we lived there (in San Jose). We went there at the right time and the right place.

"We sat down and ordered. And he brought the food to the table."

"He" was Hien Tat Chu, who had started working at Tu Do Restaurant at the corner of North First and St. John in San Jose, two days before.

"How could I ever forget that face! When I saw him I just couldn't believe it. I was shocked. Both of us recognized him.

"I looked at him then I just stared at him, but I didn't say anything. My husband looked up and we looked at each other and we knew. My husband made a quick decision, and he went outside and called the police, and told them what was happening. But I sat there looking at him, worried, like nothing is happening yet. I sat there and tried to pretend I was calm."

Huy was outside on the sidewalk, flagging down a patrol car. Officer Mike George pulled over at 6:45 P.M., and listened to the man's story. The policeman entered the restaurant and asked the waiter to step outside. Calling himself "Chhom Chhuy" of Oakland, the man claimed that he had never been to Oregon, then allowed the officer to look through his wallet. Inside was a Eugene phone number on a scrap of paper, a card from an Oregon bank, a Pacific Northwest phone bill, and several snapshots. The officer showed the pictures to the accusing couple. They pointed to Bonnie Rich, saying, "That's the girl he killed."

The waiter agreed to accompany the officer to headquarters for fingerprinting and a photograph. Portland police sent Chu's prints and description, including the tattoos "Lam Com Chua Tra" on his right arm and "An Nghia Sinh Thanh" on his left arm. They were a match, and Chu was booked into the Santa Clara County Jail.

On April 25, Chu, who had pleaded no contest

to the shooting, was sentenced to life in prison. Multhomah County Circuit Judge Robert P. Jones said Chu "was too dangerous to be in society" (*The Oregonian*, April 26, 1989, p. D9). On May 30, Chu's parental rights to his two children were terminated. He declined a request to be interviewed for this book.

"If he'd spent more time (in prison) on the first murder he committed maybe this wouldn't have happened," Bonnie's brother, Stan Rich, told the judge.

The Wildest Chase

Lewis Wesley Barnes, 32, was one of those fugitives who thought he could outrun the law. At least he tried, after being on "America's Most Wanted," in a wild chase involving officers and agents from five different agencies.

On April 24, 1988, Barnes escaped from the Marion County Jail in Florida. He was there awaiting trial for the slaying of David and Betty Branum at the Wayside Antique Shop in Ocala, on June 26, 1984. Police said that Barnes and an accomplice handcuffed the couple to the store safe and shot them before stealing a half million dollars in jewelry and antiques.

Half the goods were recovered in Las Vegas by July 1987, and were traced to Barnes. Two months later, he was spotted by Texas drug agents on a stakeout. They chased him, and he was captured after a gun battle. He was convicted already of trying to murder the officers, and was awaiting trial on the Branum killings when he escaped.

Barnes might have spoken softly, almost like a little boy, but under his coat he would probably have an automatic weapon, even an Uzi.

After his profile on the September 18 broadcast (#32), viewers in San Antonio tipped off police to his being there. A viewer even provided the tag numbers off Barnes's car to the FBI, allowing them to trace him to a San Antonio apartment complex on September 25.

When Barnes left the complex in his car, FBI agents called for backup and left in pursuit. The agents tried to stop Barnes by sandwiching their two cars against his—one in front, the other behind. But he reversed, ramming the trailing car and speeding off in the opposite direction.

In the high-speed chase that followed, Barnes fired a .25-caliber automatic pistol at the pursuing agents. They returned fire and hit the radiator of his car, disabling it, and forcing Barnes to flee on foot.

By now, the search involved dogs, helicopters, light aircraft, Texas Rangers, deputies from both Bexar and Medina Counties, and SWAT teams from the FBI and San Antonio Police.

Barnes barged into a house in the neighborhood, took the keys to a van, and drove off at high speeds. He crashed into a ditch, then raced into a nearby woods. At 6:15 P.M., search dogs found Barnes in the woods under a log pile. He had buried himself in mud, and was crying as the cuffs were put on him, FBI agents said.

On his person, agents found the pistol and $10,000 cash. Maybe he had seen his profile, since he had just had $4,000 worth of dental work done to hide the telltale gap between his front teeth, as mentioned in his AMW profile.

Surrenders

As of December, 14 fugitives had surrendered to authorities after being profiled on "America's Most Wanted." Some admitted that seeing themselves or hearing about their profiles was a factor in giving up. Others claimed it was a coincidence.

Stephen Baughman was the first fugitive to sur-render to authorities, as mentioned previously, on April 3, 1988 in Houston, Texas.

Stephen Randall Dye became the second when he flagged down a San Diego police car on June 20. (More on AMW's aid to John Mikrut in a later chapter, "Victims.")

On the eve of their AMW profile on August 14, accused murderers Kevin Kelly and Kenneth Shannon, announced that they would surrender to New York City authorities the following day. Members of the "Westies" gang, an Irish organization accused of loansharking, union extortion, gambling, and murder, they were wanted for the 1985 killing of construction worker Michael Holly.

Accused cop killers Raylene Brooks, 17, and Kirkton Moore, 27, turned themselves in to Los Angeles Police four days after their AMW profile on October 23, 1988, through the efforts of local newsman Warren Wilson. The pair were being sought for the drive-by shooting of L.A.P.D. officer Daniel Pratt on September 3. Pratt and his partner, Veronica DeLao, were observing a liquor store when they heard automatic rifle fire nearby. Pratt fired ten rounds at a car allegedly driven by Brooks. Police said Moore fired at Pratt, striking him in the head and killing him instantly.

According to L.A.P.D., Wilson said that Moore's mother, Julia Hill, had contacted him on October 26, saying her son was willing to give up. Wilson and a KTLA camera crew flew to Las Vegas, but couldn't make contact with Moore. Wilson drove back there with Moore's mother and sister, in communication with police. The entourage arrived at the TV station at 4 A.M., and the pair surrendered to police a half hour later.

Moore told police that he watched AMW every week, and had watched it in his Vegas hotel room. He was also aware that there was a $40,000 reward (AMW does not offer any rewards for tips), and his photograph was all over California.

"Even my mother would roll me for $40,000," Moore reportedly told L.A.P.D. "And they (AMW) always get their man."

Another accused killer, Clarence Swanigan, also sought the aid of a trusted journalist in making his surrender after his AMW profile. Wanted for the 1988 slaying of a Chicago cab driver, Swanigan, 23, saw himself on the March 12 broadcast (#56), at a home he shared with a girlfriend in Flint, Michigan.

Swanigan fled to a hotel, where he called his mother in Chicago. She called their pastor, who contacted TV reporter Russ Ewing to help. Eight tips to the AMW hotline after the profile had placed Swanigan in Flint, one giving his exact address.

On Monday, March 13, Ewing flew his own plane to Michigan to meet the fugitive. They talked for several hours, then returned to Chicago the next morning. On the drive from the airport to a police precinct, Ewing said, two undercover officers pulled their car over, and escorted them to the station. Swanigan surrendered at 12:30 P.M. If convicted of shooting cabby Steve Rzany, he could face the death penalty.

Convicted conman John Joseph Frank arranged for his surrender to the FBI in New York after seeing himself profiled on August 20 (#79). Frank had allegedly run up huge bills in Orlando, Florida, while pretending to be a Hollywood producer. His trip violated his Florida probation terms, having previously pleaded guilty for another spree in February in Orlando, which cost $4,174. He had also agreed to pay back $2,076 for his fun in Miami in January when he pretended to be part of an NBC Sports crew covering the Super Bowl.

During the show, Frank called the AMW hotline and spoke with Metro-Dade (Florida) Detective Hugo Gomez in Washington to arrange his surrender four days later in New York.

On September 23, 1989, John Brent Johnson, wanted by police in Edmond, Oklahoma, gave himself up after reading a newspaper account that said AMW was only planning a segment on him.

"There was nowhere left for him to run or hide," an Edmond detective said after the surrender.

Shortly after his segment aired on the West Coast on October 1, 1989 (#85), Roberto Urbaez, 38, walked into the main San Diego jail to turn himself in to authorities there. Apparently, a friend or relative on the East Coast contacted Urbaez in San Diego earlier that evening to tell him he was being featured on AMW.

According to police in Washington, D.C., Urbaez killed his former girlfriend, Mona Shiferaw, 19, a junior college student, and her brother, Tesfay, a Howard University graduate student, on January 29. Police said Urbaez had threatened several times to kill the woman and her family after she broke off their relationship around Christmas 1988.

A San Diego police spokeswoman said that the fugitive simply walked in and said that he had just been on AMW and wanted to surrender. Coincidentally, the night before Urbaez surrendered, a crew for Fox's show "COPS" was filming bookings at the same desk where he gave himself up.

Two fugitives have offered to surrender by communicating with "America's Most Wanted," one by mail, the other through his attorney.

Prison escapee Stephen DeLorenzo, 39, wrote to

AMW in July 1988, offering to turn himself in under certain conditions.

DeLorenzo had escaped from the Massachusetts Southeastern Correctional Facility in Bridgewater on May 4, 1987. From 1971 to 1974, he was convicted of four assaults on women, involving one that broke a woman's neck. On March 18, 1977, he went to an ex-girlfriend's house in Brockton, Mass., to work on her car. Police said he entered her house and shot her four times, twice in the head, with a .22-caliber revolver. She survived. He was captured in 1984 in New Orleans and sentenced to 14 to 20 years for assault with intent to murder.

In his letter, the fugitive wanted a guarantee of a good lawyer and a reexamination of his case in Washington State. During the July 31 broadcast (#31), host John Walsh invited DeLorenzo to call the AMW hotline where FBI agents were willing to speak with him. A few calls came from men claiming to be DeLorenzo, but the FBI and Massachusetts authorities were not satisfied that any of them was the real fugitive.

The family of Gregory "The Terminator" McQueen, wanted in New York City for attempted murder, third-degree robbery, and assault on a police officer, reportedly contacted famed attorney William Kunstler to negotiate a surrender through AMW. McQueen had been profiled three times on the show, and as of December 1989, he had not given himself up.

Already in Jail

As demonstrated in the case of federal bank robber Mark Goodman, wanted fugitives can sometimes hide in jail, and often be released by using an alias. But three AMW fugitives, two of them in Canadian jails, had their cover blown when correctional officers recognized them from their profiles.

A guard at the Vancouver Pretrial Services Center was shocked when he was watching AMW at home on the evening of July 9, 1989 (#73, live from San Francisco). On the screen were pictures of an inmate he knew as Daniel Alexander Maitland. But AMW said he was Teddy Unterreiner, 34, wanted by Oakland Police for 15 counts of lewd and lascivious acts with children, four counts of molestation, and two of willful cruelty. The guard contacted Oakland Police through the AMW hotline, while another guard and several inmates called the Vancouver Police Crimestoppers hotline.

The inmate's true identity was confirmed by fingerprints on Monday, July 10. Unterreiner had been arrested there on March 23, 1989, and was charged with sexual assault on a minor. He is currently awaiting trial in Canada, then will await trial in California.

Eighteen days later, on July 28, Kendall Quinn Northern, wanted for escape from a Utah prison, was identified as inmate John Wesley Hampton in Okalla Prison in Burnaby, south of Vancouver. Northern had been arrested a week before for possession of cocaine with purpose to traffic. He pleaded guilty and was about to be released on his own recognizance. Vancouver Crimestoppers had made the connection that Hampton could be Northern from AMW viewer tips. He was detained and identified by FBI fingerprints faxed to Vancouver from Salt Lake City. Northern had escaped on October 8, 1988, where he was serving five years to life for murder and robbery in 1980.

(Following Northern's profile and capture, his father, Donald Northern, owner of a small manufacturing company, called AMW to say he thought the information broadcast was "inaccurate."

"I didn't really see the program, but I can tell you what I've been told," Northern said. He stated that the man with his son on the night of the murder, Robert Phillips, had changed his original confession from saying that Northern was in the front seat and had no idea that Phillips was going to kill the cab driver, Everett Hamby, Jr.

Northern's father has never questioned his son's guilt in the crime. Under Utah law, if you are involved in a crime during which a person is killed, you are guilty of second-degree murder, he pointed out.

"You (AMW) definitely misrepresented the aspects of the thing. And you know, there were a lot of people hurt over that. Ken comes from an extremely large, prominent Utah family. You can go into any town in the state and find a relative. And that [profile] was just a glorification as I understand it. There were a lot of people hurt, really up in arms."

(AMW based its profile on information received from the Utah Department of Corrections.)

On July 30 (#76), a "John Doe" booked that afternoon into the Spokane County Jail in Washington, was identified as California fugitive George Leroy Schleuder, 30, thanks to an alert corrections officer watching AMW that evening. Schleuder, wanted by Mendocino County for rape, sodomy, and burglary, had been arrested in Spokane on charges of second-degree malicious mischief, taking a motor vehicle, and third-degree theft. He had refused to give his name when booked into jail and was listed as a John Doe.

Officer Dean Vercruysse recognized the man on AMW as the one he booked that afternoon. Mendocino officials verified his identity through fingerprints. He is accused of breaking in to the home of an 81-year-old woman in Ukiak, California, and repeatedly raping her.

International

AMW has reached over into Canada and Mexico to help nab fugitives during the past two years. As of December 1989, six fugitives were apprehended in Canada, and one in Mexico, as a direct result of viewer tips.

The most sensational capture over the northern border was convicted murderer Joseph Kindler, who had escaped from two prisons to avoid the death penalty in Philadelphia. Kindler was on death row there after being sentenced for the July 1982 beating death of David Bernstein, whose relatives brought the case to AMW (see "Victims"). In 1984, Kindler escaped from the Philadelphia Detention Center with another inmate. Once in Canada, he was arrested on burglary charges in Montreal. He didn't stay there long. In October 1986, while awaiting extradition, Kindler got some fellow inmates to boost him and another prisoner through a skylight. Using bedsheets, Kindler climbed down 13 stories and fled. The other escapee fell to his death when the rope broke.

Kindler then fled as far as he thought he needed to go. It wasn't far enough. During his second AMW profile on September 4, 1988 (#30), a viewer watching the show via satellite dish in St. John's, New Brunswick, recognized a man named Robert Cordato who was working in a local repair shop. He was arrested there on Tuesday, September 6, at 10 A.M., local time.

Frederick Merrill was the second AMW fugitive arrested in Canada, almost as far away as Kindler.

A career criminal and escape artist, Merrill, 41, escaped from prison in Connecticut in August 1987. He had previously been convicted of burglaries, auto theft, and escape, and was awaiting trial on charges that he beat and sexually assaulted a 55-year-old woman. He got his nickname "The Peanut Butter Bandit" from when his mother smuggled a gun to him in prison inside a jar of homemade peanut butter. She served two years for that offense.

Following Merrill's AMW profile on July 10, 1988 (#23), a viewer in Toronto recognized him and contacted police. As a result, they were able to link the fugitive with some local burglaries during which he stole the ID papers of a John Sisam. That name was entered as an alias for Merrill in the national crime computer.

During the early afternoon of September 22, the Royal Mounties responded to a disturbance call in an apple orchard in Hampstead, New Brunswick. One of the officers checked the identity of an employee there named John Sisam, and the computer indicated the bearer could be a fugitive from the United States. An officer in plain clothes put on a picking bag and went into the orchard to find Merrill. He was arrested without incident.

Viewers in British Columbia, particularly in the Vancouver area, have been credited with four captures. Michael Cooper, a suspected serial rapist wanted in Portland, was arrested in New Westminster on November 20, 1988, three days after his AMW profile. Part of his scam to lure women to rob and rape them was posing as a San Francisco 49er football player. Vancouver Crimestoppers received six calls saying Cooper had been living in the area and working in local restaurants. One tip even provided an address, which led police to arrest him as he was coming out of his apartment.

Rudy "Mike" Blanusa was nabbed by a Vancouver Police Strike Force in Burnaby on January 23, the day after his AMW profile. Son of a California sheriff, Blanusa, 35, was wanted in Stanislaus County, California, for kidnapping two brothers, transporting them to a remote field, and killing them with a shot to the head. He had been living in the area for about 8 months, going by the name of Robert Davies. When police pulled him over on Monday afternoon, he denied his true identity, until they rolled up his sleeves and found his telltale tattoos: a castle on his right shoulder, vikings on his right upper arm, and a bear on his right elbow.

The fifth and sixth fugitives to be arrested in Canada were Teddy Unterreiner and Kendall Quinn Northern, as previously mentioned.

"America's Most Wanted" is currently being broadcast on five Canadian independent stations in Calgary, Regina, Saskatoon, Winnipeg, and Hamilton. Many Canadian viewers also watch the show via satellite transmissions, cable systems, or from Fox affiliates close to the Canadian border.

Several fugitives profiled on "America's Most Wanted" have been captured south of the border in Mexico, but only one as a direct result of viewer tips.

On November 17, 1989, Ernesto Traslavina, wanted by U.S. Customs for drug smuggling, racketeering, and escape, was arrested by authorities in Mexico City, due to AMW viewer tips. He was turned over to U.S. Customs agents two days later and is being held in Chicago.

Agents said that Traslavina, who had recently moved to Mexico City, was at the international airport to meet friends arriving from the United States. He was arrested while waiting for a taxicab at 4 A.M. Eastern Time. Using the name of Charlie Gomez,

Traslavina had been living in Queens, N.Y., for about 18 months, working as a consultant to a company that remits currency to Colombia. He had altered his appearance, but continued his flashy lifestyle. Arrested by agents on June 13, 1987, in the largest drug bust in Nevada history, he escaped while working as an informant on a drug buy the next day in Manhattan Beach, California.

Though not a direct result of viewer tips, U.S. Marshals credit AMW in helping gain information for the arrest of William "Pops" Pegram in Belize, Central America, on September 11, 1988. The elderly fugitive was arrested without resistance on a remote resort island off the Belize coast in cooperation with local officials. The entire arrest was videotaped by U.S. Marshals and broadcast on AMW on September 18 (#32).

Fugitives often go out of the U.S., thinking they'll never get caught. One fugitive left civilization, so he thought, by going up into the Bitterfoot Mountain regions of Montana and Idaho. But the mountain man's eagerness to pose for photos for two backpackers, who just happened to be AMW viewers, led to his capture.

Steven Ray Allen, 41, was wanted for the 1986 killing of a 3-year-old boy in Castle Valley, Utah. He was featured on the July 2, 1989 (#72) episode of AMW. During the summer, two backpackers hiking in the Bitterfoot wilderness spent a week with Allen and showed two rolls of photographs of him. Seeing the July 2 broadcast, the two alerted the FBI. They showed agents their photos and directed them to the remote area where they saw the fugitive.

On August 4, the FBI and the Utah Attorney General's Office began a publicity campaign about Allen in that area. They circulated the new photos on fliers among hunters, campers, rangers, and law enforcement agents. It worked. A week later, two U.S. Forest Service workers returned from work in the Bitterfoot area and saw the Allen fliers. They recognized the man they had seen two days earlier near Thunder Mountain Road at the west fork of the valley.

Alerted by the Rangers' Station, Ravalli County Sheriff Jay Printz, assisted by six deputies, the Forest Service, and Minutemen Aviation Services, launched a massive airborne search. On Friday evening, Allen's horse was spotted in a clearing at the top of the Continental Divide. The pilot, Minutemen's Mike Mamuzich, saw a campfire in the trees nearby.

The next morning, Saturday, August 12, Sheriff Printz and four deputies helicoptered back to the site. Spotting the horse again, the sheriff and his men were dropped along a nearby trail. They tracked Allen to a new campsite, four miles from the top of the Continental Divide near Porcupine Springs, Idaho. They arrested him without incident, being the 59th AMW fugitive to be captured by viewer tips— and the first on the Continental Divide.

Watch Those Tattoos

Every wanted poster or description of a fugitive notes the individual's tattoos. Whatever the fascination that a criminal type has with these emblems, they often wind up turning in the owner. Such was the case with several AMW fugitives—some in bizarre fashion.

Convicted murderer James Ray Renton, 50, had escaped from the Arkansas State Prison on July 12, 1988, along with three other inmates. He had a long criminal record, arrested at age 14 and convicted at age 18, including a conviction for capital felony murder of an Arkansas police officer, Patrolman John Hussey, 23, in December 1979. He had previously been convicted for post office burglary, possession of narcotics, parole violation, forgery, and counterfeiting foreign securities. Having used some 25 aliases, Renton was a skilled printer, and had worked as a painter, photo engraver, and advertising director. In Arkansas, he was serving life without parole for murdering the police officer, whom he had kidnapped, handcuffed to a tree, and shot three times in the head with his own .357 magnum.

On the U.S. Marshals Top 15, Renton was also a strong candidate for the FBI's Top Ten List, having been on it for 13 months, from April 1976 to May 1977.

As for his tattoos, there were several. On his left forearm, there was a wreath of flowers; on his upper right arm, "J. R."; "Smiley" or "Shirley" on his right forearm; his Army serial number, RA18458712, on his outer left forearm; and the initials "O.N." on his left wrist.

The Marshals had some leads that Renton had headed south into Texas when the fugitive was profiled on AMW on August 21 (#29). About 200 tips were received on the case. A police informant in Austin, Texas, saw Renton on the show. Apparently, the fugitive also caught the show.

At midnight on September 6, the informants contacted police, saying that a man looking like Renton was registered as William Hall at a Salvation Army shelter a block from the police station. At 3:07 A.M., five officers sneaked through the dimly lit dormitory where some 120 men were sleeping. They looked from cot to cot before they found Renton. He offered no resistance. They seized a loaded sawed-off 12-gauge shotgun, a flare pistol altered to fire shotgun shells, a hunting knife, burglary tools, and a costume makeup kit from the fugitive.

The night before, Renton told police, he had attended a Freedomfest concert at a nearby park, but left because too many officers were around and he was afraid of being recognized. He must have been very afraid. Sometime between his profile and arrest, Renton had drastically altered his appearance. He cut off his mustache, cropped his brown hair to burr, and shaved the center of his head to appear bald. He also knocked out four front teeth. And he had covered those tattoos with gauze bandages and a watch.

Renton and Kindler were caught on the same day, September 6, and were among six AMW fugitives caught within seven days—September 4 to 11—who still show records. Another AMW fugitive, Terry Lee Johnson, an FBI Top Ten, was arrested on September 8 by viewer tips in San Diego. Also caught that week, but not directly from AMW tips, were Ted Jeffrey Otuski, another FBI Top Ten, apprehended in Guadalajara, Mexico; "Pops" Pegram in Belize; and Jack Dean, Pegram's companion, in Stevenson, Alabama.

Tattoos also helped nab two other AMW fugitives, who should have covered them up. One got caught by a bunch of cherries, the other by her teddy bear.

An AMW viewer in Alvin, Texas, got a shocking surprise from a man who was cutting carpet at her window tinting business on the afternoon of July 3, 1989, about ten miles south of Houston. On the man's left arm she recognized a tattoo of a bunch of cherries that was featured on the July 2 (#72) updated profile of accused murderer Thomas "Possum" Dixon,

wanted for the 1987 slaying of his ex-wife in Lee
County, Alabama. Pam Cundiff also remembered
from the profile that Dixon had been a carpet layer
in Georgia at the time of his wife's death.

At 1 P.M., she quietly called local police, who sent
over a plainclothes female detective, pretending to
be interested in window tinting. He had obviously
attempted to hide some of his tattoos since his first
AMW profile on February 26 (#54) by tattooing a
scorpion over the word "Possum" on his left hand,
and burning off "Love" from his right knuckles.

No arrest was made that day, but the information was relayed to the FBI. At 3 P.M., Wednesday,
July 5, FBI agents and Alvin Police arrested Dixon,
still laying carpet at Ms. Cundiff's business. He was
not armed and offered no resistance.

On July 10, 1989, AMW profiled alleged brothel
madam Kelly "Sunshine" Loyd, along with Unterreiner, from its live remote from the hills of San
Francisco. She was wanted by San Francisco Police
for prostituting underage girls, and had been indicted by the grand jury for pimping, pandering,
keeping a house of prostitution, and furnishing narcotics to a minor. Among her alleged clients was local
politician Roger Boaz, a mayoral candidate, convicted for having sex with teenage girls.

Police said Loyd and her husband, Patrick Roberts, who was already in custody, used a white 1953
Bentley to pick up young runaways on the streets of
San Francisco. They would allegedly dress them up
as little girls and force them into prostitution.

Loyd liked tattoos also. She had a "Libra" removed from her left ankle, and another "Libra" with
scales on her left bicep taken off, but both scars remained. On her right buttock was a teddy bear.

Within two hours of her profile, FBI agents were

responding to tips in South Carolina that Loyd had been seen at "Buddy's Truck Stop" on state Route 52 near Bennettsville. They found two women apparently engaged in prostitution, but neither was Loyd.

They continued to investigate at the truck stop, until they were tipped off to an alleged third prostitute. Going to the home of the truck stop owner in Hartsville, they arrested Kelly "Sunshine" Loyd at 2 A.M., Monday, July 10 without incident.

It was her teddy bear that turned her in. When phoning the AMW hotline, one caller specifically mentioned seeing Loyd's right buttock tattoo.

Helping with the Hype

In at least two cases, an AMW profile might not have helped find a missing person, but it pressured local authorities to continue their search. In two other cases, it helped a witness to come forward and a mother find her son.

"America's Most Wanted" has not found the success it wished in helping locate missing persons. But it has helped draw attention to cases in the local and national media by its presence.

The show traveled to Sacramento for a June 19 (#20), 1988 profile on a missing youngster, Candy Talarico. She was recovered safely on July 18, not as a result of viewer tips, but local observers noted that AMW's interest in the case kept the pressure on local authorities to find her.

The outcome was not so happy in the case of Mark Kilroy, the missing Texas college student, whose case made international headlines.

Kilroy, a junior at the University of Texas, disappeared on March 14, 1989, while on spring break in Matamoros, Mexico. He and three friends were spending their break on South Padre Island, near Brownsville, Texas, when they crossed into Matamoros for the evening. They visited several nightspots before heading back toward the border. Kilroy disappeared at 2 A.M., having been last seen talking to a Mexican man some 3 blocks from the bridge.

The search for Mark Kilroy dragged on for weeks with little progress, despite pressure from American officials on Mexican police. In desperation, Mark's father, Jim Kilroy, contacted "America's Most Wanted" in hopes that the show would profile his son. The father spoke to John Walsh several times during the week of March 19, with Walsh offering what help he could.

An AMW crew filmed in Brownsville and Matamoros during that week, with Kilroy's three friends playing themselves. The filming was swamped with local and national TV news crews covering the case. The segment was broadcast on March 26 (#58), and some 150 tips were called in to the studio, but none led to any serious breaks in the case. Fox also produced a 20-second PSA in Spanish and English which was distributed to local TV stations for broadcast.

Kilroy's mutilated corpse was discovered on April 11, along with the ravaged remains of 13 other victims at a ranch in Mexico called Rancho Santa Elena. The brutal slaughter would become known as the "Matamoros Cult Killings." It was led by a charismatic madman, Adolfo "El Padrino" Constanzo, killed at his own request by his followers on May 6, as police closed in in Mexico City, and his high priestess, Sara Aldrete, who was arrested at the shootout with four others.

In his book, *Cauldron of Blood: The Matamoros Cult Killings*, journalist Jim Schultze noted two "very interesting sidelights" brought by AMW's visit to Matamoros.

In the first place, it allowed them to see into the Mexican side by tracking what the Mexicans were doing with tips from the show. For the first time, the Americans could see that the Mexicans were seriously running down each tip and that there seemed to be strange signs of cooperation between the Mexican agencies. Comandante Benitez Ayala in particular was out there and definitely on the muscle.

The other was more general. "America's Most Wanted" was big-time American TV, almost Hollywood as far as Mexico was concerned. News crews—that was one thing. But Hollywood! If Mexico had real reverence for any expression of America it was Hollywood. There, in the not so inaccurate Mexican view, was the real center of power in the United States.

That this big TV show had come looking for Mark Kilroy and that the story of Mark Kilroy had been broadcast on American national television, in full Hollywood treatment, with directors and actors and story boards and the pretty girl assistants, was persuasive evidence that the Mark Kilroy case was not destined to fade away fast.

The heat was on. At long last, the heat was really on...

(Avon Books, September 1989, p. 181)

Though fugitive Percy Harris, wanted for murder in Baltimore, had already been arrested before his profile could be aired, police requested that it be broadcast to encourage witnesses to come forward. It was on June 5, 1988 (#18), and within two weeks two key witnesses to the case did come forward, according to the FBI in Baltimore.

Viewers of AMW also helped police in Scottsdale, Arizona, positively identify an alleged amnesia victim and accused murderer "Joshua Stone" as Kelly Luckadoo, after his May 7 (#64) profile. Luckadoo, 18, had disappeared from Morganton, North Carolina, in December 1987, the day after he was questioned about the theft of a 1984 Porsche. Nancy Beck of Morganton, who claimed the boy was her son, said he was sick with fever when he disappeared. The last time she heard from him was by postcard from San Diego.

According to police, Luckadoo collapsed in a San Diego mall in December 1987. He claimed to have amnesia and thought he was 16 years old and named Joshua. Authorities got him treatment, but were unable to determine his identity, so he was given a last name and a birthdate. He was assigned to a foster home in Santee, a San Diego suburb.

Six months later, Luckadoo was arrested in Santee for possession of a stolen Corvette. On July 29, he was charged with killing Scottsdale, Arizona, printer Frank Storaci, the car's owner. He was extradited to Arizona in August to await trial. Using dental records, police positively identified "Stone" as Luckadoo following his AMW profile.

Advance publicity for an AMW segment helped arrest Fernando Garcia, wanted in Dallas for the murder of a three-year-old girl, even before his segment was aired. Garcia, 31, was scheduled to appear on the show on July 31, 1988 (#26). His segment was postponed to the following week, however, when AMW received a letter from prison escapee Steven DeLorenzo.

For several months in 1988, the *Star* Magazine featured a photo and description of upcoming AMW fugitives. A woman who had dated Garcia in Bangor, Maine, called the AMW hotline after seeing the fugitive's photo in the magazine. He was arrested on August 1, in Bangor, where he had been living for three months, the FBI said.

Garcia was the second fugitive arrested by *Star* readers. Denice Stumpner, wanted as an accomplice in a 1983 murder in Green Bay, Wisconsin, was arrested on a horse farm in Golden, Colorado, on June 30, 1988, as a result of both viewer tips and a reader. Stumpner, a motorcycle gang member known as "Bobber," was later convicted for his role in the beating, rape, and murder of Margaret Anderson, whose body was found dumped in a snowbank with her throat slit. Three other men were also convicted in the case.

Another AMW fugitive tried to make his own hype, which led to his arrest. Charles Russ, 39, a former California businessman, was suspected of runing over his wife with her own Mercedes in February 1987. He was also wanted for defrauding his mother-in-law of her life savings.

He was profiled twice on "America's Most Wanted," and viewer tips helped police track his apartment in Phoenix on May 7, 1989, but he had already fled a few hours after his profile.

On August 6 (#77), Russ was profiled again with updated information from his last sighting. He was now living in Hollywood, Florida, working for telemarketing firms. The FBI stated that Russ probably bought a paper that morning and read that he was going to be profiled again, because he suddenly packed and left his apartment.

But when the alert owner of a Hollywood hotel was cleaning out a room, he noticed something suspicious. He called police, who examined the personal belongings and determined they belonged to Charles Russ. According to sources, among the items left behind was a journal Russ kept on the run, a how-to book for fugitives. In it, sources said, he bragged about being among the country's best, since he had escaped from "America's Most Wanted." Not for long.

Russ's photograph had been widely distributed on fliers throughout the area. At 4 A.M., on August 24, patrolman Bill Zito recognized Russ from the fliers as he walked along a Hollywood beach. Calling in additional help, Zito questioned Russ, then accompanied him back to his Hollywood apartment, where officers found a Virginia ID car under Russ's alias, Patrick Donovan.

He was arrested and turned over to the FBI, held without bond, pending his extradition to California.

While Russ might have enjoyed being on AMW, at least one other fugitive decided to turn himself in because he feared the publicity.

According to the *Tucson Citizen* (October 7, 1989, p. 1), James Edward Henderson, 42, found out that he might be profiled on AMW. Henderson was wanted on charges of attempted first-degree murder of an ex-wife in April 1988. According to deputies, he is accused of kidnapping the woman, then hitting her with a lead pipe. Pima County detectives had also gotten another ex-wife of Henderson's arrested on suspicion of hindering prosecution. Both factors convinced the fugitive to surrender on October 6.

"He got word of it, and also that we were going

to put him on 'America's Most Wanted,'" Detective Rudy Turner told the *Citizen*.

But it was only a ploy.

"He was not going to be on the show," said Pima County Sheriff's Deputy Marty Lepird. "It was just a ploy that was used to get him to turn himself in."

A Cop Turned Bad

The top brass at the U.S. Customs Service were "real skittish" about bringing the case of fugitive Charles Jordan to "America's Most Wanted," William Green, its Internal Affairs chief, would later recall. Jordan was a popular Customs supervisor of the Key Largo office who was wanted on RICO charges, including drug smuggling.

Jordan was a Customs officer, and viewers of AMW usually expected to see hardened criminals on the show. Customs officials weren't sure how the public would react to a cop gone bad. But they decided to go with it.

According to Green, Jordan had close to a "charismatic personality," and was extremely popular with his agents. He was a self-styled "ruler of the Keys." Some were still very loyal to their former boss.

Linder sent segment producer Michael Cerny down to the Keys to film the Jordan segment in late November 1988.

Part of the filming involved pushing bales of "marijuana" out of a moving plane into the ocean below. Jordan had allegedly overlooked some of those drops for a good payoff. The Customs agents advising Cerny had never done it, so they were not exactly sure how it was done.

But they did find a convicted smuggler in prison who was willing to help out the producer. The convict offered excellent technical advice, plus a great on-camera interview.

"He was great," Cerny recalled. "He says, 'You've got to fly 100 feet off the water, go 104 knots, and make the bales 35 to 40 pounds. Throw out three bales, not four at a time, because the fourth will hit the vertical stabilizer. They can't be too heavy, because they'll explode when they hit the water.'"

And how would the plane find the boats?

"He told us to string out about 600 feet of underwater lights, something we hadn't thought of."

Jordan was originally profiled on December 4, 1988 (#43), and on several updates during the coming year. An AMW caller led agents to raids on homes of Jordan's relatives in South Carolina and Florida. They obtained recent photographs, postcards, and a videotape showing the tag numbers of the van and trailer the fugitive was driving. He also had a seven-month-old child now, which would slow down him and his wife, Dolores, on the run.

By early June, agents followed Jordan's trail to Essex Park, Colorado, a little town near Denver. He was gone, but it was the closest they had been to him in two years. They also discovered he was going by the alias of "Charles Sisson," his wife's maiden name.

With all-points bulletins issued on Jordan, especially in campgrounds, a state trooper spotted the trailer near Jackson Hole and the Grand Tetons. Agents scrambled from Colorado to Wyoming, and started checking out the local campsites using both ground and air surveillance.

At 11:15 P.M., June 15, agents from Customs and DEA, as well as local and state police closed in on the Jordan trailer in a campground. He was arrested without incident, and immediately admitted his true identity.

As former Customs Commissioner William Von Raab said, crediting the show in aiding Jordan's capture, "This closes a chapter on a dirty cop."

Shooting It Out

After AMW viewers led FBI agents two fugitives tried to fight their pursuers and were both killed in separate incidents within three days of each other.

On September 19, 1989, nine days after his AMW profile, FBI agents spotted David William Polson, 41, a one-time flight instructor, at a restaurant near Santa Nella, California, at Interstate 5 and state Route 152. Polson was wanted for the murder of an acquaintance, Janice Anderson, around Christmas, 1986, by stabbing her 11 times and dumping her body alongside a road 20 miles north of Las Vegas. He had nearly been caught in Culver City, California, from viewer tips just a few days before.

According to the FBI, Polson sped away from the agents, and began a high speed chase at 8:40 A.M. He made numerous attempts to evade the agents, then finally rammed his car into a haystack on a farm off the highway. Though he was surrounded by officers from the California Highway Patrol and FBI agents, Polson produced a weapon and began firing. He was hit several times, and pronounced dead at the scene. No law enforcement officers were injured.

Convicted murderer Leroy Chasson, 41, wanted for escaping from a Massachusetts prison in 1982, aided by his wife, Kathleen, was spotted by viewers in Denver following an update of his original profile on August 13 (#78). With information developed from the tips, FBI agents determined where the Chassons were living in Denver.

On September 22, 1989, at 5:15 P.M., agents approached a house at 1305 East 10th Avenue in downtown Denver on the pretext of asking for an address. Chasson came out of the house into the front yard, and the three agents identified themselves. He lifted a small-caliber revolver from his waist belt, which was hidden by his shirt, and opened fire on the agents. One agent was grazed on the forearm by one of Chasson's shots, but not seriously injured.

Chasson was pronounced dead at a local hospital. His wife, 42, was arrested at a Denver medical center where she was working, and was held for extradition to Massachusetts.

11

The Critics

While "America's Most Wanted" grew in pop-ularity with viewers and law enforcement, it also had its adversaries.

Some TV critics applauded the show as a great public service, while others lumped it in the lowly category of trash television. They complained that it was exploitative, and it tried to titillate viewers with violence, blurring the line between reality and entertainment.

Criticisms also came from the legal community with concerns for the rights of those profiled, particularly in the area of pretrial publicity. Others claimed that the show turned viewers into vigilantes, by encouraging them to snitch on their neighbors.

The initial reaction of the press was mixed when the show debuted on the O&O's in February, then nationally in April.

Some critics favoring the show used a play on words, calling it "arresting television," as a probable compliment. Most praised the new show, noting its public service aspect. For example:

- "'America's Most Wanted' has succeeded because it understands what Americans feel most: to feel that they matter," David Friedman, *Newsday*.
- "'America's Most Wanted' is a crime-buster and a hit for Fox," *USA Today*.
- "... It is stylized and graphic enough to provoke armchair G-men to action," Steve Weinstein, *Los Angeles Times*.
- "(AMW) is the first time law enforcement agents and a television network have collaborated on a nonfictionalized program aimed at apprehending fugitives," Cheryl Wetzstein, *Washington Times*.
- "Fox Television's 'America's Most Wanted' has become the best thing since post office walls for law enforcement.... (It's) a unique mix of documentary, news, public service and interactive television," *The Boston Herald*.
- "Fox... may have found a foolproof way to generate interest," Aljean Harmetz, *The New York Times* Syndicate.
- "The show has the blessing of the cops. It's a show that feels, looks and sounds like a cop. It works like a cop," Michelle Greppi, *Atlanta Constitution*.
- "The kneejerk reaction to a program like 'America's Most Wanted' is to label it as sensationalistic and a threat to the justice system. But then you stop to consider: the series works; it puts escaped felons back behind bars and it brings murder suspects into court. So the knee drops a little and you sit back to think some more," James Breig, *The Tidings* (Archdiocese of Los Angeles).

The most complimentary note was from *TV Guide*'s "Insider," which gave the show a "Cheers," saying:

"To the launching of Fox's resourceful project

'America's Most Wanted,' a new weekly series targeted toward capturing dangerous criminals...it's nice to see television playing watchdog."

But others had a problem with that idea. For example:

• "Still, you have to ask yourself whether 'America's Most Wanted' is really a public service it purports to be, or is merely another effort to titillate our unhealthy preoccupation with crime," Steve McKerrow, *Baltimore Evening Sun*.
• "While arm-chair crime-busting with 'America's Most Wanted,' it's easy to forget that these criminals being portrayed by look-alike actors are not some cop-show bad buys, but real people, who, like it or not, have constitutional rights," Joyce Millman, *San Francisco Examiner*.
• "'America's Most Wanted' is surely a swell public service, but it leaves a lot to be desired as prime-time entertainment," David Rosenthal, *San Jose Mercury News*.
• "This could have been and should have been an entertaining show and been a public service as well. No such luck...'America's Most Wanted' is so plodding, so stupid and so infuriatingly dull..." Bill Mann, *Oakland Tribune*.

At the annual gathering of TV critics on January 12, 1989, sponsored by the Television Academy of Arts and Sciences (the Emmy Awards), to discuss trends in the medium over the past year, AMW was put in the tabloid trash mold by several critics on the panel and attacked by name. Along with other shows in this so-called genre, the show was called "sensationalistic and exploitive."

"There are a lot of business pressures in television today," said Michael Hill of the *Baltimore Eve-*

ning Sun. "Trash television is a result of panic to find an audience." (*Emmy Magazine*, March/April 1989). Some critics, such as Eric Mink of the *St. Louis Post-Dispatch*, suggested that critics exercise judgment over how much publicity to give such shows.

One of the first writers to use the term "tabloid" in regard to television was Dennis Kneale of *The Wall Street Journal* (May 18, 1988, p. 1, 18). In a front-page, column-one story, he examined the problem of "titillating channels" which focused on "sleaze" to find profits and ratings. He noted that AMW was a show that counted young women, ages 18–49, among its loyal viewers, a highly prized demographic to advertisers, since they control a sizable part of the family budget. Advertisers don't seem to raise objection to the sex or violence of tabloid TV, he wrote, "as long as the shows deliver the viewers."

He also noted that tabloid TV, including AMW in that category, hadn't caused much reation among critics of violence and sex on the medium.

Curiously, for all the gore, tabloid television hasn't sparked much of a reaction among the most vocal critics of sex and violence on television. The National Coalition of Television Violence, a group that records every fictitious violent act on television, says it sees no need to track tabloid television. Indeed, the Coalition's Dr. Thomas E. Radecki praises "America's Most Wanted" for its role in capturing fugitives at large.

Apparently, the Coalition changed its mind over the next year. According to the November 18, 1989 edition of *Newsweek*, AMW was listed as the most violent prime-time show over the past year, according to the Coalition, with 53 "violent acts per hour."

(Since AMW is a half hour show, that would make 26.5 "violent acts" in each broadcast.)

During FBC's presentation to the Television Critics Association on July 26, 1988, an AMW press conference was attended by more than 100 TV press from across the country. From AMW were Michael Linder, John Walsh, and Tom Herwitz, while Bob Leschorn from the Marshals represented law enforcement. The discussion was lively. Some excerpts:

Question: ... couldn't you get more information out if you didn't want to create these cinematic gems that draw a large audience ... ?

Linder: We have found through our experience in answering telephone calls that there seems to be an information overload if we present too many fugitives in one particular episode.

Question: Have you gotten any negative comments from them (victims) that they'd really rather not see this crime reenacted?

Linder: ... There are many, many cases to pursue, and the last thing we want to do is hurt a family that has already been hurt by crime.

Walsh: I think we are very sensitive to that because I've been through it. ... I get a tremendous amount of mail from people who have been crime victims asking us to do their stories, if the story is unresolved.

(Later in the discussion)

Leschorn: May I add something, if I might. The cases that we give to Fox for "America's Most Wanted" are picked from 14,000 cases we receive each year. ... I don't want you to think that we just arbitrarily give them cases ... My agency spends up to a million dollars to hunt down a fugitive. So this is just the best thing that has ever come along. And it is great for us to participate all around . . . it is great for society and it is great for us.

Question: Mr. Walsh, one of the criticisms of the show is that there is an overabundance of violent crimes against attractive women that gives more voyeuristic than journalistic edge. Your response to that?

Walsh: I think we are learning, I think that we have evolved. I think that we have toned down the graphic re-creation. . . . I remember at a couple of press conferences at the FBI headquarters, that the FBI urged and said very strongly that these re-creations must be strong, that the public must realize that this is not "Miami Vice." This is not some screenwriter's nightmare. This is the nightmare and harsh reality of what has happened to American citizens, the 40 million Americans who were victims of violent crimes last year. . . . I think we've learned that a lot of the people watching our show are children. A lot of women watch our show. And I think we have learned from the feedback.

Question: . . . What concerns me about the show is the message that can be delivered which is sort of an "us" versus "them"—us being the good guys, them being the bad guys . . . the mentality that there are good people and there are bad people, which I don't think is the message that you want to deliver, but it sounds like one can come through.

Walsh: Well, you're a critic, and you're certainly entitled to your opinion, and the way we approach the show is yes, there are a lot of gray areas, and I have never said in all my public addresses that everyone needs to be incarcerated forever; first offenders, there are lots of people that need to be rehabilitated . . . I'm not saying that AMW is a quick fix or the solution, all we are saying and I have been saying is it is one tool in the arsenal, one small simple tool in the arsenal to aid law enforcement to bring these people to justice.

Question: You're saying you're not encouraging vigilantism, but when people get caught up in catching criminals, or identifying criminals, they can cross the line without realizing it, and feel that they are sort of part of the law, and maybe step beyond and insure themselves in the process.

Walsh: I say every week on the show that these are dangerous fugitives, please do not in any shape or form try to be a hero or get involved yourself. We have face-to-face dialogue on the show, every week we talk about it, that you can call for free, you can make a difference, you can remain anonymous ... It is America, anything is possible, but we say, we just don't present the facts, we say and caution people to be concerned, to be deliberate, be cautious, and call anonymously and assist, let law enforcement professionals do their job."

In an interview for this book, Pulitzer Prize-winning critic Tom Shales of the *Washington Post* commended the show for its "pro social aspects."

"There aren't many TV shows that have a direct cause-and-effect relationship," he said. "It seems largely to be a positive one, so who am I to say that this is not worth doing. I think it is worth doing."

But Shales noted that "in terms of production standards" AMW has helped popularize reenactment segments, particularly in network and local newscasts.

"I think as a practical and ethical matter, reenactments are wrong in most cases (on newscasts)," Shales said. "They are right in this case (AMW), but

unfortunately with the popularity of the show, anything that succeeds on television is going to be imitated at least four hundred times, and the
popularity of the show has led 'to an outbreak of re-
enactmentitis.

"And it's the kind of thing that TV critics have
to deplore because people are confused enough about
what is real and what is fake over the tube. And this
only adds to the confusion."

According to a Gallup poll conducted for Times-
Mirror, half of those surveyed believed that AMW is
a news program, while 28 percent believed it is entertainment. (*Los Angeles Times*, September 10,
1989, "Calendar," p. 7.)

"Younger people, who are lighter consumers of
news and who were weaned on television rather than
newspapers, were more apt to perceive . . . 'America's
Most Wanted' as news and not entertainment," the
study stated.

AMW is "breakthrough" TV from the aspect that
it invites the viewer to participate, Shales noted.

"I suppose what it's calling upon in the viewer
is a greater sense of concern about the society in
which we live, which is good because too much of TV
encourages complacency. Now it would be nice if we
had a show like 'America's Most Wanted' which
would encourage the same kind of concern for social
issues, not just crime."

Shales was concerned about the vigilante aspect
of the show, standing by his report that two actors
were turned in by their neighbors after appearing
as criminals on the show.

"Tom Herwitz called me up to say it wasn't true,
but it did actually happen. I talked to an agent, and
he said this happened," Shales said. "I'm sure you
would say that these are the occupational hazards
of doing a show like this, and not enough damage

has been done in that regard to offset the good that has been done.

"The whole idea that a viewer should be a vigilante, even though they caution that you should not try to apprehend criminals, there is still that underlying tone that you should go out and search the streets for somebody in a blue Toyota, and that's troubling."

There have been two reported cases of mistaken identity as a result of viewer tips to AMW during the past two years. In June 1988, a man in Mount Pocono, Pennsylvania, was detained for two hours by local police when he was mistaken for Carmine Esposito, wanted for murder by New York City police. In November 1989, a man was arrested for a brief period by Los Angeles Police, after workers at a Sherman Oaks restaurant mistook him for Richard Church, wanted for murder in Illinois.

When asked about the Mount Pocono incident on "Nightline," Linder apologized to any viewers who are mistakenly arrested.

"It's just one of those things we hope they understand is necessary in fighting crime," he said.

At the TCA press conference, Leschorn, a veteran lawman, noted that law enforcement officers often check out leads involving look-alikes, some resulting in mistaken arrests. Those don't only come from TV shows, he noted, but from usually reliable informants.

"During the course of investigation, investigators often come across look-alikes," he said. "When I say look-alikes, I'm talking identical. We very rarely arrest the person, we talk to him, and most times they're very cooperative. They realize that they're a dead look-alike for the fugitive, so we haven't had a problem with that."

James Fox, a criminal justice expert at Northeastern University, warned in a front-page story in *USA Today* on AMW (April 27, 1988, p. 2A) that the show could breed distrust.

"The downside is simply what it does to society," Fox said. "It causes us to look at everybody twice—friends, total strangers. Put a mustache on them and you think, 'Jeez, that's the guy I saw last night.' It can really change the nature of relationships."

ABC's "Nightline" (November 11, 1988) devoted an entire show examining "TV crime shows that try to turn their viewers into police informers." The primary show featured was "America's Most Wanted." A "Nightline" crew taped the AMW filming a reenactment of a prison escape by fugitive Alvin Jackson at the Baltimore City Jail. Among those interviewed prior to the show were Stanley Morris, Director of the Marshals; Professor Alan Dershowitz of the Harvard Law School; Gary Bennett and David Paulin, victims of mistaken arrests; and Sergeant Greg Lefcourt of the Honolulu Police Department.

On the live broadcast were Michael Linder, the FBI's Milt Ahlerich, and TV critic Ron Powers, moderated by Ted Koppel.

In discussing the show, Powers called it "a new kind of pornography, a pornography of violence," and didn't think the show "served a useful purpose." Linder and Ahlerich defended the show. Linder denied that the show segments were "gratuitously violent." (In interviews, Linder has often cited the segment of accused murderer Marlin Chin, after which D.C. Police chided the producers privately for not depicting the fugitive as being violent as he really was.)

Koppel asked Ahlerich "to be part law enforcement officer and part television critic" in his answer. As a spokesman for the FBI, Ahlerich declined to discuss "actual content," but said that the segments were accurate, being based on information supplied by the Bureau.

During the discussion, Koppel admitted having not seen the program under consideration ("... and I confess to you, I've not seen the program ... "). He declined to be interviewed for this book about the fact that he would moderate a discussion without having reviewed the product, nor would he comment on the development of "America's Most Wanted."

Among the critics on the legal side is the American Civil Liberties Union. An ACLU spokeswoman, Colleen O'Connor, who was quoted as criticizing the show in an article in *The New York Times Sunday Magazine* (September 25, 1988, p. 68), later reprinted in *Reader's Digest*, said that AMW often depicts crimes of suspects, not convicted criminals.

In a later interview, she explained that the ACLU's major concern was the "troubling effect" of presenting a crime from one point of view, especially a very prejudicial one. That could seriously affect the ability of an individual to get a fair trial after being profiled, she said.

"Their guilt has not been proven in a court of law," said Ms. O'Connor, director of public education for the ACLU. "They're under indictment or suspected of doing it. But having people portray it has a powerful impact, and there's something in these portrayals that gives a ring of truth to them.

"The camera gives credibility in a way that simple words don't. In many cases you use 'alleged' or 'the police say,' but the depiction of the crime has the same feel to me as an appearance before a jury or a grand jury, in which they are acted or told in great detail. And it gives the appearance of authority."

The ACLU also accused the show of "blurring the line between entertainment and journalism," which happens often on television today, especially in docudramas, Ms. O'Connor added.

"It's just kind of a general nervousness," she said. "What license do people in the entertainment business have as they portray themselves as credible journalists?"

Ms. O'Connor also noted the danger of prejudicial pretrial publicity in the show, and the danger of journalism becoming "too comfortable in its connection with the police."

"We all have our jobs, and apparently the ACLU is distinct from both journalists and the police," Ms. O'Connor said. "When the two seemed combined, I worry about the objectivity of news reporting. I mean what is its role here?"

"America's Most Wanted" did delay the broadcast of a segment on accused Mafia drug kingpin Gregory Scarpa, in July 1988, prior to the sentencing of his eight coconspirators in Brooklyn, New York.

Having been advised by the defense counsel that the Scarpa segment was going to be rebroadcast, Federal Judge I. Leo Glasser of the Eastern District of New York, asked AMW to "simply delay it or substitute some other segment."

"What I was essentially communicating to them was that I understood their First Amendment right to run it, and I simply adverted to the tension that existed between the First Amendment and the Sixth Amendment, the right of a defendant to a fair trial.

"I had no intention of attempting to enjoin them or taking any other legal action, since they did have the First Amendment right. I simply appealed to their sense of fairness, given the enormous amount of time, money, and effort that the government had put into this prosecution. It would be a rather unhappy event if a mistrial was declared because it was suspected that some juror on the panel had seen that rerun."

The show opted to delay the rebroadcast at Judge Glasser's request.

"He certainly was not going to tell us not to put it on, since we had every right to put it on," Herwitz said. "We thought to ourselves, is what we're really trying to do is help in the apprehension of these people, or are we trying to do it for some other purpose? And if it's trying to cooperate with law enforcement, putting it on isn't the right thing to do."

The Scarpa segment was later rebroadcast on July 24 (#25), after the trial. As a direct result of viewer tips from that broadcast, he was arrested by U.S. Marshals and DEA agents at 2:10 A.M., Monday, August 29, in a motel in Lakewood, New Jersey, where he was staying with his wife and baby. He was wanted on federal racketeering charges in connection with a Staten Island marijuana operation.

And those already behind bars don't appreciate the show either, since it discourages the chance of a successful escape.

"There's no place you can really run anymore," Jesse Barr, 51, told *USA Today* (April 27, 1988, p. 2A). He is currently serving 18 years for bank fraud at federal prison in Lexington, Kentucky.

"With shows like 'America's Most Wanted,' you can't go home again; everybody's waiting for you at home."

12

Helping the Victims

Forty million Americans, nearly a quarter of the population, were the victims of violent crime last year, according to a Department of Justice survey on violence.

There are more frightening facts:

• A 12-year-old child now has an 83 percent chance of being the victim of a violent crime within his/her lifetime;

• One out of every 12 American women are the victims of rape;

• Your odds of being murdered in the U.S. are one in 133. Last year there were 23,000 homicides in this country (size of a small city), versus 580 in Canada and 96 in West Germany.

While "America's Most Wanted" has tried to help reduce those figures by aiding in the arrest of dangerous fugitives, it is also concerned with the victims of crime. And in many cases, the show has been able to help them in their quest for justice.

* * *

Before producing a fugitive profile, AMW has always considered the effect the broadcast will have on the victims of his alleged or convicted crimes, or the survivors of those victims, who still feel the pain after many years. Many victims of crime have written the show to ask help in resolving a still open case. They are given careful consideration, but sometimes painfully turned down for various reasons— no suspect, poor images, lack of police cooperation, and others.

Even before AMW debuted on the seven O&O's, the families of four victims were already given some ray of hope that David James Roberts, the man who was convicted of ravaging their loved ones with murder, rape, or kidnap, would be caught.

According to Indianapolis P.D. Detectives John Larkins and Jerry Quackenbush, the sister of Roberts's victim in the kidnap-rape-murder convictions was afraid to let her children out of the house. She feared that the fugitive would track down the family for revenge.

The family of Bill, Anne, and Heidi Patrick had similar fears. Patsy Patrick, Bill's older sister, had adopted her brother's surviving daughter, Anna Marie, in her senior year of high school when Roberts escaped. She never told her daughter that the man who killed her parents and sisters was out until after he was caught.

Patsy wasn't going to sit patiently and let the system catch up with Roberts. In October 1987 she offered a $2,500 reward for tips leading to his return. The *Indianapolis Star* quoted a radio interview in which Ms. Patrick reportedly offered to double it "if they bring in his body." (October 27, 1987, p. 1.) The story also noted that by that time, the Indiana State Police had exhausted its leads. She also lobbied Indiana's Crime Stoppers to feature the Roberts case, but they declined, she said, citing her "vigilante over-tones."

The Patrick family in New Whiteland worried that Patsy's actions could endanger her. Later, she would admit that she was worried for Anna Marie and the family. She thought of hiring a security guard to accompany Anna Marie to her senior prom. For herself, Patsy didn't care if Roberts heard her. Down deep inside, she was even willing to confront him face-to-face; sometimes, she wanted to meet him to vent her bitterness.

When Linder and the MW crew visited New Whiteland in July to film the Roberts segment for the pilot, it was too painful for Buddy Patrick to talk about the tragedy on camera.

As Anna Marie grew up, Patsy only mentioned her parents' death if her daughter brought it up in conversation. But she was afraid of the dark, and wouldn't come into the house unless a light was on. She knew that her parents came home to a dark house. There were bits and pieces of the tragedy embedded in her mind.

Buddy told Patsy about this new show coming to profile Roberts. If it worked on these seven stations, the show would go national, he said. But it wasn't going to be broadcast in Indiana when it first went on the air. The closest would be Chicago.

Following the O&O debut, Patsy called Michael Linder in Washington, looking for a copy of the tape. Three days later, he called her to offer to present the tape in person. He was asking her to appear on the show announcing Roberts had been apprehended.

"I was ecstatic," Ms. Patrick said, remembering Linder's call to tell her of Roberts's capture. "I had said my prayers, and this one I had a receipt for. In the back of my mind, I said, 'There's got to be a way. Somebody out there has got to know this person.'

"I didn't know whose idea this was, who thought of it. But that's the person to whom I want to say, 'Hey, you did a good job.'"

Patsy Patrick did appear on the second AMW broadcast, as well as the first anniversary special. She got to see Roberts on the studio monitor, as Walsh interviewed him from Indiana State Prison. The interview brought her to tears.

"Roberts being out was a cloud over our heads," she said afterward. "His capture won't bring back anyone, but at least he won't do what he did to my family to anyone else."

Claire and Steven Berstein had hounded the FBI for almost two years to capture the man who was convicted of killing Steven's brother. Joseph Kindler had escaped from Philadelphia's death row on September 18, 1984. He was arrested in Montreal, but escaped from there on October 21, 1986.

Kindler was convicted of beating David Berstein to death with a baseball bat in July 1982. He was murdered the day before he was scheduled to testify against Kindler in a burglary case. His body was dumped in the Delaware River.

To Steven Berstein, it seemed as if Kindler "was trying to laugh it off all the way, that he could beat it.

"He was picked up within 12 to 14 hours after he murdered my brother," Steven remembered. "They had him in custody all that time. He got a lawyer and looked like a clean-cut college kid in court. He'd sit there and be very respectful. Then the jury would walk out of the room and he'd laugh, or grin. Sometimes, he'd actually break out into laughter, like it was some kind of joke between him and his lawyer.

"It seemed as though he thought he was invulnerable. At one point, when the jury went out, he turned and looked at me. He just grinned at me, as if almost to say, 'No problem, I'll get out of this, and I'll kill you too.'"

Steven Berstein had met Kindler twice before his brother's murder. David had gotten into some trouble in the past, but the thing that bothered Steven was that his brother seemed impressed by Kindler.

"I just remember begging my brother—'Stay away from this guy!'"

Kindler was convicted, but escaped from death row with the help of some inmates.

Every month, the Bersteins followed the progress in the hunt for Kindler. They even moved in fear that Kindler would seek his revenge. They met with the Philadelphia FBI agent assigned to the case, "Bud" Warner. An assistant district attorney told them that Kindler was as good as caught. "He'll track him down no matter where the hell he is," they were assured. The man was right.

During the hunt, Warner would keep the Bersteins informed when he could. Both being professionals—Steven a scientist, and Claire, an audiologist—they knew what it was like to work in a bureaucracy. They also had very high standards.

The second time around they weren't as pleased. The investigation seemed stalled, and the FBI admitted they didn't have any good leads. A different agent was now on the case, and he didn't share as much as Warner did before. They reached the point where they couldn't deal with the frustration anymore.

"Nothing had happened on the case in a year and a half, and as the world goes on, there's less chance of it happening," Claire remembered. "My husband and I looked at each other and said, 'Well, we're not stupid people, and Kindler might be shrewd, but there's got to be a way.'"

They thought of sending posters around Canada, putting ads in newspapers up there. Maybe they could put up a reward, or hire their own detective. Because Canada didn't have a death penalty, Kindler had gone there the first time, but he might not have stayed there. During his extradition hearings, his case became a *cause célèbre* for the opponents of capital punishment in Canada. This time out, he could have gone anywhere, such as Hungary, since he knew the language.

By January, the Bersteins were running out of ideas. They often read *The New York Times*, and one Sunday, it had their solution. Steve showed Claire an article about this new show called "America's Most Wanted." They looked at each other, and said, "This might be it."

They spoke to Nan Allendorfer at the show, who said that they were the first to call in with a story. She assured them that the show would give the case careful consideration and asked them to send some information. They sent newspaper clippings, which Linder studied, then decided to do the segment. It might only air in seven markets, however, which would not include Philadelphia, they were cautioned by Margaret Roberts.

The case was Michael Cerny's second AMW profile. Meeting the family of the man Kindler killed intensely motivated the producer.

"We interviewed the mother of the victim," Cerny remembered later. "That attached something special to it. It changed the whole focus of the episode. I wanted to make it as strong as possible, so people would remember this guy, and help catch him."

The Kindler segment was first broadcast on the second national show. Leads did come in, but he wasn't caught. With the help of an attorney friend, the Bersteins met with AMW for other ways to use the segment. They also wrote to the attorney general, the governor, the mayor, senators, congressmen, and the Justice Department. Perhaps, AMW could rebroadcast the segment, or arrange to have it shown in Canada.

Meanwhile, the Bersteins knew that Kindler had plenty of time to dye his hair, change his looks, and sink in somewhere. Maybe he would try to start a new life for himself with some substance to it, so he didn't have to run from place to place. He was also in another country, and who would even know him? Unless he was picked up for another crime, there wasn't much chance of the Mounties just stumbling over him. Kindler was smart, and he had beat them all, Steve thought. One of Kindler's lawyers told Berstein that his client always thought he would get off. Getting convicted came as a shock, or was it?

Steve Berstein was right about one thing—Kindler had gone about as far as he could.

The Kindler segment was rebroadcast on AMW on September 4, 1988.

When the Bersteins arrived home from work two days later, Nan Allendorfer had left some good news on their answering machine. A viewer in St. John's, New Brunswick, recognized the fugitive as a man working in a repair shop nearby. Two days later, Kindler was in custody. He was all the way at the end of Canada, separated from the other English-speaking provinces.

The capture gave the Bersteins the "satisfaction" that justice could be done, and put their lives "back on the right track." They appeared on the

show's first anniversary special to say thanks to the
show and "that brave man in New Brunswick."

"Some might call it (AMW) sensationalism, like
these people who go on the air and say, 'My son needs
a liver,'" Steve said in an interview. "All the other
people might be disgusted, but if it gets the liver for
the kid, that's a life that otherwise might not have
been saved.

"So my feeling is sensationalsim has its value.
If it hadn't been for 'America's Most Wanted,' I don't
think he ever would have been caught."

By some miracle, John Mikrut survived being
shot twice in the head at point-blank range. His life
was even more shattered by the experience itself.

After his recovery, Mikrut, 31, went into virtual
seclusion, both physical and mental. He had worked
on construction sites before, but now any loud noise
would terrify him. He didn't want to have any friends
because he couldn't bring himself to trust anyone.

On the night of October 19, 1986, Steven Randall
Dye, 40, and John Bianchi, 28, were drinking in a
bar in Parsippany, New Jersey. Bianchi said that he
thought John Mikrut was responsible for his girlfriend leaving him. At 12:15 A.M., they arrived at
Mikrut's trailer with a six-pack of beer under the
pretense of celebrating Dye's birthday. The three
lived in separate trailers at the Brookwood Swim
and Campground on Route 46.

While in the kitchen, Dye placed a .22-caliber
revolver to the back of Mikrut's head and fired one
shot. Mikrut turned around and Dye fired again,
striking him in the forehead. Dye and Bianchi fled.

At first, Mikrut thought he had been shot with
a BB gun. Two neighbors took him to the Parsippany
Police Department. An ambulance was summoned
to the station to rush Mikrut to the hospital, where

he had two bullets removed from his head.

Dye was stopped by the New Jersey State Police on Interstate 80 on a motor vehicle violation. Troopers arrested him for possession of a .22-caliber revolver. The shooting alert hadn't been issued, so he was released after posting 10 percent of his $2,500 bail, and he fled. Bianchi, meanwhile, was arrested, tried, and convicted.

Dye was also wanted for shooting a Cleveland man in 1981, after a traffic accident. He was added to New Jersey's 12 Most Wanted List.

Darryl Neier of the Morris County Prosecutor's Office brought Dye's case to "America's Most Wanted" in March 1988. Mikrut had moved to South Carolina by then, having spent a week in the hospital. He had "hung out" with his family for a while, and was slowly getting back to work and life.

"When Darryl first called me up, I didn't know anything about the show, because it hadn't been on that long," Mikrut remembered later. "He (Dye) probably thought I was dead. So I had nothing to lose, and I definitely wanted to have him caught. But I was a little leery about how well this show would work."

Mikrut spent a week with the AMW crew in Parsippany, even at a trailer park close to the one he was almost killed in. Going through that experience wasn't that difficult since he had plenty of time "to talk it out" with his family. He agreed to be interviewed on-camera for the segment.

"He must be awfully coldhearted, for one," he said. "I don't know how to explain it. Just cold, cruel, uncaring. There's a lot of words used to describe him."

The first time Mikrut saw the segment was when it aired on May 8, 1988 (#14).

"It was incredible, because it was so similar to

what I could remember of what happened that night," Mikrut said.

Twelve days after the broadcast, Dye flagged down a police car in San Diego and surrendered. He knew that he had been profiled. As for his surrender, he told a police officer later, "I have been thinking about this for a while."

Nyer called Mikrut with the news. At Dye's trial, he would testify for seven hours on two separate days. He would also appear on AMW's first anniversary special.

"Now I can continue my life, what a burden off my shoulders," Mikrut told John Walsh. "I can now continue with my life. I've confronted the person that shot me, and I've seen him come to justice."

Dye was convicted of attempted murder and sentenced to the maximum term of ten years.

On September 11, 1988, AMW took a bold step. For the first time, the show profiled a wanted child molester.

Kids in White Ridge, Colorado, called Donald Parsons "Uncle Don." A wealthy real estate salesman, he would take boys to the zoo, bowling, or swimming. Mothers would love his token gifts and his father image. His home was a mecca for kids: lots of games, toys, a punching bag, and a pool table.

But in September 1987, Parsons, 59, fled Colorado. He was avoiding trial and more than $1 million in bonds on several charges of sexual molestation of young boys, including enticement of a child and habitual sex offense. In one case, he was accused of repeatedly molesting a 12-year-old boy during 1986, and again in September 1987, while out on bond awaiting trial. He had previously been convicted twice of similar crimes: molesting a young girl in

1980, and given probation; for sexual assault on several boys in 1982.

Parsons was profiled on AMW on September 11, 1988 (#31). He was captured by FBI agents in Phoenix on October 19, after viewer tips placed him there. In February, Parsons pleaded guilty to two felony counts of sexual assault on a child, enticement, and bail jumping. He was sentenced to 36 years in the Colorado State Penitentiary.

Police said Parsons stated that he feared for his life in prison. As he was led away, he turned to a Wheat Ridge detective, and said, "See you on TV."

The Parsons profile had another impact. A mother in Kingsport, Tennessee, watched the show that night and noted similarities with her son's relationship with a local man.

"It had showed a child sexual molester, and how he responded to his victims, buying them things, taking them places... the victims become withdrawn, and want to spend their whole time with this other individual as opposed to the family unit," Detective Lowell Adkins of the Kingsport Police told the *Kingsport Times-News* (September 16, 1988, p. 1).

"She detected that in her child, and sat him down and just started talking to him, and then he told her about what had been going on then."

Thomas Lynn Franklin, Jr., 20, was charged with seven counts of aggravated rape and six counts of aggravated sexual battery for the alleged abuse of the 11-year-old boy. Police said he had confessed to molesting another boy, whose family had left Kingsport and could not be located. Franklin pleaded guilty to 12 counts of aggravated rape. Final sentencing had not been handed down by December, although the state was recommending a 20-year prison term in a psychiatric unit.

* * *

Police officers can also be the victims of crime. In the United States, more than 30,000 law enforcements officers have been killed in the line of duty in the past ten years. They can also be victims psychologically. Dedicated to their work, they can lose sleep, never rest until a fugitive is caught.

Jean Mewbourne, a Baltimore detective assigned to the sex crimes unit, vowed she wouldn't retire until Alvin Jackson was back behind bars. With an accomplice, he had been arrested and jailed for a crime spree that terrorized quiet communities around Baltimore from August 1985 to September 1986. The rampage included robberies, burglaries, rapes, and shootings.

Leon Copeland was convicted and sentenced to life for his part. But before Jackson, 24, could be tried, he went over the wall at the Baltimore County Jail on January 19, 1987.

A task force of investigators from Baltimore County, Anne Arundel County, Baltimore City, and the FBI was formed to catch Jackson. They followed leads into Washington and south, but realized he could be anywhere, even taunting them in Baltimore. They had put his picture in the paper, on television, and in convenience stores.

"I was just so obsessed that he might be back here," she said. "I would go shopping and look at every black male that was walking toward me. I couldn't think. I couldn't concentrate."

By the fall of 1988, Mewbourne had enough. She was at "a point of frustration—where else was there to go?" One morning she was talking with some officers in the station, when one mentioned "America's Most Wanted."

"I had seen the show, and I knew that he wasn't in Baltimore," Mewbourne said. "If he was anywhere else that the show was reaching, I knew that the average citizen likes to play detective. And that was the only way I could go.

"There was no way I was going to retire and leave that undone. There were just too many victims, really suffering. Physical trauma, psychological trauma, people who couldn't sleep, couldn't enjoy their homes. I guess it was police ego, but I just wanted to say I finished it."

Mewbourne called the show, and soon Nan Allendorfer was up in Baltimore at a meeting of the task force. It didn't take long for the street-smart detective to learn what kind of person she was dealing with.

"We had lunch at this Mexican restaurant and Nan had this very nice dress on," Mewbourne remembered. "A waiter was serving large glasses of ice water, and when he stepped behind her, he dropped the whole glass down the back of her dress.

"And I started laughing, because it struck me funny. And I thought, 'What is she going to do,' because she had this look on her face."

Once Allendorfer realized it was ice water, not something that could stain the dress, she roared in laughter.

"We knew she was going to be okay," Mewbourne said. "She could fit in with cops because she could laugh. Right away we fell in love with her, and she became very important to us."

The Jackson segment was filmed in Baltimore in late October. A crew from "Nightline" filmed the reenactment of Jackson's escape from the jail and interviewed several members of the task force. Mewbourne told the producer that AMW "was the best thing to happen to police work since the helicopter."

The story ran on November 6, 1988 (#39). Within hours of the broadcast, the FBI was tracking leads in Daytona Beach, Florida. Local police and FBI agents arrested him at 12:45 P.M. at his apartment in a complex called Pine Haven. He was found hiding under a bed in a back bedroom. Unarmed, he came out upon command. Local police had previously responded to domestic calls at the apartment, but knew the fugitive as Andre Jackson.

That's how Jean Mewbourne knew they would get their man. A few hours after the broadcast, she noticed the name "Andre Jackson" on several tips sheets. That was the name of Alvin's brother, and she knew that he frequently used it.

Late on the morning after the broadcast, Mewbourne, Denny O'Neil, and two other task force members were having breakfast up the street from WTTG. Suddenly, all their beepers started going off. O'Neil went to a pay phone to call, and returned to the table with good news—Jackson was caught.

"I started jumping up and down like a little kid at Christmas," Mewbourne remembered. "I said, 'Is it confirmed? Is it confirmed?' And we all started crying. It was such a relief, after 18 months, and we had him in 17 hours with 'America's Most Wanted.'"

When the group confirmed the capture, O'Neil suggested they buy champagne for Linder and Allendorfer. Mewbourne didn't think they "should bother those people," but he was already driving her and the group to a liquor store. Champagne in hand, they walked over to the studio and asked for Linder.

"This young man (Mike Walton) came out and he recognized us from the night before," Mewbourne remembered. "We said that we had brought champagne for Nan and Michael. But he said that Mr. Linder was being interviewed by 'Nightline.'"

"So I said, 'I know he's real busy, and we just came by to say thank you.'"

Recognizing the officers from the previous night,

Walton took them back to the studio where Linder was being interviewed. The executive producer stopped the interview, opened the champagne, then, with the "Nightline" cameras rolling, made a toast.

"To the partnership," he said.

Jackson was sentenced to two life sentences plus twenty years. He'll be eligible for parole in 35 years. Mewbourne hasn't retired yet, since she'll "always" keep her hand in.

At Jackson's sentencing on March 9, 1989, she sat by the empty jury box, so she could watch his face. The sentence was read, and Jackson turned to her.

"You ruined my life," he told her.

She said nothing.

"I thought that was kind of an ironic statement," she said later. "He had taken so much of ours."

On May 14, 1989 (#65), "America's Most Wanted" dedicated a special segment essay to slain police officers called "The Thin Blue Line." The day before the show taping, Walsh was the keynote speaker at the national conference of "COPS" (Concern of Police Survivors), a group of survivors of slain officers.

"I knew it was a going to be tough, because one of the hardest things for me is to talk to the victims," Walsh said afterward. "I've walked in their shoes. I know their hurt. I know their anguish. I know there isn't a whole lot I can do for them, even if they perceive I can.

"What do you say to a room of 600 or so people who have had their loved one violently separated from them because of his job. It was very emotional for me."

After his address, Walsh was due back for voice-over tapings all afternoon. Dozens of people came up to him in the hallway outside.

"I've never tried to cut people off, you've got to treat people with dignity," he said. "You've got to give them their minute. They've come a long way to talk to you, and you've got to be a human being."

Walsh met with a group from Florida, which was anxious for him to help fight for a piece of legislation with them. He was introduced to Teresa Miyares and her two children, Emilio, 10, and Jessica, 7, from Hialeah, Florida, the survivors of Officer Emilio Miyares, killed in the line of duty on November 6, 1986.

"Meeting the kids is the toughest because it tears me apart whenever I see a child who's been hurt or injured and these kids were grieving," Walsh said. He quietly invited the family and others to watch the AMW taping the next afternoon, so they could see something positive dedicated to fallen officers.

Mrs. Miyares had brought the patch from the uniform her husband was wearing when he was killed. She didn't know if she would get to meet Walsh, much less see a taping. Her good friend, Ann Becker, another survivor, also came to the taping. Ann's father had been killed when she was eight years old.

"At the taping we looked at the little patch board they have there," Mrs. Miyares said in an interview. "Ann asked me, 'Would you mind if I give the patch to Mr. Walsh?'

"So she went over with my two kids and gave it to him."

The three walked over to Walsh during a commercial break. They said they had something to present to the show, so the host called Linder down from the control room.

"The little girl pulled out the patch that her

father had on when he was killed," Walsh remembered. "She said, 'We want you to have this for your patch board.' Linder said, 'Certainly,' and we put it right up there."

And that patch—from Hialeah P.D.—is there behind Walsh during every broadcast of "America's Most Wanted."

13

John Walsh

Who is John Walsh?

Is he a television personality? A professional grieving parent? An advocate for missing children? A crusader for victims' rights? A frustrated political hopeful? Or an obsessed father of a murdered child?

It's hard for some people to understand what John Walsh is all about. Out in Hollywood, some TV executives wonder what he wants out of hosting "America's Most Wanted." Cynical reporters brush him off as a media hound, and look for a weak point to attack him. Uninformed legislators worry he will embarrass their positions on criminal justice issues.

But to millions across America, John Walsh is a victim—and a survivor. You say his name, and people will say, "Isn't he Adam's father?"

The movie *Adam*, and its sequel *Adam: His Song Continues* told the tragic, yet powerful story of Walsh's ability to turn his grief into action after the kidnap and murder of his six-year-old son, Adam. John, and his wife, Reve, not only survived the pain and strain of losing their only child, but they have also inspired thousands of other victims with their courage. They have saved countless lives with education, lobbying, and support.

Neither of them can count the number of state and federal bills they have helped pass to protect families, missing children, and victims from the inadequacies of our criminal justice system. Once a critic of law enforcement, Walsh is now one of their strongest allies, particularly as host of "America's Most Wanted."

The wall in John Walsh's Washington office is filled with awards and photographs with celebrities and politicians. He has been named Father of the Year, a Leader for the Next Generation, and Citizen of the Year. Cities and states have proclaimed days in his honor. He receives thousands of letters a month from people looking for help, lawmen pitching their cases, or people just saying thanks. His schedule rivals that of any corporate executive as he flies more than a half million miles a year to preach his cause. On the weekends he runs between studios, rehearsals, and interviews for "America's Most Wanted." With all of this, he is away from his home, his wife, and two children nearly two-thirds of his time.

When you meet Walsh, there's an incredible intensity in his eyes, and urgency in his voice, and restlessness in his manner. He's a walking encyclopedia of facts and figures about crime in America and the injustice of the system toward victims, particularly women and children, who are the most defenseless. Yet there will always be a pain in his heart for his son, Adam, and children like him who Walsh will never meet. He has testified before Congress and state legislatures, and has addressed audiences of thousands at a time. Still, the hardest moment for him is comforting victims who look to him for help.

And his happiest is spending time with children, especially his own.

Today, John Walsh is many things. But before Adam's death, the only ones he really wanted to be were a good father, a loving husband, and a successful businessman. In July 1981, he had all three.

He was born on December 26, 1945, in upstate New York. He was the first of four children, having a sister, Jane, and two brothers, James and Joseph. In school, he was a bright student, and loved sports. In college, he played soccer and later professional softball as a pitcher. During college, he met Reve, a striking blonde, majoring in art and interior design, five years his junior. She was not only attractive and charming, but also intelligent and idealistic with a strong sense of herself.

In June 1969, Walsh had graduated from college. He wanted to be a teacher, and was thinking of going to law school. That could wait awhile. Instead, he and college buddy, Jeff O'Regan, cruised down to southern Florida to work as lifeguards for six months before settling down to the serious business of life.

One afternoon on his lifeguard chair in Hollywood, Florida, Walsh spotted a youngster stranded on a jetty. By the time he reached the terrified ten-year-old, the boy was drowning. Walsh saved his life.

The boy's father, John Monaghan, called up the young lifeguard and invited him over to his spacious home. He was president of a chain of six hotels in Florida and the Caribbean.

"I understand you're getting married, and I'd like to give you a trip to Europe for your honeymoon, and give you a job when you get back," the grateful father said. "I know your background and I know you're a college graduate just biding some time down here lifeguarding. I'd like to give you a job."

Monaghan didn't have to ask twice. John and Reve were married in July 1971. At work, his new boss groomed the young protégé in the hotel business. He learned sales, marketing, advertising, public relations, personnel, management—an incredible education. Within two years, he had a great chance to move up running the Outland Promotion Board for 60 or so hotels in the Bahamas. Walsh was 27, and a little apprehensive about moving on. Monaghan was proud of his prize pupil, and anxious for him to succeed.

Most of the applicants were seasoned veterans in their 50s, and Walsh didn't think he "had a chance in hell."

"Sure you do," Monaghan assured him. "You're the best employee I've ever had. You've got the potential. Go get that job."

He did. For two years, Walsh helped increase business to the lush area, now known as the "Family Islands," and helped introduce direct air service there. Back home in Florida, the Walshes now had a son, Adam, born on November 14, 1974.

During that time, he met a well-known marketing consultant named Warren Binder. He was willing to back Walsh as a partner in his own business. Soon Walsh founded Diversified Marketing Service, and landed 14 clients in his first year of business. He was "off and running," when three dynamic Texans—Ray Mellette, James Greer, and Mike Wallon—offered him a piece of their action.

"We're forming a management company and we're building luxury hotels," they told him. "You're a rising star and we want you."

Walsh wanted in, but didn't have a lot of money to invest in the partnership. They would accept him in the group, as long as he left his current company.

So Walsh dissolved his partnership with Binder, and joined the Texans.

The company soared. They landed the contract to build the $36 million Paradise Grand Hotel in the Bahamas. It was ten years since his lifeguarding days, and Walsh was a quarter-partner in a major south Florida hotel management firm.

He was married to Reve for ten years. They had a beautiful six-year-old son, and a lovely home in Hollywood, Florida. With his wonderful family, rising career, and comfortable southern Florida lifestyle, John Walsh had the American dream. Within his lifetime, he would probably have more children, a bigger home, his own business, and perhaps someday be a millionaire.

The sunny Monday morning of July 27, 1981 started like any other for the Walshes. John went to work, where several major meetings on the Grand Paradise were scheduled. Reve and Adam went shopping at a nearby shopping mall. Walking into a department store, Reve let Adam play in the toy department, while she looked for a lamp.

A few minutes later, she returned and looked for Adam—all over. Desperately, she ran through the store and out into the parking lot looking for her six-year-old son with his red baseball cap. She called to him over the public address system in the store, then the mall adjoining it. He never wandered off by himself. Though shy and introverted, he was a bright young boy who would never just disappear without telling her.

Reve called John.

"Adam's lost," she said. He was at the mall within minutes.

The frantic couple called the Hollywood Police. They came over to the mall, and suggested the

Walshes come over to the station so they could launch a search from there. Reve left a note in her car in case Adam came back there looking for her.

"We'll find him," John reassured her. She wondered how a little boy could just disappear. Didn't anybody see him? Didn't anybody care? Unfortunately, most just mind their own business, until it happens to them.

At the police station, Reve and John gave them a description and photo of Adam. Back at the office, Mellette and the entire staff were calling their contacts in south Florida to make sure all police agencies had the bulletin. John's brother, Joe, printed up posters, which were plastered all over Fort Lauderdale, then Georgia and Alabama. A $5,000 reward was posted for information leading to Adam's safe return. His picture and description were in the newspapers and on television and radio.

A massive ground search had begun over more than 200 square miles. Police, helicopters, dogs, psychics, and hundreds of volunteers combed fields, lakes, beaches, and streets looking for Adam. The office staff, led by John's associate and best friend, Les Davies, hounded more law enforcement agencies around Florida and neighboring states. As darkness fell, John and Reve, still at the police station, realized someone must have taken their son.

Night turned into day and there was no sign of "Kooter." John, Reve, and the Hollywood detectives continually called police agencies in neighboring areas pleading with them to help look. John called the local office of the FBI for assistance. An agent politely told him that the FBI could not get involved unless there had been a ransom note, proof of kidnapping, or some evidence that the child had been taken out of the state. Walsh could not believe that the FBI would look for a stolen car, or a missing racehorse, but not his lost son.

On Tuesday afternoon, the Walshes did their first on-camera media interview. At the police station, a local TV reporter came over and asked them to give Adam's description, and tell where he might go.

"He could be abducted, and we want him to know that everyone's looking for him," Walsh said, after giving the details.

"And Adam," Reve said. "Look for landmarks to find your way home. Don't be afraid. We love you."

In the six years since his birth, Reve had known where her son was every minute of the day and night. Now, for the first time, she didn't. At home, they could hear his voice, feel his presence, yet couldn't touch him.

John called his U.S. Senator, Paula Hawkins, for help. She promised to push the FBI to join in the search, since local police couldn't follow leads out of their area. There was one lead from a youngster who had seen a man drag a boy into a blue van, but couldn't remember a license plate number.

Through his contacts, John had gotten booked on ABC's "Good Morning America" with David Hartman. Perhaps, the national attention could help bring their son home. He and Reve flew up to New York for the show. The night before they had dinner with a producer, some representatives from "Child Find," and Julie Patz, who would also be on the panel. Her son, Etan, had been missing for nearly six years.

They told the Walshes more than they wanted to know about the frustrating problem of finding missing children. In the United States, more than 50,000 disappeared a year—where did they go? It was even harder to get media attention for these youngsters, they explained. But John Walsh could help them. Before, only mothers had appeared, and they were ignored as hysterical women. A man, a father, would be listened to.

"Be our voice, Mr. Walsh," they pleaded.

He was confused. They were supposed to help him.

Shortly before midnight, the Hollywood Police called John and Reve at their hotel. Searchers had found the unidentified remains of a small boy in a swamp canal in Vero Beach, about 150 miles from Hollywood. They asked for dental records, and John had them sent. The Walshes went on "Good Morning America" wondering if their search had come to a tragic end, or would they keep looking, and hoping, for years. They pleaded for help. They criticized the lack of organization in law enforcement to look for a missing child who has left the immediate area. They pleaded again.

When they got back to the hotel, the phone rang again. The remains were identified as those of Adam Walsh, age 6. The largest search in the history of southern Florida for a lost child had come to a tragic end. For John and Reve Walsh, their American dream had become a horrible nightmare.

The funeral mass was said by John's cousin, Father Mike Conboy. Adam's classmates sang, then gave John and Reve a poster with the words, "If his song is to continue, we must do the singing."

It would take weeks, months, before John and Reve could deal with their paralyzing grief. Everywhere they looked, they thought of Adam. Turning to each other was the only answer, but even that was painful. They went up to O'Regan's home for a "sabbatical" before John dove back into his work. But when they got home to Hollywood, Joe and John's mother, "Gram," had a surprise that would change their lives again. The garage was full of bags and boxes with more than 20,000 letters. People from all over the country had sent sympathy, hope, sometimes money. Parents wrote telling of their search for their missing children. Reve read the letters for days. There had to be someplace for these letters, these people, some kind of help. They had to be helped.

John tried to plunge right back into building hotels. Every day, however, there was another talk show request for him to tell their story. Maybe it could help others, he thought. All he really wanted to do was try and piece his life, his dreams—and his marriage—back together.

Reve had decided to make a place for those letters and people. She convinced the mayor of Pembrooke Pines to let her use an abandoned police station as the Adam Walsh Child Outreach Center. From the first day, the phones didn't stop ringing with parents of missing children, desperate for help. Reve quickly realized that the first steps were education and legislation. Parents had to learn how to make their children safe from strangers. The laws had to be changed to protect the children. They were America's greatest resource, yet they had no lobby, no voice, no vote.

The missing children's advocates asked him to come to Washington to help lobby for help. There John met Jay Howell, a Senate investigator for Senator Paula Hawkins. Now she needed Walsh's help to push some legislation she had introduced called the Missing Children's Bill. Her bill was going okay, but the version introduced into the House by Florida Congressman E. Clay Shaw, Jr., was stalled in committee. The Senate version would allow the names of missing children to be entered into the FBI's computer (National Crime Information Computer); the House version did not. The Justice Department had mounted heavy opposition.

Howell wanted the Walshes to testify before the Senate committee to tell their story, especially how the FBI wouldn't help. They agreed and faced the panel of lawmakers, who didn't seem to listen.

She needed John's business genius to help run the center. Soon he turned his office into an arm of the Adam Walsh Center. The secretaries did the typing and copying of legal briefs, testimonies before Congress, and informational packets. Here was Walsh, the father of a murdered child, trying to get justice, while trying to work and pay bills. Adam's murder left another problem: it had exhausted their financial resources. They were broke.

Walsh couldn't keep his mind on his work, though. It was torture; he just couldn't do it. Every two weeks he was flying off someplace, when he was supposed to be at a hotel meeting. Mellette often covered, but the other two partners would find out. They were right, Walsh would admit years later, he couldn't concentrate on hotels. He was so hurt, so obsessed.

He was in Washington testifying, while still drawing a salary from the firm. The Grand Paradise opened late, yet Walsh was more concerned about the progress of the Missing Children's Bill. The politics of Washington made him ill, but he used his sales savvy to sway key lawmakers in both the House and the Senate. The process was long and tedious, even though they were dealing with children, not guided missiles.

As a businessman he knows how to get to the heart of the matter and hit you in the gut. Take, for example, when he helped a recent pitch by the Fox sales staff in Chicago to a major retail chain. On the line was a major ad campaign as well as a possible AMW fugitive photograph in the company's national newspaper ad supplement.

First, Walsh detailed this commitment to "America's Most Wanted," and why he would risk his reputation being involved in such a controversial program. Next, he elaborated on the reaction he got on the road from Americans, particularly victims of crime, frustrated with the current criminal justice system. Then, he highlighted some frightening statistics about crime in America, particularly about an individual's chances of being the victim of a violent crime. Finally, he went for the bottom line.

"Suppose one of these creeps (AMW fugitive) is doing the gardening around your house, but you don't know he's wanted for murder in California," Walsh begins. "One day something triggers his craziness, and he rapes your wife, then kills her, brutalizes each one of your kids, then blows you away when you walk in the door—unless he makes you watch it all.

"But if you saw this guy in the ad supplement, it would save your life, your family's lives, and who knows how many."

The ad men went to their bosses, and a second meeting was immediately scheduled for the following week.

On July 15, 1982, less than a year after Adam's murder, John and Reve received a precious gift to ease their grief—a baby daughter, Meghan Jane. Hundreds of people, many of whom followed the search for Adam the summer before, called and visited the hospital to wish them well. There were total strangers, reporters, TV cameramen, friends, and relatives wishing them well and sharing their incredible joy. Though a month premature, Meghan was a healthy, bouncing baby.

"I'm just so glad to have some good news for you," said Reve in an interview (Fort Lauderdale *Sun-Sentinel*, July 16, 1982, p. 1). "Prince William, eat your heart out." (Lady Diana gave birth a few days earlier.)

"We loved Adam so much, he was such a great joy in our hearts, it was hard not to try to fill that void in our lives," John added.

They were even more worried that a new child, especially a son, would always have to measure up to Adam. They might be horribly overprotective, and unconsciously pass along their grief to the child. But looking into Meghan's beautiful face, all those doubts quickly faded.

Up in Washington, meanwhile, the House version of the Missing Children's bill had passed. The Senate version was still stalled with the Justice Department promising to continue its fierce opposition.

A reporter from the Hollywood *Sun-Tattler* called Walsh for a comment to a statement that an anonymous Justice spokesman made about the bill's chances.

"That couple down in Florida can go pound salt," the spokesman had said.

John had no comment—"Just let it stand as it is."

That statement made him throw down the gauntlet. He returned to Washington for a key meeting between the House and Senate committees to work out a compromise. Again, he lobbied hard—right to the heart of several lawmaker-parents. The children won.

Three months after Meghan's birth, John and Reve were meeting President Ronald Reagan in the White House Rose Garden. The President signed into law the Missing Children's Act which mandated the creation of a national clearinghouse of computerized information to aid parents of missing children. It also ordered that the FBI's NCIC be used as the clearinghouse, and local FBI offices would provide assistance to parents, especially to help deal with local police.

Reagan also signed the Victim and Witness Protection Act, which strengthened existing statutes dealing with intimidation or retaliation against victims or witnesses. It also mandated that judges in federal cases had to weigh the harm done to victims before sentencing. Judges would have to order restitution by the criminal or give a reason why not. (*The New York Times*, October 13, 1982, p. 1.)

Reagan praised John and Reve's courage by saying they have "committed their lives" to the cause of missing children and enlisted the help of thousands of others (*Miami Herald*, October 13, 1982, p. 1).

John told reporters: "We finally got something passed. . . . It might not have helped us find Adam, but certainly it would have facilitated our heartbreak. When I started searching for Adam, I found that 70 percent of the police departments in Florida didn't know he was missing. What chance did I have of getting my son back, alive or dead?" (*The New York Times, op. cit.*)

A photograph of the jubilant Walshes, including Meghan, greeting Reagan after the bill signing appeared in every major newspaper in the country, and by videotape on all three network evening newscasts.

Shortly after the bill became law, John and Reve got another phone call. This one was from producer Linda Otto of Alan Landsburg Productions in Los Angeles. Since Adam's death, they had been fair game for dozens of would-be producers, competing for their story for a television movie. They would promise them creative control, big contracts, and lots of sensitivity. But John knew how to read a phony from two thousand miles away. 'They would keep it private for now.

But Otto was different. She was sincerely moved by their story and seemed strongly concerned about children's issues. Eventually, she convinced them to let her tell their story in a television movie. She would produce it, with help from Landsburg executive Joan Barnett, formerly of NBC. Michael Tuchner would direct, Allan Leicht would write it. Emmy-winning TV star Daniel J. Travanti of "Hill Street Blues" would play John, while movie-TV actress, JoBeth Williams would costar as Reve. During the next year, they would all become lifelong friends.

It would not be easy, however. Otto and Leicht would have to know every detail of their emotional horror to write the script. Intimate personal details would be put on the TV screen for millions to see. The American public would peek right into their bedroom. Travanti and Williams would have to spend days with them to learn their habits, routines, and mannerisms. The Walshes would have to serve as technical advisors for the month-long shoot in Houston. They would have to relive every painful moment.

But John and Reve *wanted* to reach the nation. They wanted Americans to know what it was like to lose a child as they did. More than a million kids a year were missing and nobody cared. *Adam* would be a way to wake them up. It would also be a way for John and Reve to soothe their grief.

The filming was rolling on a rush schedule so it could make an October air date on NBC. Travanti and Williams were extremely sensitive to John and Reve, and admit to this day that they have never played such challenging roles. Travanti's shattering performance of John's breakdown in a New York hotel after learning of Adam's death is certainly one of the most haunting scenes ever seen in a TV movie.

The movie would also motivate the principals to be committed to the plight of victims and missing children. All the actors continue to make fund-raising appearances for the Adam Walsh Centers, and Otto founded her own outreach center, Find the Children.

On the night of October 10, 1983, *Adam* premiered across the United States. It was a difficult night for the Walsh family, but they had also won another battle. Prior to the telecast, Otto and John had lobbied NBC to show the photos of missing children with a hotline number, in hopes that some might be recovered. The network's reaction was mixed. Privately, some did not want to give up two minutes of advertising/promotion spots to a public service announcement. The movie would be enough to promote the cause. Others were afraid of the legal problems it could cause, especially in cases involving parental kidnapping. A toll-free hotline was against network policy, and would start a precedent for every cause-type film, others argued. Grant Tinker, then NBC's chief, vetoed them all—the photos and number would run. As a result, 13 missing children were recovered after that first broadcast.

The movie did capture the country's attention. It won the ratings race that night, being one of the only TV movies to beat ABC's "Monday Night Football." It would be nominated for several Emmys, including best teleplay for Allan Leicht. Today, many video stores offer the film as a free rental to help promote child safety.

Adam would be repeated twice more, on April 3, 1984, and April 29, 1985, with roll calls. Out of more than 200 shown, 65 children were recovered as a result of the three airings and the film's sequel, *Adam: His Song Continues*, broadcast on September 29, 1986. Again, the film called more attention to the plight of missing children, and put more demands on John's time—away from the business.

As dramatized in the sequel film, John decided to leave the hotel business and devote his full-time energies to lobbying for missing children legislation. It was a painful decision, since he had devoted ten years of hard work to become a full partner in a multimillion-dollar operation. But he really "didn't give a damn" about the hotel business—children were his priority now. And he was going to make America safe for them. He and Reve had another surprise, meanwhile. She was pregnant with their third child.

In 1984, Walsh helped pass another child protection law, the Missing Children's Assistance Act, providing funding for the National Center for Missing and Exploited Children. It created a toll-free hotline (1-800-THE-LOST) for parents to get assistance by having the names of their missing youngsters entered in the NCIC and photographs distributed nationally. Walsh agreed to become a consultant to the center and the Department of Justice. Among his successful efforts was putting the photos of individual missing children on milk cartons, grocery bags, and direct-mail advertisements.

For three years, Walsh was one of five civilian advisors to the VI-CAP (Violent Criminals Apprehension Program) Task Force, which established a network among investigators to track and trap serial killers. Among the others serving on the panel was Ann Rule, author of the best-selling book *Stranger Beside Me* about mass murderer Ted Bundy. The effort also helped him mend fences with the FBI and other federal law enforcement agencies, which Walsh had previously criticized.

Just after the first airing of *Adam*, John and Reve had another shock which reopened their wounds. A serial killer named Ottis Elwood Toole confessed to Adam's murder. The media had a field day with the story, even camping out on the Walshes' doorstep for a comment on "their feelings." Originally, Florida authorities believed Toole, 36, who was already convicted on several other murders and was sentenced to life in state prison. Despite the possibility that he could have been trying to capitalize on the publicity surrounding the TV film, detectives thought he knew too much about the murder to be lying. He had also previously confessed to a cell neighbor about the killing. Toole later recanted, then reconfessed and recanted. Both Walsh and Florida officials now discount his possible connection with Adam's death. The mystery remains unsolved; his killer unpunished.

"We may never know who killed our beautiful little boy," Walsh said at a press conference after Toole's original confession. "We still grieve. But there are things that we can do to stop people who kill children and teach our children what to do."

But Walsh's work was not without criticism. Critics complained that the photographs of missing children scared youngsters, and made parents overprotective. Others challenged the estimates given for the number of America's missing children, some 1.5 million annually, as overinflated. (Nearly 2,000 unidentified bodies of children are buried each year in the United States, Walsh says.) Some local and federal law enforcement officials still didn't like this pesty father of a murdered child telling them how to run their offices. Some lawmakers resented him coming into *their* states to change *their* laws.

In addition to fighting for federal laws, Walsh took his agenda to the states, which he considers "fifty feudal kingdoms" with their own set of priorities and traditions. First, he won in his home state of Florida, which was the first to set up a statewide clearinghouse for missing children. Next, he moved on to California, New York, Illinois, South Carolina, Ohio, where significant child protection laws were passed over the next several years. He has been interviewed by nearly every major newspaper and magazine in the country, and been a regular guest on every network and syndicated news and talk program. In constant demand as a speaker, Walsh has keynoted numerous national conventions for labor unions, law enforcement groups, and private organizations.

To date, Walsh has testified 17 times before congressional committees, and before lawmakers in every state but Hawaii, North Dakota, and South Dakota. There are relatively few governors, senators, and congressmen he hasn't met. Over the years, he met with President Reagan five times in the Oval Office (on one visit Meghan got jellybeans) and participated in cabinet meetings about children's issues. Though his efforts have resulted in two federal laws and hundreds of state statutes, he and Reve celebrate still every new law with a champagne toast. Yet there is still work to be done.

"The children are the silent, helpless majority with no power, no vote, no platform, and no money to provide for their needs," Walsh said in a full-page ad in *USA Today* to promote *Adam: His Song Continues* (*USA Today*, September 29, 1966, p. C7).

"It is up to us, the adults, to provide not only for their needs, but also for their safety. They are the country's greatest resource and its future. They look to us for direction as we will look to them when they will determine our future."

With his experience in the TV industry from *Adam*, Walsh consulted on two more programs about missing children, HBO's "How to Raise a Street Smart Child" and PBS's "Parents' Greatest Fear." In both cases, Walsh points out, some company officials were hesitant to broadcast the shows, but both won critical acclaim, ratings success, and several awards. They are also often offered as free rentals in video stores.

Despite his successes on the road, Walsh's work was starting to take a toll on his family life. They were not living in the standard that his hotel partnership had afforded them. Reve and Meghan weren't comfortable living in a new city, Washington, D.C., away from their family and friends in Florida. They soon had another addition to the family, when Callaghan Drew was born in 1985. Their joy was nearly turned into tragedy, as he struggled through the first week of his life with a serious infection known as "wet lung."

Today, there are four branches of the Adam Walsh Child Resource Center in West Palm Beach, Florida; Orange County, California; Rochester, New York; and Columbia, South Carolina. The nonprofit centers depend entirely on private and corporate contributions, especially through fund-raising events hosted by Walsh throughout the year across the country. Three centers, in Boston, Cleveland, and Alexandria, Virginia, were closed for lack of funds. Among its significant corporate sponsors are Digital Equipment, Bristol-Myers, Advo-Systems, Mony Financial Services, Western Publishing, K-Mart, Product Moves, American Home Food Products, and Alloette.

The centers are a national organization dedicated to making America safer for children. Their aim is to prevent the abduction and molestation of children and to effect positive changes in the systems that serve children. As a primary source of information for parents, the centers provide safety tips for protecting children and give direct assistance to families of missing and exploited children.

As for legislation, the centers constantly monitor state statutes, particularly where outdated laws no longer serve the needs of today's families. It makes a set of ten model child protection statutes available to lawmakers upon request. In the area of education, the center, in cooperation with Digital, has developed a safety program called "Kids and Company: Together for Safety." Geared to children five to 12, the program uses games, songs, and puzzles and other interest-holding activities to teach them to be smart and aware, not antisocial. It can be used in schools, as well as any adult-led community group of children.

Walsh's work has earned him recognition from hundreds of state and national groups. Among his numerous awards are: 1982 "Man of the Year" National District Attorney's Association, 1984 "Outstanding Citizen Award" Association of Federal Investigators, National PTA's Lifetime Achievement Award, Presidential Advisor on Child Advocacy, 1986 American Legion's Commander's Public Relations Award, 1985 "Father of the Year" in the "Everyman's Father" category by the National Father's Day Committee, the 1988 U.S. Marshals "Citizen of the Year," and a plaque from the FBI in 1988 for outstanding service in the public interest. He was also named by *Esquire* magazine as a young American who is changing the country, and was included in the CBS American Portrait Series as one of 160

Americans who have made outstanding contributions throughout U.S. history

On the legislative front, Walsh continually battles for state laws to protect children and all innocent victims of crime. Among the priorities in his agenda are:

• Videotaping of children's testimonies instead of open court testimonies, especially in molestation and abduction cases, and protecting the privacy of child victims by not publishing their names in the media;
• Getting police agencies to communicate with each other in cases involving missing children, especially where there is suspicion that the child has been taken out of the local area;
• Increased criminal penalties and sentences for crimes against children;
• Strict, mandatory jail sentences for repeat offenders, especially convicted child molesters;
• Background and fingerprint checks for teachers, social workers, and child-care workers;
• Protect victims and witnesses from harassment during criminal investigations;
• Require officials to provide victims with a card informing them of their constitutional rights, somewhat similar to the Miranda rights read to suspects;
• Guarantee restitution to victims, including giving them any profits a criminal may earn by selling movie, television, or book rights to his/her story.

Though Walsh is best known for his work with missing children, he has also been a staunch advocate for victims' rights. In talking to victims of crime and their families, most feel abandoned by the system. Victims and relatives of victims often write letters to judges and parole boards only to be ignored when repeat offenders are released or given leniency in sentencing. Only within the last few years have victims or their relatives been allowed to testify at parole board hearings.

Today's criminal justice system is in chaos. The only order is on sterile library shelves of cases and statutes. Among the lowest priority is the victim, as in case after case, the system has placed more emphasis on the rights of the accused than the person injured. Too often, the more violent the crime, the more a defendant's rights are protected, in contrast to the needs of the victim.

The system's concern for the victims often varies between jurisdictions. Some states have victims' rights statutes, while others ignore them. The needs of victims linger on for years, and have a devastating effect on everyone close to a case, including law enforcement officers, counselors, and doctors. All too often, the system is more concerned with the rehabilitation of the criminal, or the attempt at that sometimes impossible endeavor, than the victim's prolonged need for fairness and retribution.

Just because there is strong evidence in a case does not guarantee a conviction. As reported in *Time* magazine (August 14, 1989, p. 61), people get away with murder in about 30 percent of the 20,000 homicide deaths in this country each year, while others go undetected due to foul-ups in the investigation and evidence procedures. So in cases where no one has been brought to trial, victims will often pursue cases for years, having solid evidence but getting no justice.

All types of criminals, from car thiefs to murderers, get released after serving a fraction of their sentences, even if authorities suspect he/she will commit another crime after being paroled. For example, the average time served for first-degree murder in this country is seven years.

Some other examples of recent horrible crimes, and the amount of time those convicted served:

• Lawrence Singleton, convicted of raping a 15-year-old girl and hacking off her forearms with an ax, was slated to be released in 1987, after serving only 6½ years. His victim was maimed for life. Public opposition was so strong that Singleton had to be housed in a trailer on the San Quentin Prison grounds, before being released and kept in hiding.

• Kenneth Parnell served only five years of an eight-year sentence for kidnapping and repeatedly molesting Steven Stayner. He locked the youngster up in his house and subjected him to unspeakable sexual abuse for seven years, yet served two less for his crimes. Stayner was killed in a motorcycle accident last September at age 24, and his family and friends said he never fully recovered from his ordeal. Parnell is alive and free.

• Charles Rothenberg poured kerosene over his son, David, and set him afire in a Buena Park, California, motel room in 1983. He is expected to be released this year, having served only seven years for his heinous crime. His son, who miraculously survived, will be disfigured for life, though he has demonstrated incredible courage in his struggle to be a normal youngster.

• A New Jersey court sentenced Stephen Randall Dye to a 10-year maximum sentence for attempting to kill John Mikrut by shooting him twice in the head, as featured on "America's Most Wanted" last year. It took Mikrut nearly three years to trust anyone as a friend or go back to work on construction sites. Dye might only serve a few years more than that for his crime. Televangelist Jim Bakker got 45 years for his crimes, which didn't involve murder.

What has being the host of "America's Most Wanted" done for Walsh and his crusade?

The show's weekly production schedule puts demands on time he would rather be spending with his family or on his agenda. He often spends two weeks on the road without a day home. But being the spokesman of a national show also has benefits for a children's lobbyist.

It has helped him "an awful lot," especially when addressing legislatures or law enforcement groups. When making appearances to promote Fox and AMW, Walsh can spend half the session speaking about the show, then devote the rest to children's issues. It is also a great forum to give him "a higher profile" to convince lawmakers that child protection and victims' rights laws are important. Before he was known as the father of a murdered child, and now he is the host of a national crimefighting television show, which makes news every week with its captures.

One criticism Walsh has voiced about the American law enforcement community is its inability to communicate and forget petty rivalries. Working as the host of AMW, Walsh has been pleased to foster cooperation between jurisdictions on several cases. On several nights, he has watched federal agents and state or local police meet together for the first time, though they have both been looking for the same fugitive.

As for his personal quest for justice for Adam's death, Walsh has never wanted to get an Uzi and hunt down his son's killer. That would never bring him back, which is what he constantly tells vengeful parents. Being the host of AMW has helped him mentally and emotionally deal with his continuing grief without being a vigilante. For the past seven years, Walsh has suffered with the agony of seeing thousands of other children raped and murdered, but never being able to do anything to help catch and punish the criminals involved. AMW gives him that opportunity—as long as the system will keep repeat offenders off the streets once they are caught.

With "America's Most Wanted" Walsh can see "concrete results" of his work. For seven years he has tried to make Americans aware of the level of violence in this country. Now he gets letters from viewers saying, "I didn't know that could happen in those little towns. What can I do about it?"

On the negative side, hosting the show takes more of Walsh's precious time with his family. It is also emotionally draining to get the kinds of letters he does from victims, begging the show to take their story, find their missing loved one, or help them get justice. If the stories do not meet AMW's criteria, all he can do is write back some words of condolence. For example, one 10-year-old girl wrote him about a neighbor who was stabbed 22 times, and she was a witness to the crime. Yet with no clear suspect, the show couldn't accept the case.

During his two years with AMW, Walsh has been able to suggest cases and offer direction to Linder and the show staff, based on his own experiences as an advocate and a victim. He is especially concerned about child abductors and molesters, exploiters of women and children, and serial killers. When victims contact the show, he can often offer advice and comfort. For example, when Jim Kilroy was desperately searching for his son Mark, Walsh urged

Linder to take the case to pressure the Mexican authorities to find him. The show's exposure of the case did put the pressure on, though Mark was later found dead. The show also tried to cover the case of a missing Arizona girl, but arrived there the day the girl's body was found. Walsh understands the grief these parents feel, yet points out that many other parents will never know what happened to their missing son or daughter.

There have been times when the show has been able to help victims, such as John Mikrut, Patsy Patrick, or Steve and Claire Berstein. In those cases, and many others of people who are just comforted, Walsh finds satisfaction.

One Sunday night a woman called the show, saying she was the wife of one of the police officers killed by a fugitive caught by AMW. Dorothy Eilers Seiles just wanted to say "thank you" to Walsh and AMW, for helping catch Wilson Lee Brook. He had escaped from a Wisconsin prison where he was serving a life sentence for the 1962 murder, and was captured by AMW viewer tips on September 13, 1989, in Las Vegas. Brook told FBI agents that he had seen himself profiled twice on the show.

As a victim himself, Walsh is concerned about what it does for them. Justice is resolution. It might not bring a loved one back, but many times a capture is a resolution, a final chapter of a horrible event. It doesn't end the pain, but it puts some closure on it.

"Maybe those people won't lapse into suicide or alcoholism or divorce, like so many people I've seen drunk and on the verge of divorce," he said. "When I meet those people and they say, 'He's captured; my life can go on,' there's nothing like it! There's nothing that can compare to that kind of satisfaction."

With the show's popularity, Walsh receives some 60 speaking requests a month, ranging from major conventions to local organizations. Considering the AMW taping schedule and his Adam Walsh appearances and lobbying (scheduled a year in advance), there isn't much time for such engagements. Thus, most must be politely, and graciously, turned down.

How does he handle being a celebrity—requests for autographs, photographs, and swooning females? As for the latter, he's an extremely happily married man with two children. For the former, it makes him uncomfortable as a person. But if it calls attention to missing children and might make people want to make a difference, okay.

"I don't look at myself as a celebrity in any means," Walsh said. "I don't think that the average person thinks of me in that way either. But there are a few who in a frenzy ask me to autograph their arm. Others say we watch your show, we think you make a difference, or is there something I can do, and that's important to me.

"Adam was the victim and I'm the father of a murdered child," said Walsh, who carries his dead son's picture and frequently has his moments of grief alone.

"I'm still battling back and this is a great forum for me and for my mental stability. Yet I've seen so many victims and it still tears me apart. It destroyed our lives, but we've tried to rebuild."

Though some people will make "unusual" requests, Walsh tries to have time for everyone, as long as they're respectful and sincere. It's difficult to cut someone off, especially when you've got a plane to catch, he says, since you've got to give people their moment. Many times they've come a long way for it, especially the victims.

"One of the hardest things for me is to talk to the victims, because I've walked in their shoes," Walsh explained. "I know their hurt; I know their anguish. I know there isn't a whole lot I can do for them, even if they perceive I can. But if it helps them to talk, then fine."

Sometimes the media can ask some "weird" questions. Some ask why Walsh doesn't drive a Rolls-Royce, or live in a Hollywood mansion. Others inquire about how many marriage proposals he gets or how many women ask for photos with his shirt off. Walsh is a very private person and has never sought out celebrity status. So he often bristles at reporters who constantly question his motives. They just don't believe that he didn't dream of being in the entertainment business, and doesn't intend to seek political office.

The only time he calls a press conference is to push a children's bill or to call attention to an injustice. Yet some members of the media still can't accept that he's an honest man. In 1984, when a Florida TV critic was asked if he wished to interview Walsh in connection with the second rebroadcast of *Adam*, he said, "No thanks, John Walsh is pretty much available all the time. He loves the limelight."

Yet Walsh understands the workings of the media, and how individual personalities can affect a story.

"The public doesn't understand that critics are made to critique, to criticize. And when something's topical, and something's new, there will always be that critic who wants to get his/her byline out there, or wants to write the most controversial article to raise his/her own status. Sometimes there's a hidden agenda. Some criticism of the show is good, others are biased. But it's a person's opinion and the critic is entitled to it."

Despite the criticisms from the show's detractors, and the pressure of being a celebrity, Walsh knows the show is worth the effort when he gets letters like these:

> I really want to let you know that I do enjoy watching your program. Watching those criminals go behind bars is a great job well done by yourself and the viewers. I really do want you to know that God is surely on your side. Please keep up the great work, and I will always watch "America's Most Wanted." God bless you and your family, S.O., Galeta, California.

> My name is M.G. (withheld). I'm writing you to improve my grammar. I like your show "America's Most Wanted." My teacher saw the movie *Adam* and has told us about it. I sort of wish he hadn't of. I'm sorry about what happened. Sincerely, M.G., Cleveland, Ohio. Age 10.

> I am writing to let you know how much I enjoy your program. I feel that your program makes all of America more aware of the crimes that are being committed every day. One big reason I enjoy your program is that it shows that all violent crimes are not committed by black males. Being a black male and a former social worker, I got the impression that most Americans think violent crimes are committed by black males only. I am glad to see your program will show anyone who is wanted, no matter what the color of their skin is or age, or what crime they committed. Keep up the good work, and good luck on catching the wanted. Sincerely, L.W., Fresno, California.

> I cannot express the feelings that came over me the week when the four-year-old Candy (Talarico) was found, safe and sound. I could not hold back

the tears of joy. I think about your son, Adam. My two girls, Sarah, 5, and Beth, 6, both talk about Adam, your work with lost children, and "America's Most Wanted." Well, thank you isn't enough. I know it's touching millions because if it didn't those animals captured would still be out on the streets. Keep up the good work. L.F., Buffalo, New York.

After watching your show for a year now and other shows that have appeared about solving crimes, I decided to write an article based upon the impressions the local authorities have of national crime shows. You will be happy to know that everyone I interviewed was most impressed with national shows that attempt to locate fugitives—so much so that many local law enforcement agencies in the metro Atlanta area are putting on shows of their own to capture local fugitives...You have proven that one person can make a difference—and I wish you and yours much joy and fulfillment. Out of tragedy has come much action—and positive results....I am glad to see that television, which is cluttered with so much junk, has finally come up with a truly worthwhile program as "America's Most Wanted." Sincerely, C.D., Atlanta, Georgia.

I saw on TV how your son died and I am sorry you lost your son Adam. I know you will always feel love for Adam. You are doing real good on your job finding all the bad criminals and having them all put back in jail. I don't even know you, and you are well accepted off your show, but I think you are nice and polite too. Thank you for listening to my letter. Your best friend, T.S.G., Denver, Colorado.

How nice of you. I am delighted to have your picture—you are a sweet man. I hope your mother is alive and caring that you are trying to make a difference. Anyway, I am a 69-year-old mother, and I am PROUD to have even this slight contact with you. John, you can really count for something important. It is a wonderful example—yours—for young and old, for people touched by tragedy and the lucky ones, unscathed so far. You show us genuine concern for our "fellow travelers" and a way to do something. Have you noticed what a trend you've started with all the TV unsolved crimes shows? Be proud! Always, best wishes, J.B.L., Austin, Texas.

I applaud you and your wife for your forthrightness, for your strength, for taking Adam's murder and making it speak to the most heinous crime in our society today. I'm grateful that your dedication to your son's memory has reached out to so many who might have fallen by the wayside otherwise. There is no more precious gift than life, and no more marvelous gift than a child in which to place it. . . . Thank you for setting the positive example you do, and for expressing courage when it would be far easier to do nothing. In Him, M. & C.C., Decatur, Illinois.

I would like to thank you for the great job you are doing on "America's Most Wanted." This is a program that I watch every week. I wish it would be on longer. Don't let what Mr. (David James) Roberts said tonight stop you. You don't convict them. If they can't do the time, they shouldn't do the crime. Please keep up the great job. Thanks again to you and the others. God bless each one of you. Mrs. B.H., Alburtis, Pennsylvania.

I had the pleasure of meeting you in 1984 in Charlotte, N.C., at a seminar on child abuse. My son, Trey, and I sat in the front row and had an opportunity to speak with you during the other presentations. We admired your courage and strength then and we still do...Thank you, B. and J.P., Charlotte, North Carolina.

I am 14 years old and watch "America's Most Wanted" every Sunday night. I'm really glad you made up the show. It makes me more aware of things. I think you are such a great person for going in front of millions of people and saying things about missing children. I know when the police find other people's children, I know you are happy. You must wonder why didn't they find Adam in time? I just wanted to tell you that you are the most courageous person I can think of. Well, I just wanted you to know and other people with missing children that someone out there really cares. Your friend, S.A., Phoenix, Arizona.

And just how can a person make a difference, according to John Walsh, a man whom people say has tried to do just that?

He offers a few suggestions:

• Register and vote—yours does count. Find out who your legislators are, then write and call them to find out how they stand on crime, and the rights of victims, women, and children.
• Be aware of the criminal justice system and how it can affect you if you are the victim of a crime.

Make sure you understand your rights as an individual.
• If you are a parent, be aware of the problems and dangers facing children. Make them safety conscious, which can be done without scaring them.
• Volunteerism is not dead. Find a local group, especially one dedicated to children, and especially ones without parents. Give a few hours of your time—you'll be amazed at the results and how good it will make you feel.

Since his son's murder, John Walsh has always believed that one person could make a difference. For years, he was struggling for legislation to help children and victims. "America's Most Wanted" has made a "tremendous" difference in his quest for justice. It is an asset for law enforcement, but it needs the American public to be aware of the impact crime and violence can have on their lives.

Certain show segments have destroyed Walsh emotionally, and certain ones have passion for him. But most important for him, "America's Most Wanted" has helped many helpless victims of crime find justice. And long after the show is just an item in the TV history books, those people will never forget.

The song of young Adam Walsh does continue. Every day it's sung by his father, his mother, his sister, and his brother—and millions they have touched, but will never meet.

14

||||||

TV Crimefighting: Past, Present, Future

European viewers have been helping catch fugitives for more than two decades, thanks to a brainstorm from West German producer Eduard Zimmerman.

Back in 1963, Zimmerman, a veteran police and crime reporter, was building a new house in a small village in West Germany. He paid for the house to be built, but when he was ready to move into his dream home, one thing was missing—the roof. The contractors pulled out their crafty contract, and the seasoned journalist realized that he hadn't been an informed consumer. He had been ripped off by some con artists.

Doing some research, Zimmerman uncovered other scams that had been defrauding the unwary for years. He developed a show titled "Vorsicht Falle," literally translated as "Attention: Trap." The show has been "immensely popular" for more than 25 years, saving consumers millions of marks.

The success of that show and his experience working with police led Zimmerman to produce another show, "Case XYZ: Unsolved," which debuted in 1967. He reconstructed the unsolved crimes in the same way that he showed consumer ripoffs on his other show. West German police agencies supported the idea from the beginning, and frequently suggest cases to the show. They also cooperate when the show calls them with a case they have uncovered from the media or other sources.

Zimmerman was the first to use reenactments in a crimefighting program, but he wasn't the first to produce a show in which police asked for help. For some 28 years, London Weekend Television has broadcast a weekly 20-minute program, "Police Five," in cooperation with Scotland Yard and London Police. The show appeals for the help of viewers in the cases described, but no reconstructions are used.

Zimmerman's show is produced in Munich, and broadcast at least once a month on West German station BZF, the largest station in Europe, the creator said. It is also seen by viewers in Austria and Switzerland. In 22 years, on more than 200 broadcasts, the show has presented some 1,788 cases, and takes credit for solving 734, or 41 percent. Each hour-long show features between 10 and 12 cases.

It is broadcast on Friday nights at 8:15, ten times a year, taking a month off in the summer and March. That day and time period is considered the best for European TV viewing, Zimmerman said. He not only created the show, but he also serves as producer and "narrator." In 1970, he wrote a book about his experiences and the creation of the show.

A second, shorter "update" broadcast follows later in the night. In 15 to 20 minutes, viewers are told what has happened since the broadcast, whether cases have been solved or new clues have come in. Similar to AMW, the alleged crimes are reenacted by actors based on police information. The actor's full profile is never shown on camera to avoid viewers turning in the actors as fugitives. The show examines cases involving known fugitives as well as those in which there is no clear suspect. Viewers with tips either call the studio in Munich or the individual police agencies assigned to the case.

Though Zimmerman maintains he originated the idea, it has spread to several other countries since 1967.

"Crimewatch: UK," based in London, started five years ago from the BBC. The 45-minute show covers about 15 cases on its monthly live broadcast, usually the first Thursday of the month at 9:30 P.M., "when most children are in bed," according to the show's current producer Anne Morrison. It is followed by a 10-minute update later in the evening.

"Crimewatch" was brought to the BBC by a group that adapted it from Zimmerman's concept. It needed the cooperation of the UK's Association of Chief Police Officers, which quickly voted its approval. The show works closely with police all over the United Kingdom, but maintains editorial control, Morrison noted.

The show's crime reenactments are "tame" in comparison with those on AMW, the producer observed. Usually only three cases a show feature reconstructions, which take up only half of the program. There is no violence or close-ups of any weapons. Many cases are covered in less than a minute, using footage from video surveillance cameras, or in interviews with the investigators involved.

Once the "appeal" for information is made, "viewers immediately ring in." The show averages about 500 calls to its 20 studio lines, while police agencies get another 500 or so a broadcast.

In 52 programs (as of September 1989), there have been 52 broadcasts featuring just over 500 cases. There have been 215 arrests attributed to the show in its five-year history, Morrison said. "Crimewatch" concentrates on "serious crimes," such as murder, armed robbery, terrorism, and rape, but is very careful about "sensationalizing" the crimes with reconstructions. The show announces arrests and convictions in cases it has helped solve.

According to audience research data, the "chart" of people watching the program matches almost exactly the population of TV watchers in the United Kingdom.

In the Netherlands, "Opsporing Verzocht," translated best as "Wanted," has been a regular program since November 1982. Its creator, producer, and narrator, Will Simon, tried out the show twice in 1975, and twice in 1976, before convincing the country's police to cooperate. A TV journalist of some 28 years, Simon based his concept on the London and West German shows.

In its seven years on the air, the program has profiled 267 cases, and has helped solve more than 50 percent of them, and aided in many more not featured on the show (223 solved in all). "Wanted" uses "reconstructions," not reenactments, produced at the locations where the crimes occurred. Either police, witnesses, or the narrator tell the story, illustrated with weapons, evidence, and clues if necessary. The show is not allowed to use actual photographs of fugitives, only those taken during the actual committing of a crime, such as from video surveillance cameras. Any other images must come from artist composite sketches, not photographs of suspects.

"Wanted" is broadcast once every five weeks for 45 minutes, featuring up to 5 cases, depending on their complexity. Seen on AVRO Television, its broadcast night varies from year to year. Last year it was telecast on Thursdays at 9:30 P.M., while this year it is seen on Mondays at 10 P.M. The program usually gets up to 22 percent of the available audience, and has a high awareness level among Dutch TV viewers, Simon said.

"Australia's Most Wanted" had been in development for a year before AMW, and debuted in November 1988, produced by Grundy Television for the Seven Network, according to the show's executive producer Peter Pinne.

Based in Sydney, the show was created by Dennis Spencer, currently working for the Australian Broadcasting Commission. When Spencer was a network program manger, he did a 1984 special program on specific crimes out of Brisbane, and "it cleaned up in the ratings," Pinne explained. He decided to take the concept nationwide, and came to Seven Network with the idea.

The current hour format includes five unsolved crimes, and a section called "Case Closed," which shows police "in a good light" by highlighting exceptional police work in a particular case, not necessarily one featured on the show. It's broadcast every Sunday night at 7:30, in the most difficult slot in prime time, against the Australian version of "60 Minutes" and "Comedy Company," a local homegrown comedy show.

"We started showing unsolved crime for the whole hour, but then we found there was a certain negative aspect to that," Pinne said. "And so we wanted to put something positive, so we developed 'Case Closed.'"

There is also a "Wanted" portion, which features criminals who are wanted, tells their crimes, and shows their photographs, and a segment on missing persons. Segments are taped weeks before the broadcast, except for an update on cases solved taped two days before broadcast.

Ratings vary between states, but the show does win the ratings race in some. In 35 broadcasts (as of October 1989), the show had been responsible for solving 42 out of 150 cases, some by the end of the night.

Cases come either from police or the show's team of researchers. At any given time, there are three film crews operating in various locations around the country. One operates out of Sydney, another from Melbourne, while the third films the host's introductions. The show goes everywhere in the country, except the state of Tasmania, due to the traveling distance.

The show is hosted by Bryan Marshall, a British-born actor who has lived in Australia for the past ten years. No phone calls are taken in the studio, so the phone numbers of police agencies involved in each case are frequently shown on the screen during the show.

"He was popular but not a face that was widely known," Pinne said. "He has a good presence and good authority on the screen, that's why we went with him."

The public reaction to the show has been "very positive," Pinne said.

"It has a very high community awareness, and everyone you talk to thinks it's a worthwhile program," Pinne said. "We have gotten some flack because it's on at 7:30, which of course is a time that families are watching television, so there have been some complaints about violence. We would prefer the program to be on at a later time slot."

In addition to these three shows, there are similar crimefighting shows involving viewers in Austria, Hungary, New Zealand ("Crimewatch: New Zealand"), and South Africa.

* * *

The roots of national crimefighting shows begin with the Crime Stoppers program, founded by former Albuquerque police officer Greg MacAleese in 1976. Frustrated with growing crime in his community, MacAleese knew there were dozens of citizens with helpful information, but they were afraid or unwilling to come forward.

Supported by Albuquerque police chief Bob Stover, MacAleese founded the first chapter of Crime Stoppers, which offered both cash rewards and anonymity to callers. The first "Crime of the Week" reenactment was broadcast on station KOAT-TV on September 8, 1976, featuring the murder of a 19-year-old gas station attendant, Michael Carman, during a holdup. Thanks to a tip, two suspects were arrested. Both were convicted of six counts of armed robbery, and one was convicted of the murder.

Crime Stoppers International has grown to over 700 programs worldwide. In 12 years, it claims more than 182,000 crimes solved, over a billion dollars in drugs and stolen property seized, and a 96 percent conviction rate in more than 39,000 suspects tried.

With the local success of Crime Stoppers, network executives and producers were struggling to develop a workable national show. Another local show in Los Angeles called "WeTip," had been doing well for ten years. ABC tried, but failed, in May 1982, with four hour-long episodes of "Counterattack: Crime in America," hosted by George Kennedy.

"Basically, it seemed like the right time, but obviously it wasn't," the show's producer Robert Guenette explained.

In 1982, ABC was trying to put something against CBS's "60 Minutes," and Guenette was developing some possible pilots. Among them was "Ripley's Believe It or Not," which later had a successful network run.

"'Ripley's' beat this one ('Counterattack') out, and I would have preferred that this one go instead of 'Ripley's' because it had a bigger piece of it," said Guenette, who had been brought in by Quinn Martin Productions to develop the idea.

"I think the big reason why it didn't happen was timing," he said. Crime was up at the time, and I think it's down now so it's not so urgent. I think it struck a fearsome cord. I think it terrified people, as opposed to making them think that they could take control of it. Two, there's something abhorrent in the American system about a national snitch line. Calling your local police was something different than calling someone independent.

"It was very current, everybody was talking about shows like that, because of the success of the local shows."

The hour show featured four cases on each of its four Sunday night broadcasts from May 2 to May 23, from 7–8 P.M. Reenactments, sometimes with the actual participants, were shot on location where the alleged crimes occurred. On the fourth show, "Counterattack" featured a "happy ending" case, in which citizen participation led to the catching of the criminal. The show had a national hotline, in cooperation with "WeTip." Kennedy was chosen for the host because of his "very authoritative and strong presence," the producer stated.

Among its cases were the "Catch Me Killer" in St. Paul, Minnesota, and the "Rotten Tooth .45-caliber Thief" on Long Island, New York. The show didn't solve any cases, though Guenette said the network claimed responsibility in one case involving the murder of a Cleveland woman.

Before "Counterattack," Guenette had extensive experience with the reenactment formula by creating historic events. They were shot "newsreel" camera style as if they existed at the time being studied. One piece on the plot against Adolf Hitler was so good that the press couldn't tell if it was real or re-created. The producer has since seen some of his Hitler footage used as historic film.

There were other problems with producing "Counterattack" involving the ABC network.

"This was the first time I ever dealt with Program Practices (a network department), and the programming people really kept us on our toes," Guenette said. "Everything had to be out of a court transcript and we had to double and quadruple prove everything to them.

"We couldn't even show the faces of the actors," he said. "The program practices person on our show actually left the network to take a year off after ours because it was so exhausting."

(Linder only learned of the existence of "Counterattack" several months after the AMW premiere when he saw a segment on the sample reel of a prospective segment producer.)

NBC's "Unsolved Mysteries" first appeared as a single pilot episode on January 20, 1987 with Raymond Burr as the host. It also ran a series of seven specials with Karl Malden, followed by current host Robert Stack. Following the popularity of "America's Most Wanted," the show became a regular series in the 1988–89 season, ranking 16th nationally. It is produced by John Cosgrove and Terry Dunn Meurer.

In addition to some fugitive profiles in cooperation with law enforcement, "Unsolved Mysteries" primarily focuses on noncrime mysteries, such as disappearances, missing heirs, mysterious legends, lost loves, and amnesia. The toll-free hotline was added only after the show became a regular series. The show takes credit for helping solve close to 50 cases (as of December 1989), including noncrime mysteries, according to an NBC publicist.

Even NBC programming chief Brandon Tartikoff acknowledged the success of "America's Most Wanted" and its strength in Fox's Sunday night line-up.

During a press conference with the TCA last June, Tartikoff discussed the show, both seriously and in fun.

"I kidded with Barry (Diller) and said, 'You know if a scientist came along and developed something that could be put into the water system of America that could eliminate crime, he'd be dark on his two nights programming with 'COPS' and 'Most Wanted' and whatever.'

"That's kind of a generalization, but I do think the one thing positive that I can say beyond the acknowledgment that they have carved out a very consistent and well-selling demographic for them—they've become a factor particularly on Sunday nights—is that at least they are awake."

Later in his remarks, he added:

"But they are a factor, particularly from 8 to 9 because they have been taking out 16 to 17 share points. And I don't know how long that 'Most Wanted' program can run. But I know it has to be challenged because it's not going to go away, if we don't put some decent competition against it."

With its success, "America's Most Wanted" has become a national cultural phenomenon, coming up in daily conversation as the cure-all to one's problems. For example, in a Los Angeles deli, when a waitress complained that a customer had run out on a check, another patron quipped, "Call 'America's Most Wanted.'"

The show was featured in the comic strip "Shoe,"

as well as on the TV shows "Cheers," "Alf," and "Head of the Class," which revolved an entire episode around AMW. It has also been parodied on "Late Night with David Letterman," twice on "Saturday Night Live" (including "Iran's Most Wanted"), and on the Disney Channel's "The Mickey Mouse Club" as "America's Least Wanted." (John Walsh's own daughter informed him that he had been imitated on the Disney show.)

Success breeds imitation, especially in the entertainment industry. Since AMW premiered, as many as 18 similar shows, mostly for syndication, have been announced for development (*Los Angeles Times*, September 18, 1989). Among those making it on or close to air were "Crimewatch Tonight" with Ike Pappas, "Crimes of the Century," "Crimestoppers 800," "Missing: Reward," "Next: Lost and Found," and "Reunion."

On the local level, some Fox affiliates, including West Palm Beach, New York, Sacramento, Kansas City, and Denver, have developed their own "Most Wanted" shows in cooperation with local law enforcement. AMW has been copied by stations affiliated with other networks in Atlanta, Cleveland, Idaho, and Salt Lake City. (The host of the Salt Lake version even asked John Walsh to tape a promo spot during AMW's July location there. He graciously consented.)

Noting the success of AMW, Los Angeles County officials include photographs and descriptions of wanted criminals in a special bulletin to the county's 75,000 employees. At least one arrest has been attributed to the program so far. A similar bulletin is mailed to the 38,000 city workers by Los Angeles officials.

In the future, AMW viewers can expect the show

to continue its remote locations, such as its successful shows in San Francisco, Jacksonville (Illinois), Salt Lake City and Las Vegas in July, and New York and Chicago in November.

Being away from the "nerve center" can cause production problems sometimes.

For example, during the November 5 filming in Chicago, the crew was bouncing on the city's L train out of Quincy Station late Saturday afternoon, when the mobile phone rang. It was the Washington office calling to say a fugitive had been captured. The script had to be revised and a previous segment reshot.

The crew got off the train and boarded another one headed back into the Loop. The phone rang again—another report of a capture!

The show's ending, which had been taped Friday afternoon in downtown Chicago, had to be reshot. The sun was fading fast, and Linder and Kavanaugh had to catch a flight back to Washington to edit the show Sunday morning. With the production van's headlights shining on John Walsh in the twilight, the show was finished—with about a minute of sunlight left.

"America's Most Wanted" will also be going international, going to the scene of the crime all over the world. AMW plans to produce shows in cooperation with its international TV crimefighting show partners overseas during the coming year.

The show will also cover more breaking crimes, especially those which have paralyzed a community, state, or the nation, in fear. The show has been effective in producing segments on developing cases within a few days, such as the murder of DEA agent Everett Hatcher, the disappearance of Mark Kilroy, and the Singing Santa Claus bandit in Pennsylvania. It will also be looking at some cases of environmental crime and white collar criminals, such as some fugitives involved in the Savings and Loan scandals.

What has made "America's Most Wanted" a success, besides ratings, publicity, and captures?

"People watch for those timeless tales of man's inhumanity to man," Linder said. "But on a higher level, I think we're able to show people exactly what the criminal fugitive is all about—how relentless they are. We show how many criminals can't stop committing crimes despite their best efforts, and the best efforts of society.

"If we're able to wise up America and show them exactly what they're up against, we're going to be on the way to making some very positive changes in our system of law enforcement, and show the American people, as John Walsh says, how thin 'The Thin Blue Line' really is, and how it's going to take the cooperation of all of us to make a difference."

If he had it to do over again, Michael Linder admits he wouldn't "approach it with so much enthusiasm and optimism" as he originally did.

"None of us realized that it would be a 7-day, 24-hour operation," the executive producer said. "Or that a television production would become a police precinct in its own way."

The show handles a tremendous load of paperwork with fugitive files, viewer tips, and case followups. It takes about 150 people to put a broadcast on the air each week—from 30 staffers in D.C., 24 phone operators, dozens of actors, producers, technical staff, and FBC employees.

"If I were a producer trying to emulate 'America's Most Wanted,' I'd think twice before trying it," Linder said. "It's an extraordinary amount of hard work. And the techniques we use are still highly experimental. No movie company in its right mind, no TV network would make a movie of the week or launch any kind of dramatic television with as simplistic an approach as we did.

"There's a good reason for that. It's easy for a segment to turn out badly because we're operating without the big production company ammunition that goes into making a feature film.

"We hadn't figured out a lot of things: what kind of people in the TV community can direct a segment, what kind of cases can we do, what kinds of tips lead to the apprehension of a fugitive. There were a lot of things that we figured out only by experience and trial and error."

Their instincts proved correct.

Michael Linder continues as AMW's executive producer, while he develops other show ideas for Fox. With the success of "COPS," Stephen Chao has brought another hit to Fox from his programming laboratory. Following the death of WTTG station manager Betty Endicott, Tom Herwitz assumed her duties, while staying on top of the show's legal affairs. Still directing AMW on weekends, Glenn Weiss is also director of Joan Rivers's daytime show. When he's not hosting "America's Most Wanted," John Walsh is flying somewhere in the United States in his fight for the rights of victims and other innocent Americans, as one man trying to make a difference.

Appendix A
AMW's Captures and Convictions

Captures Resulting from Viewer Tips
As of January 1, 1990

Broadcasts: 96
Fugitives Profiled: 215
In Custody: 136
Directly from AMW Viewer Tips: 86

Fugitive:	*Profiled:*	*Captured:*
David James Roberts	*2/11/88*	*2/17/88*
Wanted for:	Prison escape, FBI Top Ten	
Prior Convictions:	Five murders, rape, arson, kidnap	
Capture location:	Staten Island, NY	

Current Status: Six life sentences and 10 years for escape (six in solitary), Indiana State Prison, Michigan City.

Donald B. Adams, Jr.   *3/13/88*   *3/16/88*

Wanted for: Erroneous prison release
Prior Convictions: Rape, armed robbery
Capture Location: East Boston, MA
Current Status: Serving original sentence plus 10 years escape, MCI, Cedar Junction.

Paul Steven Mack   *3/20/88*   *3/22/88*

Wanted for: Warrant for murder
Capture Location: Murray, UT
Current Status: Awaiting trial in Sacramento, CA; charges pending for murder in Ohio.

Karl Dunstrom   *3/13/88*   *4/9/88*

Wanted for: Assassination of five members of a crack gang in Landover, MD
Capture Location: Brooklyn, NY
Current Status: Sentenced and serving five life terms without parole in Maryland.

Kirkton Bruce
(Unidentified
Suspect)

3/13/88   4/15/88

Wanted for: Same as Dunstrom
Capture Location: New York City
Current status: Bruce sentenced to five
                       death penalties plus 120
                       years in Baltimore;
                       subject to positive ID,
                       suspect awaiting
                       extradition from New
                       York and Maryland trial.

**Curtis Ray
Morgan**

3/6/88   4/21/88

Wanted for: Murder in Sun Valley,
                       CA
Capture Location: St. Petersburg, FL
Current Status: Trial pending for 2/90,
                       being held at Los
                       Angeles County Jail.

**James Charles
Stark**

4/24/88   4/25/88
(promo)

Wanted for: Murder, kidnap, rape
Prior Convictions: Three-time convicted sex
                       offender
Capture Location: Ann Arbor, MI
Current Status: Extradited from
                       Michigan, awaiting trial
                       in separate cases in
                       Banning and Hemet, CA

Mark Goodman	*5/16/88*	*5/17/88*

Wanted for:	Escape, bank robbery, U.S. Marshals 15 Most Wanted
Prior Convictions:	Burglaries, escapes
Capture Location:	Jupiter, FL (in jail in West Palm Beach at time of broadcast)
Current Status:	Pleaded guilty and serving 35 years for bank robberies, 5 for escape, in federal prison in Lompoc, CA

Stephen Randall Dye	*5/8/88*	*5/20/88*

Wanted for:	Murder and attempted murder
Surrender Location:	San Diego, CA
Current Status:	Sentenced to 10 years maximum in New Jersey, murder case pending in Ohio.

William Joseph Walker	*5/15/88*	*5/20/88*

Wanted for:	Armed robbery
Capture Location:	Detroit, MI
Current Status:	Trial pending in Circuit Court of St. Charles County, being held in St. Peter's, MO

Jack Farmer   *5/29/88*   *5/30/88*

Wanted for: Murder, extortion,
                         narcotics
Capture Location: West Palm Beach, FL
Current Status: Sentenced to 40 years in
                         federal prison system;
                         Judge James Holderman
                         strongly urged that he
                         serve the full term.

(Farmer was captured the day after FBI Director
William Sessions announced on AMW his addition
to the FBI's Top Ten Fugitives.)

Denice Delyle   *6/19/88*   *6/29/88*
Stumpner

Wanted for: Murder accomplice,
                         Green Bay, WI
Capture Location: Golden, CO
Current Status: Convicted and serving 50
                         years in Wisconsin State
                         Prison.

Ronald Jenkins   *6/26/88*   *7/1/88*
Bridgett Green

Wanted for: Jenkins for murder;
                         Green for accomplice to
                         murder in Atlanta, GA
Capture Location: St. Louis, MO
Current Status: Jenkins convicted and
                         serving life sentence in
                         Georgia State Prison;
                         Green acquitted.

Robert Wayne Fisher	_7/17/88_	_7/17/88_

Wanted for:
Capture Location:
Current Status:

Murder, Lake Charles, LA
El Centro, CA
Convicted of second-degree murder, sentenced to life without possibility of parole, computation of sentence or pardon, serving at Louisana State Prison, Angola.

Kevin Kelly Kenneth Shannon	_8/14/88_	_8/15/88_

Wanted for:

Surrender Location:
Current Status:

Murder, attempted murder, racketeering
Manhattan, NY
Kelly convicted in Manhattan federal court on 11/16/89, sentencing slated for 2/7/90; Shannon pleaded guilty and sentenced to 20 years.

Leroy Carter	_4/3/88 & 8/21/88 (By pre-broadcast promos)_	_8/18/88_

Wanted for:
Capture Location:

Fraud, con artist
Harlem, NY

Current Status:
: Sentenced to 3.5 to 7 years in the New York State prison system in 6/89, ordered to make half-restitution in con case involving $12,000; cases also pending in New Jersey, Georgia, and Chicago.

Gregory Scarpa
: *3/6/88 &   8/29/88*
  8/24/88

Wanted for:
: Racketeering
Capture Location:
: Lakewood, NJ
Current Status:
: Convicted on six counts, sentenced, and now serving 20 years.

Joseph Kindler
: *4/14/88 &   9/6/88*
  9/4/88

Wanted for:
: Escape
Prior Convictions:
: Murder in Philadelphia, PA
Capture Location:
: St. John's, New Brunswick, Canada
Current Status:
: Fighting extradition to Pennsylvania, where he faces the death penalty; case before Canada's Supreme Court.

James Ray Renton
: *8/21/88   9/6/88*

Wanted for:
: Prison escape, Arkansas
Prior Convictions:
: Murder of a police officer

Capture Location:	Austin, TX	
Current Status:	Returned to maximum security unit at Arkansas State Prison to serve original life sentence without parole plus four years for escape.	

Terry Lee Johnson *6/12/88* *9/8/88*

Wanted for: Prison escape, FBI Top Ten
Prior Convictions: Murder
Capture Location: San Diego, CA
Current Status: Returned to state prison in Huntsville, AL to serve original life sentence plus ten years for escape.

Frederick Merrill *7/10/88* *9/22/88*

Wanted for: Prison escape, while awaiting trial on assault charges
Prior Convictions: Escape, auto theft, burglary
Capture Location: New Brunswick, Canada
Current Status: On trial for escape and burglary charges in Canada; subject to extradition to Connecticut to face charges.

Lesley Wesley Barnes   *9/18/88*   *9/25/88*

Wanted for:
:   Murder, escape from Florida prison
Prior Convictions:
:   Attempted murder
Capture Location:
:   San Antonio, TX
Current Status:
:   Pleaded guilty to two counts of murder and sentenced to life in prison, received 40 years on additional counts; returned to Texas for 40 years for attempted capital murder of police officers.

Donald Bruce Parsons   *9/11/88*   *10/21/88*

Wanted for:
:   Child molestation
Prior Convictions:
:   Twice convicted sex offender
Capture Location:
:   Phoenix, AZ
Current Status:
:   Pleaded guilty, sentenced and serving 36 years in Colorado State Prison.

Kirkton Moore Raylene Brooks   *10/23/88*   *10/27/88*

Wanted for:
:   Moore for murder; Brooks for accessory to murder of Los Angeles police officer
Surrender Location:
:   Los Angeles, CA

Current Status:

Trials pending; Moore
being held in L.A.
County Jail, Brooks in
juvenile hall.

Richard Yoshino   *10/30/88   11/6/88*

Wanted for:

Prison escape from
Hawaii

Prior Convictions: Murder
Capture Location: Gardena, CA
Current Status: Extradited to Hawaii
State Prison to serve
original life sentence;
escape trial pending.

Alvin Jackson   *11/6/88   11/7/88*

Wanted for:

Prison escape from
Baltimore while awaiting
trial on rape, burglary,
attempted murder, and
armed robbery

Capture Location: Daytona Beach, FL
Current Status: Sentenced and serving
two life terms and 20
years in Maryland State
Penitentiary.

James Malloy   *10/9/88   11/17/88*

Wanted for:

Forgery, theft in Atlanta,
GA

Capture Location: Tampa, FL
Current Status: Case pending.

Michael Cooper   *11/20/88   11/23/88*

Wanted for: Rape, robbery in
                               Portland, OR
Capture Location: New Westminster,
                               British Columbia
Current Status: Extradited to Oregon;
                               pleaded guilty to four
                               counts of first-degree
                               rape, sentenced to 120
                               years (60 years actual,
                               30 years minimum).

Steven Ray Stout   *11/27/88   12/8/88*

Wanted for: Two counts of murder in
                               Utah, FBI Top Ten
Capture Location: Gulfport, MS
Current Status: Pleaded guilty to capital
                               homicide and second-
                               degree homicide, serving
                               life in prison at Utah
                               State Prison in Draper.

William Hewlett   *7/10, 9/4, & 12/19/88*
Rebecca Hewlett   *12/18/88*

Wanted for: William for fraud, rape,
                               parole violation, and
                               questioning in murder,
                               U.S. Marshals 15 Most
                               Wanted; Rebecca for
                               fraud, 12/18 broadcast
                               only
Capture Location: Pearlington, MS

| Current Status: | William pleaded guilty to murder and Social Security fraud, sentenced to 60 years; Rebecca pleaded guilty to Social Security fraud and received 5 years probation. |

Harold Hummel   *12/18/88   12/22/88*

Wanted for:	Prison escape, armed bank robbery
Prior Convictions:	Paroled from three life sentences for murder; tried in absentia for assault and kidnap
Capture Location:	Syringa, ID
Current Status:	Convicted of escape and sentenced to 2.5 years and $4,038.23 in restitution for damage to jail; returned to Pima County, AZ, for 1/9/90 trial on armed robbery charges.

Stanley Faison   *12/4/88   12/24/88*

Wanted for:	Second-degree murder, assault, FBI Top Ten
Capture Location:	Detroit, MI
Current Status:	Convicted of second-degree murder and assault with intent to do

great bodily harm, sentenced to 55–90 years and 12 months in Michigan State Prison at Jackson.

Rudy "Mike" Blanusa   *1/22/89*   *1/23/89*

Wanted for: Murder, kidnapping in Modesto, CA
Capture Location: Burnaby, British Columbia
Current Status: Extradited to California; in Stanislaus County Jail, CA, awaiting trial.

Frederick Raskin   *10/30/88*   *2/1/89*

Wanted for: Murder in Augusta, GA
Capture Location: Tampa, FL
Current Status: Extradited to Georgia, awaiting trial in Augusta.

Gene Wasson   *2/12/89*   *2/13/89*

Wanted for: Murder in Sulphur, LA
Capture Location: Roselle, NJ
Current Status: Pleaded guilty to manslaughter, serving 21 years in Louisiana State Prison.

Darrell Lynn   *2/19/89*   *2/24/89*
Templeton

Wanted for: Kidnapping, assault, and
                         rape in Tucson, AZ
Capture Location: Miami, FL
Current Status: Pleaded guilty, sentenced
                         to two years and an
                         additional sentence for
                         parole violation.

Clarence   *3/12/89*   *3/14/89*
Swanigan

Wanted for: Murder in Chicago
Surrender Location: Chicago, IL
Current Status: Trial pending, being held
                         at Cook County Jail,
                         Chicago.

Vernon Earle   *1/29/89*   *3/17/89*

Wanted for: Prison escape, U.S.
                         Marshals Most Wanted
                         15
Prior Convictions: First-degree murder
Current Status: Returned to Lorton
                         federal prison in Virginia
                         to continue original 65-
                         year sentence; pleaded
                         guilty to homicide and
                         escape for an additional
                         20 years.

Ronnie Hill   *4/2/89*   *4/5/89*

Wanted for: Burglary, parole
                                 violations in Denver, CO
Prior Convictions: Sale of stolen property
Capture Location: Chula Vista, CA
Current Status: Pleaded guilty, sentenced
                                 to 32 years combined for
                                 counts from three
                                 jurisdictions, serving at
                                 Colorado State Prison.

Hector Fragoso   *4/16/89*   *4/21/89*

Wanted for: 12 murders in Mexico
Capture Location: Three Points, AZ
Current Status: Awaiting trial for
                                 narcotics charges in U.S.,
                                 subject to deportation to
                                 Mexico to face multiple
                                 murder charges.

Robert Charles   *11/6/88 &*   *4/25/89*
Witt   *3/5/89*

Wanted for: Prison escape,
                                 Portsmouth, VA, while
                                 awaiting trial for
                                 burglary
Capture Location: Albuquerque, NM
Current Status: Extradited, being held in
                                 Portsmouth, pending
                                 trial.

Michael Taylor	*4/9/89 &* *5/20/89* *5/7/89*
Wanted for:	Escape from Orange County, CA, jail, while awaiting trial on armed robbery
Capture Location:	Rapid City, SD
Current Status:	Extradited, being held in Orange County Jail, pending trial on armed robbery in 1/90.

Joshua Stone	*5/7/89* *5/27/89*
Wanted for:	Amnesia victim accused of murder
Identified:	By mother in North Carolina, and confirmed by police in Scottsdale, AZ
Current Status:	Awaiting trial in Maricopa County Jail, AZ.

John Emil List	*5/21/89* *6/1/89*
Wanted for:	Five counts of murder in Westfield, NJ, since 1971
Capture Location:	Midlothian, VA
Current Status:	Awaiting trial in spring 1990, being held at Union County Jail, NJ.

John D'Ambrosio	*12/4/88, &* *5/28/89*	*6/10/89*

Wanted for: RICO, drug charges
Capture Location: Palmyra, NJ
Current Status: Convicted and sentenced
                         to 50 years in federal
                         prison.

Mauricio "El Gato" Aldana	*6/4/89*	*6/15/89*

Wanted for: Murder in Los Angeles
Prior Convictions: Selling narcotics
Capture Location: Tijuana, Mexico
Current Status: Tried and convicted in
                         Mexico; sentenced to 20
                         years.

Charles Jordan	*12/4/88*	*6/15/89*

Wanted for: Conspiracy, narcotics,
                         former U.S. Customs
                         supervisor in Florida
Capture Location: Jackson, WY
Current Status: Trial pending, possible
                         plea expected.

Carl Burns Kimberly Edwards	*6/25/89*	*6/27/89*

Wanted for: Rape of a child in
                         Cleveland, OH
Capture Location: Fort Pierce, FL
Current Status: Pleaded guilty, sentenced
                         to three life terms for

child abuse and two
years on other charges.

Thomas "Possum" Dixon	2/26/89 & 7/2/89	7/5/89

Wanted for: Murder in Alabama
Capture Location: Alvin, TX
Current Status: Fighting extradition from
Texas, trial expected by
2/90.

Teddy Unterreiner	7/9/89	7/9/89

Wanted for: Molestation in Oakland,
CA, and molestation and
escape in Colorado
Capture Location: Recognized as inmate in
Vancouver Jail, British
Columbia
Current Status: Extradited, facing 20
felony counts, possible
guilty plea; led police to
additional child
molestation suspect.

Kelly Loyd	7/9/89	7/10/89

Wanted for: Pimping, pandering, and
running a house of
prostitution
Capture Location: Hartsville, SC
Current Status: Awaiting trial in San
Francisco.

Michael Lee Price   *7/23/89   7/24/89*

Wanted for: Parole violation,
                            suspected abductor in
                            Copperas Cove, TX
Capture Location: Rockport, TX
Current Status: Pleaded guilty, sentenced
                            to life term in Texas
                            penal system.

Kendall Quinn   *7/23/89   7/28/89*
Northern

Wanted for: Prison escape in Utah
Prior Convictions: Second-degree murder,
                            robbery
Capture Location: Vancouver, B.C.
Current Status: Extradited to continue
                            term of five years to life;
                            awaiting trial on escape
                            charge.

George Schleuder   *7/30/89   7/30/89*

Wanted for: Rape, attempted sodomy,
                            burglary, interstate flight
Prior Convictions: Burglary
Capture Location: Spokane, WA, already in
                            jail under alias for
                            malicious mischief and
                            theft
Current Status: Extradited; bound over
                            for trial in 3/90; being
                            held in Mendocino
                            County Jail, CA.

Steven Ray Allen　　2/19/89 &　　8/12/89
　　　　　　　　　　　　　7/2/89

Wanted for:　　　　　　Murder in Utah
Capture Location:　　　Porcupine Springs, ID
Current Status:　　　　Extradited; trial set for
　　　　　　　　　　　　2/26/90, continued from
　　　　　　　　　　　　12/89; being held in
　　　　　　　　　　　　Moah, UT.

Edwin Maldonado　　5/29/89　　　　8/23/89

Wanted for:　　　　　　Weapons violations
Capture Location:　　　New York City
Current Status:　　　　Being tried in New York
　　　　　　　　　　　　for federal weapons
　　　　　　　　　　　　charges, then in Texas
　　　　　　　　　　　　for more federal
　　　　　　　　　　　　violations, including
　　　　　　　　　　　　RICO.

Ray Warren　　　　10/9/88, &　　8/25/89
　　　　　　　　　　　　3/19/89

Wanted for:　　　　　　Murder in Billings, MT
Capture Location:　　　Phoenix, AZ
Current Status:　　　　Being held without bond
　　　　　　　　　　　　for pending trial in
　　　　　　　　　　　　Yellowstone County
　　　　　　　　　　　　Detention Center, MT.

Charles John　　　　5/7, 8/6,&　　8/24/89
Russ　　　　　　　　8/13/89

Wanted for:　　　　　　Fraud, grand theft in
　　　　　　　　　　　　San Diego, CA, and

prime suspect in wife's
slaying

Capture Location: Hollywood, FL
Current Status: Extradited; bound over
for trial on murder
charge possibly in 1/90.

**John Joseph
Frank**   *8/20/89*   *8/24/89*

Wanted for: Probation violation in
Orlando, FL, and
defrauding an innkeeper
Surrender Location: New York City
Current Status: Being tried in Orange
County, FL, then faces
charges in Miami.

**John Patrick
Eastlack**   *9/10/89*   *9/11/89*

Wanted for: Two counts of murder,
burglary, theft, arson,
escape in Tucson, AZ
Prior Convictions: Fraud involving stolen
credit cards
Capture Location: El Paso, TX
Current Status: Awaiting trial in Pima
County Jail.

Wilson Lee Brook   *2/5, 2/12, & 9/13/89
8/6/89*

Wanted for: Prison escape in
Wisconsin
Prior Convictions: 10 years for burglary,
felony possession of a

weapon, possession of stolen property, and life for first-degree murder of a police officer

Capture Location: Las Vegas, NV
Current Status: Pleaded guilty to escape and operating a vehicle without owner's permission; continuing life sentence plus additional consecutive sentences.

Alan Buck Jones, Jr.   *8/27/89*   *9/18/89*

Wanted for: Burglary in Columbia, SC
Capture Location: Ft. Lauderdale, FL
Current Status: Fighting extradition; being held in the Broward County Detention Center, Ft. Lauderdale; South Carolina authorities expect his return in 2/90 to face charges.

David William Polson   *9/10/89*   *9/20/89*

Wanted for: Murder in Las Vegas, NV; embezzlement and parole violation in California
Prior Convictions: Grand theft

Capture Location:	Killed in shoot-out with FBI agents and California Highway Patrol officers near Los Banos, CA.

Leroy Chasson
Kathleen Chasson

2/28, & 6/12/88, 4/23, & 8/13/89   *9/22/89*

Wanted for:	Leroy escaped from Walpole prison in Massachusetts while serving a life sentence for murder; Kathleen allegedly aided that escape
Capture Location:	Leroy killed in a shoot-out with FBI agents in Denver; Kathleen arrested later
Current Status:	Kathleen extradited, and facing charges.

John Brent
Johnson   *9/23/89*

Wanted for:	Burglary, rape, and murder in Oklahoma
Surrender Location:	Oklahoma City, OK (prior to broadcast when learned of AMW profile)
Current Status:	Preliminary hearing in 12/89, bound over for trial in Oklahoma County Jail.

Jerry Whittington	*3/5, 7/23, & 9/29/89*	
Diane Armstrong	*9/10/89*	

Wanted for:

Whittington for felony theft in four states, and Armstrong as his accomplice, in Louisiana

Capture Location: Dawson City, CA

Current Status: Pleaded guilty to interstate transport of stolen property, awaiting sentencing in El Paso County Jail, TX; Armstrong released on $250,000 bond prior to sentencing, having pleaded guilty to similar charges.

Pedro Estrada *2/21/88* *10/1/89*

Wanted for:

Seven counts of murder in New York City, FBI Top Ten

Capture Location: Harrisburg, PA

Current Status: Case pending.

Robert Urbaez *10/1/89* *10/1/89*

Wanted for:

Two counts of murder in Washington, DC

Surrender Location: San Diego, CA

Current Status: Extradited to DC; indicted by grand jury; being held in DC Jail pending trial.

James Henderson   *10/6/89*

Wanted for: Kidnap and assault on
                             former wife in an
                             Arizona desert
Surrender Location: Tucson, AZ (due to fear
                             of being profiled by
                             AMW)
Current Status: Awaiting trial in Pima
                             County Jail, AZ

Seymour   *10/22/89*   *10/22/89*
Pinckney

Wanted for: Murder, incest in
                             Paterson, NJ
Capture Location: Moon, VA
Current Status: Extradited; held in
                             Passaic County Jail, NJ,
                             pending trial.

Emilio Bravo   *10/30/89*   *11/22/89*

Wanted for: Prison escape in Miami
Prior Convictions: Murder
Capture Location: San Diego, CA
Current Status: Awaiting trial.

Steven Barnett   *10/8/89*   *10/27/89*

Wanted for: Murder, kidnapping in
                             San Diego, CA
Capture Location: Hermosillo, Mexico
Current Status: Awaiting trial in San
                             Diego.

Christopher Rambert   *10/15/89* *11/4/89*

Wanted for: Prison escape from Massachusetts

Prior Convictions: Rape, armed escape, armed robberies, and burglaries

Capture Location: West Covina, CA

Current Status: Extradited; back in maximum security facility at Walpole, MA; continuing nine life sentences and three 30- to 40-year sentences; charges pending for escape.

Samuel Earl Dillon   *11/5/89* *11/7/89*

Wanted for: Murder in Chicago, IL

Prior Convictions: Served two sentences for murder

Surrender Location: Chicago

Current Status: Charge dropped.

John Ray Bonds   *4/16/89* *11/18/89*

Wanted for: Aggravated murder in Ohio

Capture Location: Wickliffe, KY

Current Status: Extradited; being held in federal detention center in Milan, MI; being prosecuted on federal

weapons charges, then
for murder in Erie
County, OH.

Ernesto
Traslavania   *7/30/89*   *11/18/89*

Wanted for: Drug Smuggling, RICO
Capture Location: Mexico City, Mexico
Current Status: In federal custody
                               awaiting trial in Las
                               Vegas, possibly in 1/90.

Lee Nell Carter   *11/19/89*   *11/19/89*

Wanted for: Murder, attempted
                               murder in Mobile, AL,
                               FBI Top Ten
Capture Location: Detroit, MI
Current Status: Trial pending.

Preston Ronald   *9/24/89*   *11/27/89*
Jones

Wanted for: Prison escape in San
                               Diego
Prior Convictions: Burglary
Capture Location: Los Angeles, CA
Current Status: Trial pending.

Bradley Melvin   *12/17/89*   *12/18/89*
Hughes

Wanted for: In four states on counts
                               of theft, theft by
                               deception, grand larceny,
                               parole violations, false

	alarms, impersonating police
Prior Convictions:	False alarms
Capture Location:	Saco, ME
Current Status:	Pending, awaiting jurisdictional decisions.

• Portland fugitive Hien Tat Chu was to be profiled on December 11, 1988, but he was apprehended on December 7, four days before the broadcast, as a direct result of publicity surrounding his profile. Chu pleaded no contest to a murder charge and was sentenced to life in Oregon State Prison, also denied parental rights to his two children.

• Fernando Garcia, wanted for murder in Dallas, Texas, was to be profiled on July 31, 1988, but was captured on August 1, when a reader of *The Star* magazine recognized his photo in an AMW column. He was tried and found guilty of capital murder, and received the death penalty.

• The profile of previously arrested murder suspect Percy Harris resulted in two witnesses coming forward in the week of June 5, 1988.

Appendix B

John Walsh Interview with David James Roberts
Broadcast on AMW's First Anniversary Special
Sunday, April 25, 1989
Indiana State Prison, Michigan City

Walsh: Mr. Roberts, you were a fugitive from the fall of 1986 until 16 months later when you were captured. The pressure must have been tremendous. What was it like on a day-to-day basis?

Roberts: Well, the pressure at first was tremendous, you're correct about that. However, on a day-to-day basis, it really wasn't that great because I kept myself very busy.

Walsh: When you learned you were going to be profiled on "America's Most Wanted," what went through your mind?

Roberts: Immediately to flee the area. In fact, let me correct that. I did not know it was going to be "America's Most Wanted." I just knew several hours before the program was actually aired that I was going to be profiled.

Walsh: So then you decided that it was time to run?

Roberts: Oh, most assuredly.

Walsh: Without exception, everyone you worked with at the shelter said that you did fine work there. Were you trying to settle the score for the murders that you were convicted of?

Roberts: No, I had no score to settle. In fact, I believe had you done a little research on me, I'm quite sure you will find that the attitude I displayed while working for that program, in fact is the same attitude I've always displayed throughout my whole working history.

Walsh: I have to dispute that. Your record includes multiple counts of rape, the murders of four people, two of whom were children. You've demonstrated throughout most of your adult life that you cannot function in society by your record. What do you think society should do with someone like you?

Roberts: What society should do with people like me is to be sure that these people are actually guilty of the crimes that they are incarcerated for.

Walsh: Well, you've been convicted in each of those counts that we talked about.

Roberts: I most assuredly was. It took five jury trials, facing the electric chair, for me to be convicted of that. I am quite sure, Mr. Walsh, that I could take you and subject you to five jury trials. I'm quite sure that we could convict you of something, all right?

Walsh: You're serving six life sentences and you're not on the penalty of death, do you think the death penalty is a deterrent?

Roberts: Without a doubt it's not a deterrent. I don't see where anyone could possibly think that a death sentence would be a deterrent. That's ridiculous. To be predisposed to believe that I am an individual who was about to commit the act of murder, would in fact stop and say, "Hey, I better not commit this murder because this state has the death penalty." In fact, if anything the death penalty would be an inducement to an individual, I would believe, to commit murder.

Walsh: Well, let me ask you something of a personal nature. My little boy was murdered.

Roberts: I think that was heinous.

Walsh: I know the agony of that. And I can only think something worse than that would be living with the knowledge that you murdered two children, of which you were convicted. How do you live with that knowledge?

Roberts: Sir, I've lived with it because I was convicted of it, not because I'm guilty of it. In fact, which brings me to the question, may I ask you a question along those same lines? How do you feel being a part of an instrument that takes people who maybe are not guilty of such heinous crimes and really drives these individuals into prison? How do you live with it? How do you sleep at night knowing that the possibility exists that you could be making an individual suffer for something that he did not do? Have you ever thought of that?

Walsh: Absolutely. I've thought of it continually and I believe in the criminal justice system. And I believe that people are entitled to have due process. I believe that if they are wanted, they should be brought back and either proven innocent or guilty. If they have been convicted and are at large and have demonstrated the criminal activity that you have, they should be returned to prison.

Roberts: I should hope that you're not hostile toward me, Mr. Walsh. Our system does fail at times. But I'm willing to give it a chance.

Walsh: All right, Mr. Roberts.

You have just finished reading one of the first books published by Harper Paperbacks!

Please continue to look for the sign of the 'H', below.

It will appear on many fiction and non-fiction books, from literary classics to dazzling international bestsellers.

And it will always stand for a great reading experience and a well-made book.